AF541325

James Joyce

A Critical Study of His Novels, Poetry and Play

James Joyce

A Critical Study of His Novels, Poetry and Play

Soumyajit Samanta

Published by
ATLANTIC
PUBLISHERS & DISTRIBUTORS (P) LTD
7/22, Ansari Road, Darya Ganj,
New Delhi-110002
Phones : +91-11-40775252, 23273880, 23275880, 23280451
Fax : +91-11-23285873
Web : www.atlanticbooks.com
E-mail : orders@atlanticbooks.com

Branch Office
5, Nallathambi Street, Wallajah Road,
Chennai-600002
Phones : +91-44-64611085, 32413319
E-mail : chennai@atlanticbooks.com

ISBN 978-81-269-1736-5

Printed in India at Nice Printing Press, A-33/3A, Site-IV,
Industrial Area, Sahibabad, Ghaziabad, U.P.

Preface

The relevance and appeal of Joyce has always been foremost in modernist studies, i.e. if we go by literary canons. But Joyce is in many ways an exponent of both high and low, canonical as well as popular cultures. Hence, the mystery of his texts is encoded in a hybrid mix of both categories. Joyce's letters, prose writings and his drama evince ways and forms of subversion of the Logos in multiple forms.

Dismantling of authority and its re-fiction in its myriad forms have been the tenor of Joycean prose, which illuminates the hybrid forms of marginal discourse as well highlights the local, popular, regional idiosyncrasies. Joyce has wafted out of the ivory tower of aesthetics and found beauty in the ruggedness of the primary and the ordinary.

Stephen the artist is both unique as well as ubiquitous among us as we move from being to becoming. Art and its appreciation becomes a dynamic process, scintillating and arresting in its multivalent forms until it finally reaches the mind of the artist. Joyce has recast and relived the medieval in the modern, much in the tenor of Umberto Eco, albeit differing in its essentials. The Joycean artist-hero has been reincarnated in the humdrum vibrations of the average Leopold Bloom. He has even re-invented himself in *Finnegans Wake*, and his personality defies literary, historical, anthropological, mythical and popular demarcations.

In this encyclopaedic medley of narratives, it is difficult to locate the persona of Joyce as he flits in and out of contraries and parallelisms of discourses—a pulsating carnivalesque of discord and concord. The Joycean novel accelerates towards a metanarrative but more often than not, the discourse always explodes in a multiplicity of voices, resisting genres, and the closure of literary theories as well as as that of aesthetics. Joycean prose celebrates and exults in the liberation of the word and language as such.

It is often hazarded that Joyce has wrecked the novel in its classic form and nomenclature. But he has also broached a new kind of creative activity. For him any kind of creativity is consequent on an act of creative dismantling or decentring of the artist. This de-legitimization or deconstruction of the ego-centric perception of the artist may be located in the materiality of his being and in his writing. The Joycean artist is historically located in the aftermath of the two World Wars, against the ideological onslaught of logocentricism and its attendant ideology. As against the biblical enunciation—let there be light—runs the Joycean echo—let there be word and beauty was enunciated through the creation of images by the artist in hallowed moments of epiphany. Softly we tread. We dare not disturb the artist, nor the object of beauty. We only hear the waterfall or the peals of a girl's laughter or the bubbling of a gentle stream where a girl is bathing. The quintessential Joyce is incarnated in the three phases of Aquinian aesthetics: integrities, consonantial and claritas. The final impact of Joycean prose can only be a feeling of joy or radiance—a textasy or textasis.

Soumyajit Samanta

Acknowledgements

The book forms an integral part of my Ph.D. thesis and I record my gratitude to Professor Jasodhara Bagchi of Jadavpur University, Department of English, who had acted as the supervisor of my thesis and provided valuable suggestions. I am also grateful to late Professor Michael Sprinker of Stonybrook University for suggesting suitable modifications for the book to be published in its present form.

The book owes its present structure to Anindya Bhattacharya, Asst. Professor of English, my numerous interlocutors and fellow teachers in India and abroad, who suggested that the study should be so designed as to benefit both researchers as well as students of English literature. Finally, I would like to record my gratitude to my wife Chandrayee, and my son Sunny for their support and understanding during the preparation of the present manuscript.

Soumyajit Samanta

List of Abbreviations

CH	Critical Heritage
CW	The Critical Writings of James Joyce
D	Dubliners
FW	Finnegans Wake
Letters	Letters of James Joyce, 3 vols.
P	A Portrait of the Artist as a Young Man
PJJ	The Portable James Joyce
U	Ulysses

Introduction

This study seeks to place James A. Joyce (1882-1941) against the background of post-structuralist thought because of fundamental affinities in his thinking. It is curious to note that in spite of his Catholic inheritance and upbringing, Joyce questions the very basis of theocentric vision of things, raising doubts about the Logos, as immanental and transcendental. The Logos is variously referred to as the Creator, the father-figure, the matrix of discourse, the all-encompassing, pervading tyrannical authority represented by means of religion, codified morality, societal norms and rules, political and repressive institutions and traditional forms of thought, harnessing individual freedom. The validity of logocentric authority as a transcendental figure controlling the fates of individuals outside the purview of humanity and of the author as the dominating factor dictating the terms of discourse from outside the text has been questioned variously. Similarly, the immanental idea of the Logos as being present within and influencing all elements including the classical pattern of discourse, subtly informing the text with a moral meaning, thereby manipulating it towards an aesthetic closure, has also been discarded. Indeed such a study reveals that the self may be found to be resting on doubt and incertitude. As writing subjects the self to the forces of solicitation (Derrida, 1978: 6) we gain an insight into the ontological principle of *différance* which rules at the heart of things (Derrida 1978: 78, 198, 203).

Joyce makes use of art for the purpose of dissecting and subjecting the self as well as the text to the forces of deconstruction. Joyce feels a profound necessity of self-mutilation. The artist-god must submit and be crucified and he must be his one and the only arbiter. Hence the necessity for enacting multiple fictive roles which give the illusion of ego but which at the same time enable the self to form his own critique. Thus, Richard Rowan in *Exiles* not only represents his Other but such a fiction is a deeply-felt need on Joyce's part to discover what lies at the centre of his identity. Rowan's struggle with himself is also a part of Joyce's agonised conflict with his deeper self.

Dubliners focuses dispassionately on several issues and may be said to question the trace of authorship. The colourless narrative also illustrates the subject's powerlessness in controlling his world as well as the loss of linguistic ownership. Irony is often employed for the purpose of evasion and baffling of available given meanings in the text. Simultaneously, Joyce uses satire and irony to distance himself from his fiction which, however, has an ambiguous character, since his fictional characters are used to serve the purposes of self-criticism. Joyce's critique of himself is especially highlighted in *Portrait* where Stephen revolts against logocentric authority in the form of paternity, religion, politics and nationhood. But since fatherhood is found to be situated in doubt and uncertainty, Stephen's action likewise questions the authorship of texts. When Joyce doubts the validity of his own identity, he is forced to accept the ambivalence at the centre of his own self.

The same problem is variously focused in *Ulysses* and *Finnegans Wake*. In *Ulysses*, the employment of multiple myths opens up the discourse to the influence of other texts. This process of intertextuality subverts identity and fractures both Bloom and Stephen into multiple fictive roles. Here again the plethora of narrative styles in various chapters fractures the logocentrism of classical discourse and reveals the essential illusion of fatherhood, illustrating the equivocation of the central character Bloom/Ulysses, who is both Everyman and Noman.

Finnegans Wake lacks any fixed centre of discourse because it deals with the entire course of human history, reflecting the narrative movement from individual plane to 'dividual chaos' (*FW*, 186). As context is fractured into multiple positions, the two main characters, Humphrey Chimpden Earwicker and

Anna Livia Plurabelle slide under multiple identities. *Finnegans Wake* is more exploratory in nature because here the Logos is not only decentred, but also shown to be the cause of fracture. Thus, father is the cause of fissure of fatherhood and God is posited against Himself, He being responsible for His own decentring. In this way, Joyce as the teller/tailor of tales subjects identity to an endless process of fracturing, differing and perennially deferred in time.

Joyce's theory of impersonality is to be assessed in the light of his protest and transgression against the limits of his own self; against his multiple identities which form the subject of his poems. This fissuring of identity into diverse positions (Everyman) necessitates an isolation on the part of the artist in order to come to terms with the vacuity (Noman) at the centre of himself. The stasis of emotions or the arrest of pity and fear at the heart of this dramatisation of the self is the ultimate feeling of joy or claritas felt by the artist in perceiving the aimlessness and neutrality at the heart of being. Finally, this ability to withdraw the self from the fictive centre of discourse defies the classical idea of the transcendental or immanental God. Joyce, therefore, throws a challenge to his readers to find out the real personality behind his texts. And it is to his dismay that the reader finds an equivocation at the very heart of discourse where the self ought to be.

Contents

The Critical Scene

1

Richard Ellmann's classic study on James Joyce (Ellmann, 1982) has shown how the corpus of criticism on Joyce largely bears on the structure of his works. This trend may be found around the eighties. Although structuralism has been superseded by post-structuralist and deconstructionist readings of Joyce's works, critics on Joyce still now tend to focus on the textual implications of his work, on character and plot even when concentrating on the rich symbolism and polysemy of his writing. Terence Hawkins in *Structuralism and Semiotics* (1977) has indicated the importance of Giambattista Vico in his analysis of Joyce's works. Vico in his *The New Science* (1968) has explained how the history and life-cycle of society and nations reduplicates the history of man and his life. Just as an individual progresses from birth through the processes of maturity and marriage to old age and death, similarly the history of mankind follows a systematic progress from barbarism to civilisation and to culmination in glory, only to decay and decline in the last stage. But Vico had adumbrated a fourth cycle or ricorso, which may be understood as a resurgence or a process of rebirth which marks the beginning of a new cycle.

Vico in his *The New Science* has attempted to explain how God speaks through the medium of thunder to humans and frightens them to caves, where they reproduce and produce children and civilisation: "The thunder surprised some of them...and frightened copulating pairs into nearby caves. This was the beginning of matrimony and of settled life" (Vico 1968: xxvi).

Alan Roughley in *James Joyce and Critical Theory: An Introduction* (1991) has explained how Joyce uses:

> The three-stage pattern to structure the *Wake* in much the same way that he uses the three-letter groups HCE and ALP. He also uses the ricorso, and his one-hundred-letter words for thunder signify a thunder that is also derived from Vico.... In the human creation of myths and institutions Vico saw a process which is essentially the creation of *structures*. The establishment of laws and the creation of institutions is the creation of structures by which humankind civilises itself. The process is a poetic process in the radical, or root, sense of *poesis* as a making or a creating. This poetic process also helps humans to create themselves for in making institutions and social structures humans also create themselves. (Roughley 1991: 2)

It is to be noted that Joyce applies this idea in the *Wake* but he has coupled with it the Freudian concept that the development of society and most of society's creation result from a sublimation of sexual drives. "Artistic creation and the establishment of social institutions are always involved with a drive that is fundamentally sexual" (Roughley 1991: 3).

According to Vico,

> The first step in the building of the "world of nations" were taken by creatures who were still (or who had degenerated into) beasts...humanity itself was created by the very same process by which institutions were created. Humanity is not a presupposition, but a consequence, an effect, a product of institution building. (Bergin and Fisch 1968: xliv)

It is remarkable that in the *Wake* we find Bygmester Finnegan building a "Walworth of a skyscraper" its shape is unmistakable, "his roundhead staple of other days rise(s) in undress masonry upstanded" (*FW* 4, 34-36). When Jarl Uan Hoother comes out of his castle to enter the Prankquean's vagina, or "her port" their sexual union is an act of "porthery" that creates alliterative poetry or "illiterative porthery" (*FW* 23, 9-10).

In this connection, Ferdinand de Saussure's lectures *Cours de Linguistique Generale* (1974) between the years 1906 and 1911 may be said to form the linguistic basis of structuralist thought and such approach may be found to be illuminative and exploratory in an understanding of Joyce's works. Saussure actually departs from a taxonomic conception of language in which individual words act as signifiers of meanings and which may be said to develop historically and "semantics studies the historical development of meaning with a historical context which is diachronic" (Roughley 1991: 3). Against such a historical examination of the development of meaning, which emphasises the diachronic aspect of language, Saussure recognised that the meaning of words may also be established by the relationships of a word with other words in a sentence or a given context. Such synchronic relationship between words and their meanings in a given context had led Saussure to emphasise the autonomy of language which may be instrumental in understanding such a multilayered text like *Ulysses* which incessantly draws, as Hugh Kenner has stated in his *Joyce's Voices*:

> Our attention to the autonomy of language and its ability to function without necessarily engaging in a relationship with non-linguistic objects in the so-called 'real' words: "All the book, the book (insists), is words arranged, rearranged". (Kenner 1978: 49)

In other words, Joyce's play on words in both *Ulysses* and *Finnegans Wake* may be considered to be a development of Saussure's path-breaking ideas on the arbitrary relationship between words and the objects which they signify and especially of his study of language's *phonemes* or the minimal units of sound which are required to determine meaning. Joyce has used Saussure's basic linguistic structuring process which creates a system of relationships and which may lead to a difference of meaning occasioned by a linguistic difference which is essentially a *structural* difference in the relationship between words which may resemble each other. Terence Hawkes in *Structuralism and Semiotics* (1977) has explained how Joyce's writing, especially the *Wake* shows his operations of language at the phonemic level and how "every word, letter, penstroke, and paperspace is a perfect signature of its own" (*FW* 115: 7-8). Hawkes has shown that

> The notion of a complex pattern of paired functional differences ('kin' and 'bin' can be paired because of the 'in' sound which they share) is an example of binary opposition which is fundamental in both structuralist and poststructuralist theory. (Hawkes 1977: 24)

Hawkes has also pointed out that the identical and dual aspects of language and myth that are identified by Saussure and Levi-Strauss are also in accord with the discoveries made by Roman Jakobson. Jakobson's idea of language as conditioned by polarities is identical to that of Saussure. Hawkes has identified that Jakobson's polarities are partially derived from "Saussure's insight concerning the syntagmatic (linear and horizontal) and associative (vertical) planes of linguistic performance" (Hawkes 1977: 76).

Jakobson has described the relationship of words as a horizontal, linear relationship with its neighbours in the syntagmatic sequence of individual articulations. This metonymic aspect of language corresponds with Saussure's diachronic dimension and

> is characterised by the combining process which creates the syntagmatic sequences of each utterance or articulation. The metonymic is binarily opposed to the metaphoric aspect of language. The latter corresponds with Saussure's synchronic dimension and is characterised by selection and association in terms of the ways in which individual words are chosen from the repository of *langue*. Each word in a particular utterance must first be selected from a particular associative group which exists synchronically and then combined with other words in order to produce the diachronic sequence of the syntagmatic order. (Roughley 1991: 8)

Indeed, the above brief sketches of some of the insights of Vico, Saussure and Jakobson may be found to be extremely useful in understanding some of the fundamental principles that are used in structuralist analyses of Joyce's writings. Such critics as Campbell and Robinson in their book, *A Skeleton Key to Finnegans Wake* (1947) and Clive Hart in his *Structure and Motifs in Finnegans Wake* (1962) have both attempted to deal expansively with recurring narrative signifiers which often exist in structural relationship with themes and motifs. The interplay of terms like 'light' and 'dark' in "The Sisters" in *Dubliners*, the symbol of the rose and the bird in *A Portrait* or the 'potted meat' in *Ulysses*, the multidimensionality of words like 'tea', 'tree', 'rainbow' in *Wake* are prime examples of Joyce's usage of 'motif' or 'leitmotif' which actually refer to small semantic units or "short verbal construct(s), characterised by certain easily recognisable patterns of rhythm, sound, form and sometimes, sense" (Hart 1962: 20).

Joyce's method may be sometimes likened to the so-called primitive bricoleur who collates diverse materials and "carefully and precisely orders, classifies and arranges" them into "improvised" or "made-up" structures "by means of a logic which is not our own" (Hawkes 1977: 51). This has reference to Derrida's definition of "bricolage" as the use of "tools" such as "means", "collected or retained on the principle that they may always come in handy" (Derrida 1974: 104). Joyce's use of critical and non-critical materials (like popular songs, catch phrases, journalese and the kind of gush from girls' weeklies) simultaneously in his employment of puns from the basic structural unit of the *Wake*. Indeed, Hart's "insight into the importance of context and the preparation of the reader in the operations of the pun are like the kernels of Umberto Eco's later analyses of the *Wake's* paronomasia (Roughley 1991: 9-10).

Umberto Eco, who was tremendously influenced by Joyce, has explained his interest in *The Aesthetics of Chaosmos: The Middle Ages of James Joyce* (1982) where he has stressed Joyce's interest in medieval aesthetics as well as his preoccupation with Italian art and literature. Eco's semiotic study of *Finnegans Wake* had appeared earlier in *The Role of the Reader* (1979) but in his later book, Eco becomes particularly interested in the "permanence of a medieval model" (Eco 1982: vii) in both Joyce's early and later works, and he assesses the *Wake*, in particular, as offering itself as a model of language, as "an excellent model of a Global Semantic System" (Eco 1979: 68). Echoes of Joyce's *Wake* may also be perceived in Eco's later work, *Foucault's Pendulum* (1989), where Soapes writes the "incomprehensible message": "river run, past Eve and Adam's..." (Eco 1989: 416).

In *A Theory of Semiotics* (1979), Eco makes a distinction between open and closed texts and cites Joyce as being the model author of open texts. According to Eco, authors who produce texts aiming at exciting a precise response paradoxically produce a "closed" text. On the other hand, Joyce is considered an exponent of open texts since he asks his readers to consider the interplay of possible interpretations foreseen by Joyce in his portrait of Shaun in *Finnegans Wake*. Roughley interprets that

> Open texts generate 'productively ambiguous messages' which 'leave' the reader 'free to reconsider the whole of (his or her) semantic universe', but simultaneously bind the reader 'to the indecomposable unity of...alternative interpretations. (Roughley 1991: 59)

In *Finnegans Wake*, Joyce terms the perfect reader of his text as "that ideal reader suffering from an ideal insomnia" (Eco 1979a: 120, 13-14). Eco cites this as an instance of the author "foresee(ing)" the model reader as one who is "able to master different codes and eager to deal with the text as with a maze of many issues"(14). The most interesting point at issue is that the reader is unable to use the text as he or she desires. He can only obey the dictates of the text and be guided by it. In the end, the matter at issue is "not the various issues (raised by the text) in themselves, but the maze-like structure of the text" (Eco 1979a: 9).

Again, Eco uses Joyce's *Ulysses* to illustrate his distinction between the reader of closed texts and that of open texts. Authors of thrillers like a Fleming novel or a *Superman* comic strip always have in mind a selective audience, while if one goes through Joyce's text, one can "extrapolate the profile of a "good *Ulysses* reader" from the text itself since the "pragmatic process of interpretation" is not an empirical process of cognition" independent of the text qua text, but a "structural element of its generative process" (Eco 1979a: 9). Eco's view gets credence from his semiotic analysis of *Finnegans Wake* in his essay "The Semantics of Metaphor" in *The Role of the Reader* (1979b), where he shows how Joyce's use of puns in the *Wake* is heavily dependent on a greater cultural code. Also that Joyce's employment of puns demonstrate a semiotic process which the reader can follow in order to decode and understand his puns and thereby "participate in the role of a model reader in the *Wake*'s textually generative process" (Roughley 1991: 60). Finally, Eco considers the importance of Joyce's text in its presentation of itself as, among other things, "an excellent model of a Global Semantic System" (Eco 1979b: 68). This is because it "posits itself, quite explicitly, as the Ersatz of the historical universe of language"(68). Again, Joyce's model is of particular interest in a semiotic investigation of semantics because it stages a "methodological exigency of the sort found in a study of general semantics proposing to illuminate the ways in which language can generate metaphors" (Eco 1979b: 68).

Like Eco, Julia Kristeva is a semiotician, who has written on a variety of subjects and who is well known for her contributions to other areas of critical theory, like psycho-analytic studies and interpretations of literature. Her work shows significant understanding of *Ulysses* and *Finnegans Wake*. In *Desire and Language: A Semiotic Approach to Literature and Art* (1980), Kristeva follows Saussure and Greimas to develop a semiotic theory, which has an affinity with Mikhail Bakhtin's distinction between monologic and dialogic discourse. Roughley has explained her position in the following manner:

> Her aim is to produce a theory for better understanding writing which serves a subversive social purpose and she shares some of the conclusions of critics like Margot Norris who see Joyce as part of a radical and subversive tradition of writing.... *Desire and Language* also illustrates Kristeva's role as a participant in the development poststructuralist theory. Instead of looking at works of literature as discrete, self-contained texts, Kristeva considers their functions as intertexts. (Roughley 1991: 67)

According to Kristeva, any semiotic network or 'signifying practice' is a 'field', or a semiotic 'space traversed' by lines of force...in which various signifying systems undergo such a transposition (Kristeva 1980: 15). Like Bakhtin, Kristeva is quite taken up with the notion of *polyphonic* novel as a form, which incorporates 'carnivalesque structures'. It is interesting to note that Kristeva sometimes makes use of the structuralist position, which counterpoints the horizontal (diachronic) and vertical (synchronic) axes of language. She has defined the 'status' of the 'word', of language, in terms of two similar axes: "The word's status is thus defined horizontally (the word in the text belongs to both writing subject and addressee) as well as vertically (the word in the text is oriented toward an anterior or synchronic literary corpus)" (Kristeva 1980: 66).

Like Eco, who has situated the reader within the text and defines him or her as a product of the text, so Kristeva's theory sees the reader as an "addressee" who is "included within a book's discursive universe only as discourse itself" (Kristeva 1980: 66). Kristeva, therefore, along with Eco and others, declines to separate the triad of author, book and reader as separate entities. Rather, she is of the opinion that the reader is bound up with a position within the language of the text and of his position as continually being changed by the operations which language performs and which is bound to influence the psychology of the reader.

Kristeva follows the dialogical structure defined by Bakhtin in her exposition of "text" and "text-content":

> each word (text) is an intersection of words (texts) where at least one other word (text) can be read. In Bakhtin's work, these two axes...he calls *dialogue* and *ambivalence*.... (A)n insight first introduced into literary theory by Bakhtin (is): any text, is constructed as a mosaic of quotations; any text is the absorption and transformation of another. The notion of *intertextuality* replaces that of intersubjectivity, and poetic language is read as at least a double. (Kristeva 1980: 66)

It is of the utmost importance to understand Joyce's works as models of such a theoretical perspective. *Finnegans Wake*, for example, may be understood as that text's identification of itself as the work of Shem the Penman. He is situated within the text and his writing is a mosaic of "once current puns" and "quashed quotatoes" (*FW* 183: 22), or "quotations". Shem's exhaustive list of deformed quotations which appear as "piously forged palimpsests" which come from a "pelagiarist" and (plagiarist's) "pen" (*FW* 182: 2-3). In this connection, Roughley points out how

> Joyce's text also operates as a model for the notion of the poetic text as a double, and one can use Eco's model of associative chains (a model derived from the *Wake*) in order to follow a continually bifurcating chain of signifiers generated from the signifier 'Dublin', 'duble', 'doob', 'doubloons', 'doubleyous', 'doublin', etc. One could follow these chains in order to experience Joyce's text as a chain of signifiers.... (Roughley 1991: 69)

Kristeva's theory of the novel has always been centred around what she terms as "O-1" and "O-2" logic. She has critiqued the traditional idea of the sign as a unity of signifier and signified, or the notion of sign. According to her, such a notion

> is a product of scientific abstraction (identity-substance-cause-goal as structure of the Indo-European sentence), designating a vertically and hierarchically linear division. (This) scientific abstraction (is responsible for O-1 logic).... Scientific procedures are indeed based upon a logical approach...founded on the Greek (Indo-European) sentence. Such a sentence begins as subject-predicate and grows by identification, determination and causality. Modern logic...evolves out of a O-1 sequence: George Boole, who begins with set theory, produces formulae that are more isomorphic with language—all of these are ineffective within the realm of poetic language, where I is not a limit. (Kristeva 1980: 69-70)

Kristeva's aim is to transcend the "monological", the O-1 logic (Bakhtin), though the power of literary semiotics which:

> must be developed on the basis of a *poetic logic* where the concept of the *power of continuum* would embody the O-2 interval, a continuity where O denotes and 1 is implicitly transgressed. (Kristeva 1980: 70)

According to Bakhtin, literature, which operates on the principles of "realism", has a characteristic tendency to function within this (O-1) space, and hence the realist novel may be termed "monological" (Kristeva 1980: 70). Kristeva's citation of Joycean texts as prime example of a form of writing, which escapes the limitations of O-1 logic is primarily due to Joyce's creation of a form which makes use of traditional realist narrative patterns but simultaneously subverts it. Joyce's use of subversive pattern does not merely limit itself to narrative modes but also extends to themes and characterisation. Thus, in *Ulysses* we find him compressing minute realistic details of Dublin life within the compass of one day, especially 16 June 1904 but at the same time the epic parallel of Leopold Bloom's actions with that of Odysseus clarifies the subversion inherent in his characterisation, where an "advertising salesman as a middle-aged man is contained with a form that fuses Dublin's citizen with Homer's hero" (Roughley 1991: 70). It is interesting to note that Joyce's achievement (along with that of Proust and Kafka) of creating the "polyphonic" modern novel, "incorporating carnivalesque structures" actually exemplifies the operation of Kristeva's O-2 poetic logic (Kristeva 1980: 7).

Roughley in his *James Joyce and Critical Theory* explains why Kristeva has cited the *Wake* as a prime example of carnival as discourse because the *Wake* functions as a dream and situates itself outside the pale of realist narrative. Kristeva has herself defined carnival as discourse which "by adopting a *dream* logic...transgresses rules of linguistic code and social morality as well" (Kristeva 1980: 70).

Bonnie Kime Scott is another exponent of Anglo-American feminist writing and she has written two books on Joyce from her personal feminist viewpoint. In her *Joyce and Feminism* (1984), Scott has posited a set of feminist framework for possible critical approaches to Joyce and has explained the mythical, historical and cultural contexts of women in Ireland in order to understand Joyce's sketch of such female characters like Emma Clery, Molly Bloom and Issy. Scott has explained her position more clearly in her second critical study, *James Joyce* (1987):

> In *Stephen Hero*.... Emma Clery plays opposite Stephen Dedalus, whose perception of her include muse and goddess. But Emma has a set of aspirations that had been neglected in previous criticism. I have examined her educational and nationalist interests as aspects of female culture in Joyce's background. Molly Bloom...emerged in my study with several roles. As a realistic character she takes on the values and limitations of identities such as Jew, child of the Gibraltar garrison and Dubliner—in the aspects of married woman, mother and female artiste. More forcefully, she also plays an iconoclast whose complaints coincide with much of feminist consciousness-raising of her own era and of the late 1960s. Finally, I questioned the ideologies behind usual critical interpretations of her as earth mother and offered new goddess associations, particularly from the Celtic world.... The third female character...was Issy, the daughter figure of *Finnegans Wake*, and like Emma Clery, a young woman with intellectual potential. Issy uses wit, sarcasm and linguistic invention to comment upon patriarchal culture and to respond to the artist figure of the *Wake*. She also has mythical dimensions—including identification with the Egyptian goddess, Isis, and Deirdre, a fugitive from patriarchal plot in Irish myth. (xiii-xiv)

According to the perspective offered by gynocriticism, female culture is seen to be dominated by the larger, male-controlled, mainstream culture. But in this context Scott has shown how we can have a different insight into Joyce by noting how the operations and assistance of women editors and publishers of Joyce like Marsden, Weaver, Rebecca West, H.D. and Bryher (Winnifred Ellermann, allying with Sylvia Beach created a congenial environment for Joyce to enter the mainstream literary canon). The marginal as well as substantial and unconventional forms of female assistance which Joyce has received throughout his literary career may help us to understand why and how Joyce was always critical about his Jesuitic education, which functions as a sort of "male building" in his corpus of his works (Scott 1987: 18-19). This ability of Joyce to distance himself from conventional and Jesuitic modes of thought and performance shows his great achievement in questioning the rational tradition of canonised great men and their writings as well as providing alternatives to such logocentricism. Scott has examined how Joyce explored alternatives to canonised writing by drawing upon female subculture and which posed serious challenges to the classical curriculum as seen in Stephen Dedalus's growing disenchantment with the classical canon, forming the backbone of his education. This reflects his own gradual development towards those models of writing which Joyce used in the later portion of *A Portrait* and at the end of *Ulysses* as well as in *Finnegans Wake*.

In her second chapter, "The Canon: Challenges to Male-centred Literature and History", Scott explains the challenges offered by feminism to the idea of the Joycean canon. She has outlined the sexual and political implications of the process of canonisation in the following terms:

> James Joyce is one of the 'great writers'. He appears in anthologies and on course lists; he is known to educated people in the West and beyond. He has come to represent the experimental prose of the modernist period of literary history. In other words, Joyce is 'canonised'. The canon we have today is largely the product of industries and institutions dominated by men; it was composed by male writers, centred upon men's experiences and views of history, and was more readily available to men than to women. It leaves out a great deal that women have written and largely writes and conceptualises them out of history. (Scott 1987: 15)

At the same time, Scott is interested in demonstrating how Joyce's development illustrates a gradual movement from traditional canonised forms to experimental forms with which feminists may identify. Both in *Ulysses* in its use of popular literature and in *Finnegans Wake*'s approach to history, Scott has argued how the "paradigm is no longer the classical text, but comes much closer to the 'litters' of obscure, collective, working-class and even non-human origin" (Scott 1987: 45).

For Hélène Cixous, the word *exile* defines Joyce's life and his poetics. In her *The Exile of James Joyce* (1976), she has examined Joyce's life in terms of the psychological states which Joyce has experienced and considers his 'exile' as a psychological and ontological state essential to his writing (Roughley 1991: 131). Cixous has demonstrated how Joyce has revealed his indebtedness to Nora for inspiring him as an artist and a creator in his essay entitled "Portrait of the Artist", written on 7 January 1904. The role of women in Joyce's life and career occupies a place of supreme importance since it was in the company of women that Joyce felt he could be certain and sure of himself, devoid of fear and hesitation and such an idea has been worked out time and again in his novels beginning from the *Portrait* to *Finnegans Wake*.

Cixous has also noted how most of Joyce's domestic relationships have been ultimately subordinated to his role as an artist and how the conflicts in his family life, especially when Joyce's own son was born was intensified by the priority he gave to art. When *Dubliners* was likely to be published, Joyce felt that Nora was giving much more attention to his son than to his book. Cixous has also noted that how "Joyce's self-imposed exile in his written work entailed an abdication from the role of father of flesh and blood children" (Roughley 1991: 137). But much more than such considerations of exile, Cixous has focused on an important stylistic feature of Joyce's art, namely how "Language Replaces Reality" in Joyce's writing (Cixous 1976: 673-736). Commenting upon Joyce's Irish background and his family, Cixous has stated:

> The family, the economic and social problems are...both concrete elements of surrounding reality—an end in itself, but linked...(ultimately however) any realism is at once overtaken and assimilated, to become the surface of a symbolism which is made less and less publicly significant as it is more and more charged with personal

> meaning, until with *Finnegans Wake*, it becomes Joycean form of occultism, initiation to which is achieved by a progress *through* Joyce enabling one to reach reality. (Cixous 1976: ix-x)

Such differences between these realities contribute to the meanings within the texts of Joyce's works, but Cixous thinks that the "fluidity of form" to which Joyce's multiplicity of styles contribute, is a direct consequence of the "displacement of reality, or rather (of) the modifications which the notion of reality here begins to undergo" and in *Ulysses*, reality loses its "common universal objective experience" and becomes a "particular, subjective, often incommunicable experience":

> If *Ulysses* apparently takes place in Dublin...it is really only a framework and a setting. Dublin exists, but much more as an animate object, a giant body, a corporate character, than as a stage. 'The' consciousness is made up of all individual conscious minds.... (Cixous 1976: 696)

Cixous actually considers *Ulysses* as a "monsterous epiphany" revealing the "total manifestation of reality through language" (Cixous 1976: 674). Joyce has, according to Cixous, utilised the medieval concept of the "summa" like Eco and taken the concept of totality without its content, order and hierarchy, which had made the correspondence-system possible". Indeed, Joyce's use of multiplicity of styles has shifted the emphasis from the writer to reality as the "form of what is written" (Cixous 1976: 687). Cixous has shown how in Joyce's prose "form mimics reality", without any authorial comment or judgement, "it is not a technique" of "identical reproduction". Joyce uses "language and all" of its "possibilities of expression of equivalent matter" and "juxtapos(es) the work and the world with no intermediary" in order to find out the hidden meanings in the "concrete subjective". Cixous has noted in this manner how meaning in Joyce's texts has been determined in part by differences:

> ...all the meanings (of Joyce's writing) are already contained in the discrepancy or differences between absolute reality, reality as read, and reality as written. (Cixous 1976: 688)

Cixous has located the radical nature of Joyce's writing in his use of the technique of interpenetrability, which makes the apparent division between character and setting/environment nearly transparent. In other words, Joyce's multiplicity of style contributed to the "fluidity of form" where the categories of objectivity and subjectivity intermix with each other. Indeed, Joyce's reduction of chronological and objective time within the space of one single day was made possible because *Ulysses* became a "book of consciousness", where "history ceases to exist". Next, Joyce's destruction of space has been confirmed when he telescopes the text's "space of reality" into "one consciousness" which is "globally and cosmically inclusive and eliminates the distinctions between the events in outer or inner worlds" (Cixous 1976: 700). In this context, Cixous has hazarded the notion that the very nature of Joyce's polyphonic and "ex-centric" writing challenges the archetypal, logocentric world order created and dominated by God. This subversion of the theological foundation of phallocentrism is in harmony with the aims of female writing which also attempts to overcome the domination of phallocentric narratives. In this manner, Cixous indicates that Joyce's writing:

> tries to replace the imagery common to Western thought, with its implications of a beginning and an end, a here and there, a past and a present self and an other, by a world without history, a continuous world of osmosis. (Cixous 1976: 701)

Furthermore she adds,

> Even Stephen and Bloom only succeed in directing this disorder to a limited extent; their minds interpenetrate, and fantasies move from one to another, without at once being noticed.... Life and death communicate in the vertiginous movements of the dance macabre. (Cixous 1976: 701)

Thus, the conventional separation of realism from fantasy in the traditional novel has been nullified.

It is interesting to note that Margot Norris in her study of *Finnegans Wake* has explained Joyce's attack on the traditional concept of structure from the point of view of a philosophical and psychoanalytic 'event' or 'rupture' in the "history of the concept of structure", which according to Jacques Derrida "took place in the history of thought sometime in the late nineteenth and early twentieth centuries" (Roughley 1991: 270).

Roughley points out that if Norris is correct and Joyce's attack on structure which Derrida discusses in his essay "Structure, Sign and Play in the Discourse of the Human Sciences" in his *Writing and Difference* (1978) be taken as a part of the revolution in thinking about structure, then Joyce may be taken as a prime exponent of one "of those authors in whose discourse" the practice of "decentring" and the "thinking (of) structurality of structure" have "kept most closely to its most radical formulation" (Derrida 1978: 280). Roughley has shown how Derrida's readings on Joyce centres more or less on his later work, especially *Finnegans Wake* (Roughley 1991: 271-72).

In his essay "Two Words for Joyce" in Attridge and Ferrer's collection of essays entitled, *Post-structuralist Joyce*, Derrida has stated his indebtedness to Joyce: "every time I write, and even in the most academic pieces of work, Joyce's ghost is always coming on board" (Attridge and Ferrer 1984: 149). Derrida confesses to having read Joyce on and off for twenty-five or thirty years. In fact, Derrida's concern with the *Wake* is in consonance with his interrogation of the idea of totality in connection with any book whatsoever. In fact, as Roughley has explained that

> Derrida's concern with the concept of the book as a unified totality is also apparent in *Of Grammatology's* famous pronouncement that "the Outside is the Inside" (Derrida 1974: 44) and in his writing on "the End of the Book and the Beginning of Writing", Derrida contends that deconstructive writing begins with its refusal of the oppressive totality of the classical philosophical concept of the book as a unified, organic form. The end of the phallogocentric domination of writing begins with the end of 'linear writing', or what we have seen Kristeva

> call monologic writing, and Derrida states that the "end" of linear writing is indeed the end of the book, even if, even today, it is within the form of a book that new writings—literary or theological—allow themselves to be, for better or worse, encased. (Derrida 1974: 86) (qtd. in Roughley 1991: 278-79)

Finally, the delimitisation of the text as a perfect totality and the end of linear writing may be encapsulated by the opening and closing words of Joyce's "*Doublends Jined*" (*FW* 20: 15-16) which runs thus:

> A way a lone a last a loved a long the [outside of the book] riverrun, past Eve and Adam's, from swerve of shore to bend of bay, brings us by a commodius vicus of recirculation back to Howth Castle and Environs. (*FW* 628: 1-3, 15-16)

Joyce, therefore, may be seen to subject the inviolate nature of the Logos to the forces of 'solicitation', which releases the discordant notes within the self that had been locked within the linearity of discourse (Derrida 1978: 6). As the matrix of discourse suffers dislocation, the centrality of authorial self is deconstructed into several possible positions within the text. There is a vital interconnection between linguistic experiments, along with a breakdown of classical syntax (wherein there is a correspondence between subject and object) and a deep distrust, coupled with a negation of tyrannical authority in theological, political, social and aesthetic spheres in Joyce. It is within the perspective of this study to illustrate how the authorial self fractures owing to the dichotomy between the signifier and the signified.

Previous critics had aimed at an illustrative reading of Joyce's linguistic innovations without establishing their relevance in a novel discourse, which emphasises the "dividual chaos within the authorial self" (*FW* 186). Authority, authorship of texts and the artistic process in Joyce has always been explained in terms of impersonal theory of art enunciated towards the end of *A Portrait.* "The artist, like the God of creation, remains within or behind or beyond or above his handiwork, invisible, refined out of existence, indifferent, pairing his fingernails" (*P* 215).

The notion of authorial absence has been advocated by Robert Kiely in his work *Beyond Egotism: The Fiction of James Joyce, Virginia Woolf and D.H. Lawrence* (1980). Kiely's adumbration of the romantic protean self, which has a centrifugal movement, absorbing all, and finally assuming objective proportions form the basis of his critical adventure. In speaking of the three above authors, he therefore concludes:

> The steadiest, most fundamental and significant movement in the works of Joyce, Woolf and Lawrence is outward from the individual and local to the relational and universal.... In their ability to endow a transitory subjective vision with the substantiality of an objectively verifiable event, all resembled to some degree their Romantic predecessors. (Kiely 1980: 7)

Once again, if we turn to the final page of *A Portrait* we will find the basis of such a critical interpretation in Stephen's assertion: "O life! I go to encounter for the millionth time the reality of experience and to forge in the smithy of my soul the uncreated conscience of my race" (*P* 253). This orthodox notion of self as developmental, evolving and enjoying a dialectical relation with the world is due to an appreciation of such novels from the classical point of view as 'Bildungsroman'. Post-structuralist critics sharpen their claws against such smug notions of the self as developmental and progressive, revealing deep fissures within itself. Indeed, the deconstruction of self and a consequent revision of the artist's relationship to his work becomes a focal point of Joycean critical canon from the seventies onwards.

Among the most widely known exponents of the recent critical trend, mention ought to be made of Colin MacCabe, who makes language the focal point of his deconstructionist approach in his *James Joyce and the Revolution of the Word* (1978), boosting his efforts later with his edition of new critical ventures in his *James Joyce: New Perspectives* (1982). Arguments that challenge the omnipresence of logocentric or paternal authority and conduct a reading into the dismembering of identity constitute the focal point of Maud Ellmann's essay "Polytropic Man: Paternity, Identity and Naming" in *The Odyssey* and *A Portrait of the Artist as a Young Man* (MacCabe, 1982) and also in "Dismembering Dedalus: *A Portrait of the Artist as a Young Man*" (Young 1987). Colin MacCabe in his essay "The Voice of Esau: Stephen in the Library", carries on the post-structuralist tendency of highlighting Joyce's unmaking of self and language:

> Language and identity are here posed in a very specific relation: to assume an identity, to recognise and be recognised by the father, is to refuse the possibility of re-interpretation.... The escape from paralysis that threatens Stephen Dedalus...is through investigating the constitution of those discourses; deepening *A Portrait*'s concern with language to include the whole history and forms of the English language in which Stephen's soul 'frets' (*P* 194) [sci]. It is this formal re-writing that allows *Ulysses* to return again and again to its own events, refusing any final interpretation, liberating both subject and language in one and same gesture. (MacCabe 1982: 113)

The notion of intertextuality envisages a fracture of both the subject and the eluding of authorship in discourse. Jacques Derrida's essay along with that of Andre Topia, Jacques Aubert, Stephen Heath and Helene Cixous, in the collection of essays edited by D. Attridge and D. Ferrer (1984), focus on this aspect of Joyce's work. Vicky Mahaffey in *Reauthorizing Joyce* (1988) is concerned to portray the reification of authority in Joycean discourse especially with reference to *Ulysses* which, as she illustrates, delineate three forms of authority; the patriarchal (single), the binary and paradoxical (double) and the collective (multiple). The Lacanian perspective of the structure of the unconscious, being the structure of language, has been embraced by S. Brivic in his study, *Joyce and the Creator* (1985). Here also the classical subject is shown to be fragmented but in the place of the "inter-said" (Brivic 1985: 58).

The Joycean canon has always highlighted the decentring of the classical subject especially from the seventies onwards. Although M. Norris's study, *The Decentred Universe of*

Finnegans Wake: A Structuralist Analysis appeared in 1976, but its surprisingly modernist orientation sends its reverberations even down to the nineties. In this study, Norris pays special emphasis to the antisubjectivism, which is implicit in the narrative structure of not only *Finnegans Wake* but also in *A Portrait*. Any modernist or radical interpretation of Joyce is bound to take cognizance of the fact that: "Knowingly or unknowingly he participated in those intellectual currents of early-twentieth-century Europe, whose destructive impact depended on a profound revision of the understanding of language" (Norris 1976: 2). Norris points out that the implications of language not only lie in the unconscious but also in the organisation of psychic and social life based on similar unconscious laws, along with the structures that underlie various human activities related to the family, religion and social communications. In this sense:

> The local use of mythic patterns in *Portrait* expands in *Ulysses* to a massive mythic structure that ascribes the condition of the individual not merely to accidents of environment but to certain constant predispositions in his own nature and in the order of things as well. (Norris 1976: 4)

In the eighties, the Joycean connection with a continuously expanding popular culture has been explored from the Bakhtinian angle by R.B. Kershner in *Joyce, Bakhtin and Popular Literature: Chronicles of Disorder* (1989). Kershner investigates Joyce's modulation of 'popular culture' and 'literary and subliterary texts' which produce a 'critical polyphony' in his work. In a different vein Freud and Heidegger have been used in exploring the genre of the epiphanous novel in Lawrence, Joyce, Faulkner and others in *The Making of the Twentieth Century Novel* by John Orr (1987). Orr's study is interesting because he is concerned to show how the epiphanous modes gives "a substantial presence to what is conventionally absent from the analytic discourse of the society, language as the fullness of expressive voice, of the hidden voice which is normally never heard" (Orr 1989: 15). The polyphony of voices in the Joycean text has a referentiality that may extend to Irish folklore, myth, culture and also to history. This has been the focus of Joycean studies made by L.H. Platt, Collin Owens, David Mikics, A.E. Duffy, M.C. Carpenter in the nineties and by James Fairhall, Mark Osteen, Fritz Senn and others in the special issue on history in the *James Joyce Quarterly* (Summer 1991). Other critical approaches in the post-structuralist tradition include feminist criticism by Patrick McGee, Trevor Williams, G.M. Leonard, M. Norris, Luce Irigaray, Annette S. Levitt, Diana E. Henderson and others in the 1989 issue of *James Joyce Quarterly*.

One of the most important thrusts in the Joycean canon of recent years has been the analysis of the post-structuralist dimension of Joyce's texts and an exploration into the nature of the authorial self. The idea of impersonality in art has been given a new orientation with the disappearance of the author in discourse. Hong Duk-Seon's Ph.D. dissertation, *James Joyce and the Ideology of Discourse* (1993) examines the author's narrative experiments, which displace the authorial voice of the text, showing the hesitancy of meaning. The ideological implication of Joyce's textual experiment lie, according to Hong, in a radical alteration in the relation between text and reader as well as in seeing Joycean discourse as a potentially subversive semiotic force, having political implications as it "breaks through habitualised communicative structures and calls hierarchical systems of signification into question" (Duk-Seon 1993: 2825-26-A). Further, the power of disruption is also seen in dismantling or as Hong terms it the "death of the subject" in *A Portrait* where the modernist text is shown to transgress the traditional norms of "Bildungsroman". The author's relationship to his texts have been considered from various points of view as in Ian Matthew Crump's Ph.D. dissertation on *Disselving the Individuone: Joyce's Narrative Representation of the Self* (November 1991) and in Ginette Verstraete's thesis *Critical Distance: Fragmentation from Friedrich Schlegel to James Joyce* (September 1992). It is relevant to note here that the opposite interpretation, which sees Joyce appropriating or usurping the female voice, has also been current. Critics have sometimes attacked Molly Bloom's soliloquy as being artificial and expressive of a man's discourse. Scott W. Klein in his essay "Speech Lent by Males: Gender, Identity, and the Example of Stephen's Shakespeare" (JJQ, 30: 3, Spring 1993) points out, however, that:

> The inauthenticity of Molly's voice in this age of awareness of construction of gender, in short, is assumed, both by those who attack Joyce as antifeminist and by those who would claim his engagement with protofeminist issues. Consideration of "Scylla and Charybdis" in *Ulysses*, however, reveals that themes of gender, inauthenticity, the theatrical artifice are already contained within the book's aesthetic argument. (1993: 439)

It is important to note that in Stephen's lecture on Shakespeare, the poet and dramatist does not provide a patriarchal model of creativity but as will be shown in the section of *Ulysses*, he rather represents an androgynous example, open to ambiguous interpretation both by feminists and antifeminists. This is directly related to the deconstruction of logocentrism in Joycean texts. Thus, Klein comments:

> The centrifugal forces of Shakespeare's desire both the creation of the self and the self's fragmentation, the drive towards both representation and repetition undermine the possibility of achieving reconciliation within a transcendent selfhood. Even as he is defined by desire, he is subject to the categories of division with which Stephen ends his argument. (1993: 447)

In this sense, recent critical opinion concerns itself with the post-structuralist valorisation of dissonance in discourse, which emancipates the revolutionary work of Joyce from the paralyzing effects of logocentrism as well as the tyranny of binary opposites, which have been current in Western metaphysical thought.

It is indeed a formidable task to establish a post-structuralist reading of Joycean texts in the light of such an august body of critical commentary but which is felt necessary especially when one feels the ambivalence at the heart of Joycean discourse. The purpose of this study is to use the conclusions previously offered and to continue the trend by using the tools of post-structuralist approach to delve deeper into the Joycean self to illustrate how the discordant voices in the text reveal the equivocation at the heart of the author. This study reveals the origin and the effect of fractures within Joyce the narrator, showing his rebellion against the ontic determination of being by the forces of logocentric authority, both external and internal. In other words, he comes to understand his ontological limits when he faces the indeterminacy within himself. And this is consequent on the differential character of signification in the domain of discourse. The ambiguity of the Joycean author is highlighted when he challenges the tyranny of his own self which imprisons the other by allying itself with all forms of logocentrism. In the liberation of the Other in discourse lies the germ of self-transgression.

The Joycean author indulges in self-critique, self-desecration in order to transgress his own limits. Each character in Joycean discourse is confronted with his own critique. Whether it is Joyce in his letters or in his poems, fictive representations like Richard Rowan, or Stephen Dedalus, Leopold Bloom or H.C. Earwicker, all are forced to indulge in self-criticism, leading to acts of self-transgression. It is of utmost importance to note that language participates in the deconstruction of the fictive-authorial self because it has a self-reflexive character, decentring its axis in the innumerable permutations and combinations, reflecting the incoherence and uncertainty at the heart of discourse. Even the central characters who participate with their likenesses in myth, legend, history or the racial unconscious share the burden of wounding doubt, reflecting back to their creator the fundamental instability at the heart of their Being. Finally, acts of self-transgression are occasioned by the equivocation at the heart of creative activity where Joyce parallels Shakespeare in Stephen's theory (in *Ulysses*), being both the agent and patient, the man who creates and the man who suffers, in being both Iago and Othello or Shylock and Antonio.

The Decentred Self

2

Before explaining the problematics of self in Joyce in the light of post-structuralist thought, it might well be interesting to note how such an approach becomes meaningful in Romantic and post-Romantic idea of self. In fact, such issues have been highlighted by Derrida himself in his *Writing and Difference* where he is fond of referring to Kant as a seminal thinker who has focused on the principle of ego and its irreducibility to its object of perception (Derrida 1978: 120). In his study of Levinas, Schelling and Husserl, Derrida notes how this principle of ego, which also paradoxically moves towards self-transgression, form the characteristic bases of their philosophical thought.

According to Derrida, Levinas perceives the "innate tragedy of the ego" when he notes that on the one hand "the ego cannot be itself even when it ventures out toward the other" and on the other hand he remarks "the impossibility for the ego not to be itself" (Derrida 1978: 130-31).

It is very ironic that the ego is aware of this dichotomy within itself, and this knowledge which is the "first discourse and first word of eschatology" permits its separation and speaking to the Other. This fundamental principle of knowledge which is this "always-being-one-and-yet-always-other" has already been noted by Schelling (Derrida 1978: 131). Derrida confirms that no philosophy which is responsible for its language is able to renounce "ipseity in general":

> Between original tragedy and messianic triumph there is philosophy, in which violence is returned against violence within knowledge, in which original finitude appears,

> and in which the other is respected within, and by, the same. This finitude makes its appearance in an irreducibly open question which is the philosophical question in general: why is the essential, irreducible, absolutely general and unconditioned form of experience as a venturing forth toward the other still egoity? Why is an experience which would not be lived as my own... impossible and unthinkable? This unthinkable and impossible are the limits of reason in general. (Derrida 1978: 131)

It is true, as Derrida indicates that Husserl knew about the limitations of philosophy, which is the discourse of this reason as phenomenology and which fails to answer such a question by essence since "every answer can be made only in language, and language is opened by the question" (Derrida 1978: 131). Derrida significantly explains that in the admission of the "subjective *à priori*" by transcendental phenomenology lies the only plausible route to halt "the totalitarianism of the neutral, the impersonal 'absolute logic', that is, eschatology without dialogue and everything classed under the conventional... rubric of Hegelianism" (Derrida 1978: 132).

But transcendental phenomenology fails to answer the question concerning the basic premise by which the "original violence of discourse permit itself to be commanded to be returned against itself" and to be "always, as language, the return against itself which recognises the other as other" (Derrida 1978: 133). On the other hand, Derrida explains the significant departure made by Levinas who "by radicalising the theme of the infinite exteriority of the other" has thereby been successful in assuming the "aim which has more or less secretly animated all the philosophical gestures which have been called empiricisms in the history of philosophy" (Derrida 1978: 151). Empiricism becomes the true for this movement of thought to the other, "of this resigned acceptance of incoherent incoherence inspired by a truth more profound than the 'logic' of philosophical discourse, the true name of this renunciation of the concept, of the a prioris and transcendental horizons of language" (Derrida 1978: 151).

At this juncture a few observations must be made in the light of Derrida's comments on the principle of ego. Primarily, the ego reaches its own interiority with the help of something outside it. Next, the concept of otherhood is based on the metaphysics of desire which is characterised by excess. Since this notion of excess can never be consumed by any form of totality, it can never be appropriated by the ego. Thus, acts of self-transgression become continuous as the ego attempts repeatedly to overcome its own "interior difference", which becomes an "illusion" and "a play of the Same" (Derrida 1978: 93).

The focus which Kant has laid on the disparity in our very selves in the perception of the sublime reveals a deep crisis and loss of identity. Indeed, as Terry Eagleton observes in his study of Kant in *The Ideology of the Aesthetic* that the sublime actually functions as a

> Chastening, humiliating power, which decentres the subject into an awesome awareness of its finitude, its own petty position in the universe, just as the experience of beauty shores it up. Moreover, what would be threatened by a purely "imaginary" ideology would be the subject's desire as well as its humility. The Kantian sublime is in effect a kind of unconscious process of infinite desire, which like the Freudian unconscious continually risks swamping and overloading the pitiable ego with an excess of affects. The subject of the sublime is accordingly decentred, plunged into loss and pain, undergoes a crisis and fading of identity; yet without this unwelcome violence we would never be stirred out of ourselves, never prodded into enterprise and achievement.... Ideology must not so thoroughly centre the subject as to castrate its desire; instead we must be both cajoled and chastised, made to feel both homeless and at home, folded upon the world yet reminded that our true resting place is in infinity. It is part of the dialectic of the beautiful and the sublime to achieve this double ideological effect. (Eagleton 1990: 90)

Further, Eagleton points out that the interest of Kant's aesthetic lies in the power of imagination to create a meaningful synthesis, but "without feeling the need for a theoretical detour" (Eagleton 1990: 85). The viability of such an aesthetic lies in creating a harmony between ourselves and the world; a synthesis which is primarily fictional and subjective. That is to say:

> In aesthetic judgement, however, we have the curious sense of a lawful totality indissociable from our intuition of the immediate form of the thing. Nature appears animated by an indwelling finality which defeats the understanding; and this finality, in a pleasurable ambiguity, seems at once a law to which the object conforms and nothing less than the irreducible structure of the object itself. (Eagleton 1990: 85)

Whereas the external world exists outside us and is constantly in a state of flux, steeped in a movement of blind change, and irreducible to a self-determining rational will, it becomes the achievement of the aesthetic and teleological modes of judgement (as presented in *The Critique of Judgement*) to portray the empirical world in its freedom, purposiveness and significant totality (Eagleton 1990: 84). It is important to note that while certain phenomena might be seen to display a purposive unity in the artist's aesthetic, unity might not be deducible from logical conclusions in the real world.

Kantian philosophy is thus balanced between the claims of the sublime which forces the subject into crisis and that of the aesthetic which becomes "the mode of religious transcendence, of a rationalistic age—the place where those apparently arbitrary, subjectivist responses which fall outside the scope of such rationalism may now be moved to the centre and granted all the dignity of an eidetic form" (Eagleton 1990: 88). In this context, it would be meaningful to observe that Joyce refuses to languish in the precincts of such an aesthetic, which enfolds all contradictions in an imaginary totality. Rather he accepts the irreconcilable dissonances of a vibrant nature whose existence depends on conflict and tension. Such submission to the blind world of change illustrates his rebuff to the idealist metaphysics of Hegel, which finds in the reification of self a possible alternative to the dichotomies of the physical world.

Hegelian aesthetic castrates the self of its principle of ego, living it open to its consumption by a "system in which every element, being correlative to every other, at once presupposes and is presupposed by every other" implies an eternally complete consciousness as the condition of its being (Haldar 1927: 26). Thus for Bosanquet, "philosophical speculation", becomes:

> the conscious attempt on the part of the finite mind critically and systematically to read the deeper implications of both itself and its environment. In the end, he thinks, the lesson is that such a mind is guided throughout by the "spirit of the whole" which is implicit in it and its environment alike and which when made explicit is the Absolute wherein mind "comes to itself". (Cunningham 1933: 408)

It was the premise of idealist thought to illustrate that the self possesses the ability to transcend its limits through the establishment of a relation in a world of systems. Through its own self-consciousness the sovereignty and independence of the self was breached as it arrived at a consensus in terms of aesthetics, morality and politics. Further, the evolutionary aspect of the self was stressed in its acceptance of historical forces. By participating in the "conscious movements in the secular process of the eternal mind" it moves towards self-perfection (Pater 1917: 19). The principle of relativity in Paterian aesthetic was an important landmark in the history of aesthetic philosophy because it seized upon the bilateral aspects of the Romantic perception of reality and made possible the interaction of subject and object in a dialectical movement, thus moving away from the romantic idealisation of self as well as its dissolution in the impersonal world of flux. By seeking a logocentric principle in the dynamic movements of nature, Paterian aesthetics integrated the artist in a higher totality. Beauty becomes more a question of form than of truth. Perfection in prose reaches a high point in the euphonious and sensuous prose of Pater, traces of which may be found in Joyce's

A Portrait. As the intensity of the artistic process becomes highlighted, art becomes an end in itself.

Although Joyce in his early stage shows traces of Pater's aesthetic, yet there exists a radical difference between his approach to art and that of Pater's. He firmly rejects an all-embracing design of harmony in aesthetics. His antipathy to the synthesising function of art is based on his acceptance of a world of differences where the integrity of individuals is respected to such an extent that it resists reduction to a logocentric design. It is this pervasive variety in phenomena that prevents art from becoming a mere end in itself, an artifact outshining the splendour of nature. For Joyce the referentiality of the infinite world of natural forms becomes essential for this fissuring of self. Paradoxically, his aesthetic becomes violent and destructive, threatening the stability of institutions and driving the self to acts of transgression.

Joyce's innovatory and novel aesthetic might finally be seen against the background of English Romanticism. Wordsworth, ,for instance, highlights the principle of continuity as the fundamentals of self. Although Locke and Hartley deal with the problem of identity in relation to continuity, yet they fail to reach the Wordsworthian conclusion that self can be known only through experience and that its oneness may be perceived precisely in change. Robert Langbaum in his study *The Mysteries of Identity: A Theme in Modern Literature* (1982) traces strategies for reconciling self and experience and the illustration of the idea of continuity of the self in six central Romantic and post-Romantic figures like Wordsworth, Arnold, Eliot, Beckett, Yeats and Lawrence. Joyce is concerned to reverse this developmental, process-oriented perception which sees the self as continuous with nature especially in Romantic and post-Romantic aesthetics. At the same time, however, he keeps the dynamism of nature within their reckoning. Langbaum explains that:

> the empiricist philosophers try, and fail, to find a static continuity through the flux of perceptions. But for Wordsworth, Keats and the other romanticists, continuity is dynamic; it is the continuity of change, growth, the

> continuity that comes of the faith that enables us to live by absorbing the individual perceptions into an intuited whole. (Langbaum 1982: 29)

It is significant to note that in this context Keats's manner of referring to this world as the "vale of soul-making" is somewhat similar to Wordsworth's answer to the empiricist attack on the Christian concept of soul. In this respect, he uses the word "soul" in a new way. According to Langbaum:

> ...Keats says that we come into the world as pure potentiality or "Intelligence" and that we acquire a "soul" or "sense of Identity" through "Circumstances". And it is the main purport of Wordsworth's poetry to show the spiritual significance of this world, to show that we evolve a soul or identity through experience and that the very process of evolution is what we mean by soul. (Langbaum 1982: 29)

The transition from sensation to value was possible for Wordsworth because he emphasised on the creative power of the mind. In this change over from the world to the self both Wordsworth and Coleridge modify and accept the Locke-Hartley concepts of memory and association. Their interpretation of these two empirical philosophers may be witnessed in their preoccupation with the unconscious aspects of the associative process.

In Wordsworth, the terms "soul" and "imagination" are often used interchangeably because as Langbaum explains "the poet or man of imagination is being used to epitomise a psychological process" (Langbaum 1982: 42). The achievement of a transcendent self through the establishment of a relation between the self and the world becomes possible because of Wordsworth's emphasis on the epistemological process in his mind:

> For Wordsworth the self is memory and process—the memory of all its phases and the process of interchange with the external world. The movement of thought into sensation and back again corresponds to the circular movement of self into nature and back again and to the

> circular movement from the subjectively individual to the objectively archetypal phases of identity and back again. Each such circular movement, which could be conceived as starting from outside as well as inside, is a new creation, a new confirmation, of self and is impelled by joy. (Langbaum 1982: 46)

The Wordsworthian epiphany illustrates this correspondence of the self with externality and its consequent oneness by means of a momentous act of imagination (Langbaum 1982: 45) or by "archetypalisation" of the individual (Langbaum 1982: 43).

The idea of epiphany as used by Joyce show a complete change of purpose. Rather than illustrate the unity of self with objective phenomena Joycean epiphany underlines the emancipation of self from the discourse of the Other/other. In *A Portrait*, Joyce's use of the epiphanic mode is conventionally located in the well-known image of the girl in midstream at the close of chapter four (*P* 171-73). It should be noted that Joycean epiphany is primarily a product of language, which engenders a sudden transition from a portrayal of concrete reality to a hypnotic one, suggested by the rise and fall of the cadence of prose. In fact, the prose enacts a sexual release and although commentators insist that the artist as Stephen here is a detached observer, yet the rhythm of the passage belies such an interpretation. It is undeniable that Stephen participates in the sensual beauty of the girl and by this means he affirms the artist's love of life and beauty. Mention should also be made of a similar epiphany at the end of chapter two where Stephen surrenders himself in the arms of a prostitute, affirming his initial relationship with women (*P* 101). But whereas his earlier affirmation of life was a product of lust, the later epiphany does not indicate Stephen's physical relationship with the girl. And it should be noted that the opening passage in chapter five, following upon the heels of the second epiphany present a prosaic reality, harping on the ugliness and crude materiality of life.

Stephen's encounter with life through the medium of these two epiphanies present a couple of interesting issues. The first thing that strikes us is that the second epiphany of the girl is a parody and a critique of the earlier one. Not only does it mime Stephen's sexual release in the woman's arms but it illustrates the power of discourse to create the otherness as woman. It is the significant function of the Other that language enacts by forcing the subject to turn back on his own discourse, enabling him to confront his own fracture. The overflow of desire in the Other both gives to the girl a reality not to be found outside the artist's discourse and compelling him to recognise within himself his own 'interior difference' which must be overcome and not appropriated (Derrida 1978: 93). Thus, in Joyce, epiphanies are to be thought of as products of language coercing the author to confront the essential ambiguity in himself.

By insisting on this self-reflexivity in discourse, therefore, Joyce clearly dissociates himself from the incarnational aesthetics of Romantic discourse which embody the objectification of the self only to enable it to return to a more comprehensive and unified self. In Coleridge's opinion:

> This principle, and so characterised, manifests itself in the SUM or I AM, which may be variously expressed by the words spirit, self and self-consciousness. In this, and in this alone, object and subject, being and knowing are identical, each involving and supposing the other. In other words, it is a subject, which becomes a subject by the act of constructing itself objectively to itself; but which never is an object except for itself, and only so far as by the very same act it becomes a subject. It may be described therefore as a perpetual self-duplication of one and the same power into object and subject, which presuppose each other, and can exist only as antithesis. (Coleridge 1973: I, 183)

In Coleridge's terms, once again, the Logos as Creator is paralleled by the logocentric thought of the poet who resolves everything into himself. The Secondary Imagination of the artist:

> Dissolves, diffuses, dissipates, in order to recreate...it struggles to idealise and to unify. It is essentially vital, even as all objects (as objects) are essentially fixed and dead. (Coleridge 1973: I, 202)

In this sense, Joyce might be said to retain the freedom and power of the will and on the part of the self to perform its own critique but at the same time it abjures the Romantic delimitisation of self which reflects it back to itself, but only to illustrate the poet's possession of his own transcendental self. The author turns inward, the difference, however, lies in the sense of purpose. Whereas the Romantic discovers the plenitude of the universe in himself, his self being synonymous with everything outside him, Joyce discovers his essential ambiguity and uncertainty which must be transgressed time and again, thus despairing of any final knowledge about himself.

Because of its differential nature, Joyce's theory of Being defines the limits of self by its encounter with other selves and the referentiality becomes infinitely possible. In this referential pattern, self is referred back to itself, made conscious of its limits and not as in idealistic thought, which helps the self to transcend its limits and merge into a totality. As the self becomes conscious of its ontological limits, it paves the way for its own enlightenment, discovering on its own some possible modes of transgressive activity. When the individual is made aware of the tyranny of authority, which attempts to curb his freedom, he rebels against such domination. In other words, the self becomes his own critique because he needs to escape domination from both the authority of others and the social or historical roles foisted upon him by external agencies. The action of self-reflexivity not only implies a self-critique in relation to oneself but also with reference to other selves. Thus, it is at the point of intersection between the self and other selves, between the one and many that the act of writing becomes an activity of endless selving in terms of space and time, leading to a fundamental instability at the heart of beings; an absence of any centre at all.

One of the main concerns of contemporary theory is its preoccupation with the ontology of our existence hovering over the notions of human limits and freedom. In his essay "What is Enlightenment?", Michel Foucault states that:

> The critical ontology of ourselves has to be considered not, certainly, as a theory, doctrine, nor even as a

> permanent body of knowledge that is accumulating; it has to be conceived as an attitude, an ethos, a philosophical life in which the critique of what we are is at one and the same time the historical analysis of the limits that are imposed on us and an experiment with the possibility of going beyond them. (Foucault 1986: 50)

The above extract from Foucault's essay indicates that one of the main concerns of contemporary theory is its preoccupation with the ontology of our existence hovering over the notions of human limits and freedom. According to Foucault, critics are concerned with conducting diverse inquiries into the "definition of the historically unique forms in which the generalities of our relations to things, to other, to ourselves, have been problematised"(Foucault 1986: 50). He takes as his point of departure Kant's interpretation of the Enlightenment in his three "Critiques". In his essay Foucault underlines Kant's unique approach to the question of Enlightenment which does not lie in a perception of its distinctness as a major world event, or in the heralding of a new world, but in his understanding of the event in a negative manner, as an "exit" or a "way out" (Foucault 1986: 34).

In his critique of the Kantian theory of Enlightenment, Foucault is interested in a "philosophical ethos" which involves "a critique of what we are saying" thinking, and doing, through a historical ontology of ourselves (Foucault 1986: 45). This is to say that whereas Kant was preoccupied in knowing the limits which knowledge has to renounce in the act of transgression, we are much more concerned as Foucault says, "to transform the critique conducted in the form of necessary limitation into a practical critique that takes the form of a possible transgression" (Foucault 1986: 45). This shift in the historico-critical attitude entails that this work be done "at the limits of ourselves", which will submit itself to the "test of reality, of contemporary reality, both to grasp the points where change is possible and desirable, and to determine the precise form this change should take" (Foucault 1986: 46). It naturally follows, therefore, that the "historical ontology" of ourselves must be side-tracked from all global or radical projects but also that with the acceptance of the idea of change at the basic ontological level, we shall be forever despairing ourselves at any complete knowledge of our essential self which will always be at the mercy of the forces of change. As Foucault explains, the author/critic continually transgress his limits in order to come to terms with himself and by doing so constantly produces his own mystery at the heart of his ontology:

> It is true that we have to give up hope of ever acceding to a point of view that could give us access to any complete and definitive knowledge of what may constitute our historical limits. And from this point of view the theoretical and practical experience that we have of our limits and of the possibility of moving beyond them is always limited and determined; thus we are always in the position of beginning again. (Foucault 1986: 47)

The basic difference between Joyce and other Catholic writers is the way he makes use of religion to overcome and transgress the limitation of his own personality. This may be seen with special reference to Stephen's use of Catholic tenets to overcome his own limitations. Herein lies his originality which is to say, he does not accept the self as something given; predetermined by God, or as conditioned by environment as in some nineteenth-century writers. Joyce offers a unique instance of post-modernist condition in that he continually subjects the traditions of writing, whether they be Catholic, Romantic, or late Victorian realism and scientism, to a transgressive activity. Although, for example, he is sometimes influenced by classical thought, he emphatically rejects the pre-Christian notion that virtue consists in a perfect command over oneself; a sort of what Foucault terms permanent political relationship between self and self. Neither does he accept the Christian idea of self where many elements in the pre-Christian culture of self was integrated, displaced and reutilised so that personal salvation became channelised through a pastoral institution which looks after the souls of people. In the Christian scheme of things, the idea of self which had enjoyed its autonomy in the earlier era gradually perished as it was integrated in a higher totality.

Foucault in his essay, "What is Enlightenment?", explains how in Western culture up to the sixteenth century, asceticism and access to truth have been always linked and it was only with the advent of Descartes that evidence has been substituted for ascesis at the point where the relationship with the self intersects at the point of one's relationship to others and the world (Foucault 1986: 371). In Joyce, the idea of selving is primarily a creative activity carried on at the intersection of self with the world. It is at this point that the individual is confronted with his ontological limits.

The notion of absence or the fissure of self in discourse forms the crux of Foucault's essay "What is an Author?". The French critic formulates his theme by quoting Beckett: "What does it matter who is speaking?" and finds this indifference underlining "one of the fundamental ethical principles of contemporary writing" (Harrari 1979: 141). Illustrating the gradual relaxation of authorial control and manipulation of discourse, he draws attention to the process in which the process of signification has freed itself from the despotism of the signified. Today's discourse is characterised by its freedom from the dimension of expression, that is to say the process of writing carries its own meaning and is not dictated from any external point of view beyond the discourse.

> Referring only to itself, but without being restricted to the confines of its interiority, writing is identified with its own unfolded exteriority. This means that it is an interplay of signs arranged less according to its signified content than according to the very nature of the signifier. Writing unfolds like a game (jeu) that invariably goes beyond its own rules and transgresses its limits. In writing, the point is not to manifest or exalt the act of writing, nor is it to pin a subject within language; it is rather a question of creating a space into which the writing subject constantly disappears. (Harrari 1979: 142)

If the process of signification, along with the nature of the signifier determines meaning, then writing becomes a ceaseless activity which always transgresses its limits. At the same time since it is an inexhaustible process, there is no question of the author dying in order to attain immortality; the act of scripting requires the self-effacement of the author. Indeed his absence becomes all the more remarkable because the notion of authorship has been indefinitely deferred in the nature of discourse.

> Writing has become linked to sacrifice, even to the sacrifice of life: it is now a voluntary effacement which does not need to be represented in books, since it is brought about in the writer's very existence. The work, which once had the duty of providing immortality, now possesses the right to kill, to be its author's murderer, as in the cases of Flaubert, Proust, and Kafka. That is not all, however, this relationship between writing and death is also manifested in the effacement of the writing subject's individual characteristics. Using all the contrivances that he sets up between himself and what he writes, the writing subject cancels out the signs of his particular individuality. As a result, the mark of the writer is reduced to nothing more than the singularity of his absence.... (Harrari 1979: 142-43)

According to Foucault, writing creates its own laws of existence and provides its own spatial and temporal dimension. There is then something in the very act of scripting which recoils on the author and precisely this would never have happened unless the centre was subjected to the forces of dissolution. In fact, both Foucault and Derrida argue that the centre of discourse is non-existent. This would imply that the specificity of structure and discourse-pattern is discarded in favour of the free play of signifiers. Foucault points out that it is the notion of writing which has debarred us from taking cognizance of the writer's disappearance, thereby concealing as well as obfuscating the moment of the author's abdication in the text. The discourse should not only debunk the patterns of logocentricism but should enable us to "situate his recent absence". Foucault explains that post-structuralism is concerned in employing the idea of writing as distinct from the act of writing or the expression of a meaning to be expressed by somebody.

> In current usage, however, the notion of writing seems to transpose the empirical characteristics of the author in a transcendental anonymity. We are content to efface the more visible marks of the author's empiricity by playing off, one against the other, two-way of characterising writing, namely, the critical and the religious approaches. Giving writing a primal status seems to be a way of retranslating, in transcendental terms, both the theological affirmation of its sacred character and the critical affirmation of its creative character.... To imagine writing as absence seems to be a simple repetition, in transcendental terms, of both the religious principle of inalterable and yet never fulfilled tradition, and the aesthetic principle of the work's survival, its perpetuation beyond the author's death, and its enigmatic excess in relation to him. (Harrari 1979: 144-45)

Foucault cautions us against privileging of the authorial function under the *à priori* of writing and reminds us of our task in locating the "space left empty by the author's disappearance" (Harrari 1979: 145).

Foucault's analysis of the author-function in various patterns of discourse in literary history is aimed at showing how these discourses become objects of appropriation through our concern with questions of authentication of texts. He significantly points out that the legitimisation of discourse often serve to nullify the contradictions which may surface in a couple of texts by locating a fundamental or originating contradiction in the author which then provides for the resolution of disparate currents in the text.

Joyce is critical of his relationship with the materiality of writing. Being closer to the literary movements on the continent and due to his association with the Imagist movement, he had already aimed at criticising the writer's standpoint in his career. His theory of impersonality and artistic process were promulgated at an early age (1903-04) and although in later years he revised his aesthetic standpoint, a consideration of its basic assumptions is bound to throw light on his theory of writing and the role of the authorial self. Indeed, Joyce's theory of art was deliberated at the ontological limits of self. Initially, the theory of impersonality was considered somewhat akin to the detachment of the artistic process in drama, especially as in Ibsen. Joyce was always fascinated by drama since it gave free rein to the hidden forces in the psyche and to the interplay of differing levels of meanings. Also drama permits the unfolding of passion from all angles, which actually point to a revelation of truth, reflecting the comprehensive nature of human experience. According to Joyce, drama is a unique art form because it arises out of spontaneity of human life, thereby reflecting its richness and sharing in the mythical perspective of each age. It also concerns itself with truth and not beauty, because in Joyce's conception beauty is consequent upon the author's ability to control its manifestation with the definiteness of a certain form. Truth, on the other hand, is something inescapable and inalienable, confronted by the artist and which can never be changed or subordinated by the dicta of tyrannical authority represented by the forces of religion, tradition, politics, law, social hierarchy or for that matter, artistic form.

Joyce constantly presses home the fact that the artistic process and especially the activity of writing possesses an omniscience and an omnipotence which cannot only transubstantiate whatever is ugly, humble or glorious into a work of art, but can also subject everything to criticism. It is this activity of writing that frees an author from the constricting influences of both tradition and his own ego.

The notion of writing is a complex activity which takes into account similar activities which have their origin in other authors, both contemporaneous and anachronistic. Its materiality does not argue a linear progression from an author's personality but has a vertical dimension beyond time and history, although it might experience its birth at a particular moment of time. This is what Eliot meant when, he said that Joyce's parallel use of the Odyssean myth in *Ulysses* is fraught with the "importance of a scientific discovery" since it successfully gives a shape and a meaning to the futility and anarchy of contemporary history (Eliot 1975: 177). And yet Eliot was still doing Joyce an injustice when he appreciates the technique of *Ulysses* from a relativistic viewpoint and from the notion of a schematic activity. What ought to have been stressed by T.S. Eliot is the openness of the Joycean text which reaches out in multifarious directions, to myth, history, archetype, politics, religion and other areas, including the critique of language and its history of different stylistic variations.

Within the norms of post-structuralist theory, the Joycean text may be said to re-examine the privileges of the subject from the point of discourse study. Rather than legitimise the text as a product of an author, the subject is shorn of its originating function, and analysed as a variable and complex function of discourse: "How, under what conditions and in what forms can something like a subject appear in the order of discourse? What place can it occupy in each type of discourse, what functions can it assume, and by obeying what rules?" (Harrari 1979: 158).

In this manner, we tend to reverse the traditional and orthodox notion of the author.

Thus, the necessary implication is that the author is redundant and his removal is deemed necessary for polysemic texts to function so as to work towards a proliferation of meaning and discourse patterns (Harrari 1979: 160).

The notion of writing as free play of signifiers which is antagonistic to the logocentric closure of texts is also taken up by Derrida in *Writing and Difference.* In his essay "Structure, Sign and Play in the Discourse of the Human Sciences" in *Writing and Difference*, Derrida explains how the concept of structure which is actualized through an overall notion of totality as well as an immovable centre at the heart of the text permits only the play of its elements within the limitations of a significant design.

In a certain sense, the centre both provides the matrix of discourse and yet since it is not structurally related (that is to say as it is not incumbent on the elements of the text), the totality "has its centre elsewhere" (Derrida 1978: 279).

According to Derrida, therefore, the centre is not actually the centre at all:

> The concept of centred structure—although it represents coherence itself, the condition of the "episteme" as philosophy or science—is contradictorily coherent. And as always, coherence in contradiction expresses the force of a desire. (Derrida 1978: 279)

The notion of centre may be then said to be deferred eternally. From the point of view of structure it differs elementally from other textual components. Again, the "permutation or the transformation of elements" as well as the substitution of meaning at the centre is infinitely deferred. Thus the centre remains indefinitely "beyond the reach of play" (Derrida 1978: 279). The idea of *différence* or "writing" in the general sense of economy underlines Derrida's explanation of the absence of a definite centre or authorship at the heart of discourse. Thus, any form of writing involves an anxiety resulting from "a certain mode of being implicated in the game, of being caught by the game, of being as it were at stake in the game from the outset" (Derrida 1978: 279). The anxiety of production stems, therefore, from the lack of a definite centre, which may be both inside and outside and which also may nonchalantly be termed either the origin or end.

Derrida's critique is directed against both the immanental presence of the author in the text and the absolute presence of the transcendental signified outside a system of differences. This raises the question, how do we define the centrality of discourse? According to Derrida, it became necessary to think that the matrix could never be conceived as a fixed locus with a "natural site" but a

> Function, a sort of nonlocus in which an infinite number of sign-substitutions came into play. This was the moment when language invaded the universal problematic, the moment when, in the absence of a centre or origin, everything became discourse...that is to say, a system in

> which the central signified, the original or transcendental signified, is never absolutely present outside a system of differences. The absence of the transcendental signified extends the domain and the play of signification infinitely. (Derrida 1978: 280)

According to Derrida, the free play of signifiers also depends on the modulation of discourse. Following Levi-Strauss in *The Savage Mind* he introduces the notion of the bricoleur as someone who utilises "the means at hand", which actually refers to instruments put at his disposal and which he adopts by the method of trial and error (Derrida 1978: 285). This use of material, heterogeneous in origin and form becomes a critique of language known as bricolage. If bricolage refers to the need of borrowing one's concepts from a text belonging to a culture or a heritage which is facing extinction then it could might as well be used to describe mythopoetic activity, as Levi-Strauss does in *The Savage Mind* (Derrida 1978: 285-86). In effect, as Derrida points out, "What appears most fascinating in this critical search for a new status of discourse is the stated abandonment of all reference to a centre, to a subject, to a privileged reference, to an origin, or to an absolute archia" (Derrida 1978: 286). He illustrates the theme of this decentring in Levi-Strauss's *The Raw and the Cooked.* Derrida explains that the Bororo myth lacks unity or authentic source:

> The focus or the source of the myth are always shadows and virtualities which are elusive, unactualisable, and non-existent in the first place, everything begins with structure, configuration, or relationship. The discourse on the acentric structure that myth itself is, cannot itself have an absolute subject or an absolute centre. It must avoid the violence that consists in centering a language which describes an acentric structure if it is not to shortchange the form and movement of myth. Therefore it is necessary to forego scientific or philosophical discourse, to renounce the episteme which absolutely requires, which is the absolute requirement that we go back to the source, to the centre, to the founding basis, to the principle and so on. (Derrida 1978: 286)

The point to note here is that the "mythopoeic" function of "bricolage" tends to make the philosophical or epistemological requirement of a centre seem to be a historical illusion.

It is to be seen that in Joycean discourse transgression of limits occur. His writing creates this space where the process of signification operated at the limits of the ontological determination of being. This occurs at various levels. On one level it "solicits" the metaphysical foundation of beings, bringing to light their incompleteness in their very existences (Derrida 1978: 6). Their indefinite character may be apparent in their role as signifiers, attempting to signify the myriad attributes of the Creator in various ways but unsuccessfully so because the ontological limits of their being have not been clearly delineated. Further, as has just been noted, Joyce is in favour of submitting all sorts of finite perfection to the process of general dissolution. Again, no trust is placed in the self as the ultimate signified since the onus of establishing the character of signification is made consequent upon the poet's perceptive process which, however, is extremely ambivalent once it centres around the question of language. As discourse focuses on the palpability of phenomena it highlights the centrality of thisness as well as translating the potentiality of things into forms of actuality. In other words, self as the ultimate signified is placed at the mercy of the indefinite nature of signifiers and made consequent on their differential repetition, becoming eternally deferred in time and space. From this point of view totalisation becomes untenable in the classical style where one "refers to the empirical endeavour of either a subject or a finite richness which it can never master. There is too much, more than one can say" (Derrida 1978: 289). According to Derrida, this is one way of determining the limit of totalisation, which he finds in Levi-Strauss's discourse, especially in the primary importance given to the notion of play of signifiers by him in *Conversations, Race and History* and *The Savage Mind*.

The interdeterminate character of writing and the hesitancy of meaning prevents the legitimisation of discourse in the corpus of Joyce's works. Joyce's uniqueness lies in an innate awareness that the reign of logocentrism is over in discourse.

Hence, it is that even in an early work like *A Portrait* we find that the author's relationship with his other or fictional substitute is critical in more ways than one, inviting the reader to make his own responses to the text which argues for a variety of interpretations. Not only does Joyce consciously segregate himself from Stephen but the latter is handled with irony. The author is then doubly removed from portraying his actual experience. He is able to assess the effect of his actions in the past from the point of view of maturity. He is also able to form an estimate of his erstwhile experience through the narrator or Stephen Dedalus's actions and mistakes. The discourse becomes doubly ironical because it enables the author to form his critique of his own self by the abdication of his narrative self in the story. That is to say Joyce absolves himself from the tyranny of logocentric discourse by liberating himself from the power of his own past and experiences. He anticipates Derrida's quarrel with history in *Writing and Difference* where he notes that the classical preoccupation with the past has always been complicated by a teleological and eschatological metaphysics. Thus, it is that Joyce the author is absent from the discourse in *A Portrait* because the activity of writing becomes self-reflexive, turning its back on itself.

In this context, it will be significant to quote Derrida's ideas of historicity:

> The thematic of historicity, although it seems to be a somewhat late arrival in philosophy, has always been required by the determination of Being as presence. With or without etymology, and despite the classic antagonism which opposes these significations throughout all of classical thought, it could be shown that the concept of episteme has always called forth that of historia, if history is always the unity of a becoming, as the tradition of truth or the development of science or knowledge oriented toward the appropriation of truth in presence and self-presence, towards knowledge in consciousness-of-self. History has always been conceived as the movement of resumption of history as a detour between two presences. (Derrida 1978: 291)

On another level, non-totalisation may be defined from the standpoint "of the concept of play" which implies that the nature of finite language does not permit the idea of totalisation. In this sense, the finite play of signifiers ensures a field of infinite substitutions not because the field of play is too large or infinite, but due to absence of any centre which can arrest the free play of substitutions. This "movement of play, permitted by the lack or absence of a centre or origin, is the movement of supplementarity" (Derrida 1978: 289). As the sign is permitted to replace the centre, it actually supplements something which does not exist, thereby "taking the centre's place in its absence". Hence one can never hope to "determine the centre and exhaust totalisation" because the sign which is added "occurs as a surplus, as a supplement" (Derrida 1978: 289). The supplementary meaning is in the nature of an addition, performing a vicarious function, supplementing a vital lack on the part of the signified. The supplementary nature of meaning may be witnessed in the "overabundance of the signifier", which is the "result of a lack which must be supplemented" (Derrida 1978: 290).

Derrida's emphasis is on the nature of play that brings it into conflict with history and the theory of presence in discourse. Play antedates the alternatives of presence and absence and hence may be said to disrupt the notion of presence in historical discourse. Ontology is consequent on the "basis of the possibility of play and not the other way round" (Derrida 1978: 292).

Derridean notion of play shows an insecurity:

> This affirmation then determines the non-centre otherwise than as loss of the centre. And it plays without security. For there is a sure play: that which is limited to the substitution of given and existing, present, pieces. In absolute chance, affirmation also surrenders itself to genetic indetermination, to the seminal adventure of the trace (sic). (Derrida 1978: 292)

This notion of the supplementarity of meaning through the play of signifiers may be seen in Joyce who, early in his career had mastered a nonchalant and phlegmatic style that permitted the free play of signification. *Dubliners* illustrates the triumph of the epiphanic mode of writing where a focus on trivial details bring out the hidden forces in the narrative, creating a space at the heart of representation, a vertical space where hidden levels of meaning surface, turning potentiality into actuality, thus defeating the linear progression of discourse. Primarily, the use of the epiphanic mode in Joycean discourse is always aimed at permitting the free play of meaning in an object indicating its essential character during the course of the narrative and which is quite independent of the author's subjectivity. This technique of writing is perfected by Joyce in *Portrait* where epiphany is used to counterpoint the profane and the sacred nature of beauty through the terrestrial experiences of Stephen.

Joyce often affords a prime instance of what happens when the ontic determination of beings is subjected to the forces of what Derrida has called "solicitation". Derrida explains:

> Structure then can be methodically threatened in order to be comprehended more clearly and to reveal not only its supports but also that secret place in which it is neither construction nor ruin but liability. This operation is called...*soliciting*. In other words, shaking in a way related to the whole.... The structuralist solicitude and solicitation give themselves only the illusion of technical liberty when they become methodical. In truth, they reproduce, in the register of method, a solicitude and solicitation of Being, a historico-metaphysical threatening of foundations. (Derrida 1978: 6)

Instances of the "solicitation" may be found in the decentring of notions of personality in *Ulysses* and *Finnegans Wake*. In *Ulysses*, the Bloomian personality disintegrates into a host of other persona like Dedalus, Noah, the father of Prince Hamlet, Ulysses, pseudo-persona like Rudolph Virag or Henry Flower.

Molly's acentric character is also noted in her synonymity with Penelope, Callidike, Calypso, Gea-Tellus. Stephen, on the other hand, becomes a variation of Telemachus, Icarus, Japhet, Prince Hamlet. What needs to be stressed here is the almost infinite capacity of these three characters to perform at various levels of being, thereby ushering in a complex mixture of different narratives, whose origin thus remains mysterious, indefinite and perpetually deferred because there can never be fulfilment or a movement towards a telos, where the unit of self has been subjected to the forces of solicitation.

A similar fissuring and decentering is also operative in the figures of H.C.E. and A.L.P. in *Finnegans Wake*, where their mythical dimensions have been extended in such a manner, that it defies spatial and temporal categories. Earlier, in *Ulysses* the acentrality of narrative was found in the continuous change of perspectives which made the authorial stance ambiguous. In *Finnegans Wake*, the discourse becomes so omnipotent and omnipresent that it unfixes the loci of everything. It becomes uncertain and mysterious like the "chaosmos", unable to distinguish the nature of things and persona. The narrator is positioned on the void. In fact, the discourse unites itself in a flow of signifiers, leading nowhere. It is this notion of excess which defeats any attempt to locate the originary impulse of the book.

Creative imagination, poetic freedom and the production of discourse are vitally interconnected through the notion of excess in writing. Derrida explains that:

> This universe articulates only that which is in excess of everything, the essential nothing on whose basis everything can appear and be produced within language; and the Voice of Maurice Blanchot reminds us, with the insistence of profundity, that this excess is the very possibility of writing and of literary inspiration in general. Only pure absence—not the absence of this or that, but the absence of everything in which all presence is announced—can inspire, in other words, can work, then make one work.... This emptiness as the situation of literature must be acknowledged by the critic as that which constitutes the specificity of his object, as that around which he always speaks. (Derrida 1978: 8)

It is this notion of absence or inadequacy at the heart of the process of signification that gives rise to the incessant flow of signifiers. The emptiness at the centre constantly oppresses the writer so that he is always conscious that in expressing something he is actually saying nothing. The subject being indistinct, it becomes "the consciousness of nothing, upon which all consciousness of something enriches itself, takes on meaning and shape" (Derrida 1978: 8-9). As the thought revolves on the whatness of a thing, speech is formed and on this very experience a plethora of signifiers are produced, which becomes equivalent to experiencing the subject. According to Derrida, the process of writing is not a "determined pathos" although the author feels the anguish of writing because there is non "empirical modification or state of the writer". He plays upon the Latin "angustia" meaning "narrowness or distress". Thus writing becomes the

> responsibility of angustia: the necessarily restricted passageway of speech against which all possible meanings push other, preventing each other's emergence. Preventing, but calling upon each other, provoking each too, unforeseeably and as if despite oneself, in a kind of autonomous overassemblage of meanings, a power of pure equivocality that makes the creativity of the classical god appear all too poor. (Derrida 1978: 9)

The act of writing creates and gives rise to a complex flow of signifiers and this idea of plurality of signification gives a new dimension to the authorial function, which is radically different from the classical idea of a writer expressing himself in his work. Following Leibniz, Derrida focuses upon the notion that there is only one true text, "the earth's true Bible" and therefore "the differences between individual works is simply the difference between individual interpretations of one true and established text" (Derrida 1978: 10). The multiplicity of texts does away with the uniqueness of meaning and destroys "the theological certainty of seeing every page bind itself into the unique text of the truth" (Derrida 1978: 10).

Modern criticism and aesthetics contribute to the notion of creation as being "equivocal, ontological and aesthetic" (Derrida 1978: 10). There seems to be a basic uncertainty in writing because the author is not sure whether his creation will always express "the universe, resembling and resembling it" (Derrida 1978: 10). This is because no signification can exist prior to writing. To write is to be conscious of the fact that nothing which has not been produced within literality has no existence at all. Meaning is not consequent upon a prior action of the mind but is aroused through a process of permutation and combination in an oblique manner, thus illustrating the fact that the writer does not manipulate language from without, maintaining an omniscient perspective, but rather constructs himself, and becomes in Merleau-Ponty's words, "a kind of new idiom" since his words take him by surprise and dictate his flow of thoughts (Derrida 1978: 11). In this context, Derrida also reflects Husserl's idiom in *The Origin of Geometry* where he teaches us to think that "meaning must await being said or written in order to inhabit itself, and in order to become, by differing from itself, what it is: meaning" and in this way "the literacy act thus recovers its true power at its source" (Derrida 1978: 11).

Since writing creates meaning continuously, it has an "inaugural" character, which makes it "dangerous and anguishing" (Derrida 1978: 11). The writer is at the mercy of his medium, he cannot predict the direction his discourse will take. No prior knowledge can control the act of writing "from the essential precipitation toward the meaning that it constitutes and that is, primarily, its future" (Derrida 1978: 11). There is thus no sense of continuity between time past, time present and time future because it is the momentary act of writing which matters. Moreover, the differential character of meaning as well as its equivocality necessitates a radical break with the notion of an overall design or paradigm, which in earlier literature gave writing its meaning. From this perspective writing provides the outlet "as the descent of meaning outside itself within itself; metaphor-for-others-aimed-at-others-here-and now, metaphor as the possibility of others here-and-now, metaphor as metaphysics in which Being must hide itself if the other is to appear" (Derrida 1978: 29). No meaning can proceed out of itself unless it is differential in nature.

Indeed, no meaning is imposed by any external authority and every transgression of self as well as meaning issues from the text of Joyce. Every movement of thought in the Joycean text for instance, thruts itself towards the suppression and containment of the other by logocentric authority. Such writing does not imply a culmination in itself but illustrates "a tearing of the self toward the other within a confession of infinite separation" (Derrida 1978: 75-76).

Thus, Joycean protagonists require the factor of negativity (either work or history or the traditional ethos) for its self-transgression. That is to say "simple internal consciousness could not provide itself with time and with the absolute alterity of every instant without the irruption of the totally-other, so the ego cannot engender alterity within itself without encountering the Other" (Derrida 1978: 94).

From the point of psychoanalysis, Freud has explored the "self's radical ex-centricity to itself with which man is confronted" by questioning his Otherness manifested in language (Lacan 1977: 171). Lacan in his *Ecrits: A Selection* has drawn our attention to Freud's discovery:

> Who, then, is this other to whom I am more attached than to myself, since, at the heart of my assent to my own identity it is still he who agitates me? His presence can be understood only at a second degree of otherness, which already places him in the position mediating between me and the double of myself, as it were with my counterpart. If I have said that the unconscious is the discourse of the Other (with a capital O), it is in order to indicate the beyond in which the recognition of desire is bound up with the desire for recognition. In other words, this other is the other that even my lie invokes as a guarantor of the truth in which it subsists. By which we can also see that it is with the appearance of language the dimension of truth emerges. (Lacan 1977: 172)

Lacan's formulation of the problem of identity focuses on the fissures within the self especially at the intersection where it is expressed in discourse and at the level of desire where it overflows into the Other. The mediation which is possible between "me" and the "double of myself" can only be conducted through discourse. This question of self-reflexivity in language which is at the forefront of modern literature has been noted earlier in Foucault's works. The otherness of discourse not only brings to light the hidden depths and repressions in the personality but gives credence to it by acting as the guarantor of the other which it would not have been aware of otherwise.

Derrida emphasises the otherness of Being as the fundamental of both ontology and metaphysics. The movement of the ego towards the other signals the "rupture of logos" which does not signify the inception of irrationalism but is actually "the wound or inspiration which opens speech and then makes possible every logos or every rationalism" (Derrida 1978: 98). This wound or rupture at the heart of Being is essentially creative in nature because:

> A total logos still, in order to be logos, would have to let itself be proffered toward the other beyond its own totality. If, for example, there is an ontology or a logos of comprehension of the Being (of beings), it is in that "already the comprehension of Being is said to the existent, who again arises behind the theme in which he is presented". The "saying to the other"—this relationship to the other as interlocutor, this relation with an existent—precedes all ontology; it is the ultimate relation in Being. (Derrida 1978: 98)

Post-structuralist discourse, by expatiating on the differential nature of Being explains why and how the discourse of the other creates an ontic opening signifying its non-determination. It also gives a possible explanation why both Hopkins and Joyce was against logocentrism which had so saturated Western metaphysics and aesthetics as to make itself apparent even in Eliot's modernist conception of the impersonality of the artistic process. Post-structuralist thought explains the notion of infinity as "non-determination and concrete operation" permitting the idea of the "determination between Being and ontic determination" which is to imply that the disselving of ontic closure would closely follow when the very notion of infinity would "open the question, and the ontico-ontological difference" (Derrida 1978: 150).

It is vital to understand how in modernist texts the discourse of the other creates an ontic opening, leading to the fissure of self. Especially in Joyce, the decentring of personality may be evident not only from a reading of his narratives but is also apparent in his letters, poems, and his drama *Exiles*. His letters for instance reveal an interesting psychological dilemma. It is that Joyce's passion for Nora finds its expression not in terms of classical romance where the lover idealises his mistress but in a desecration of the lady's personality in a variety of images. Although this may be explained from the point of view of a lover's desire for possession, yet in this context an alternative reading becomes necessary. Primarily, the letters illustrate Joyce's profound uncertainty and doubts about himself which he tries to neutralise by reaching out to Nora. He creates a mystique about himself by fictionalising love situations none of which conforms to the actions of a conventional lover. He had earlier confessed to his brother Stanislaus that he felt uncomfortable in the role of a lover. And yet his poems in *Chamber Music* display the tender emotions of a teenager in love. But even in his poems, Joyce as lover restrains himself from giving full liberty to his passion. It is all the more surprising to note that early in his career Joyce had concentrated on the problem of identity.

Joyce's love poems were composed during a critical moment of his life when he was overwhelmed by poverty and despair. This technique of consciously distancing oneself through fictionalising love situations as well as creating multiple images of himself in order to perplex his love in letters show Joyce's desire to escape from the limiting influence of his ego, and a deep need to confront himself, and if occasion permits to indulge, even in self-critique. This desire to liberate oneself from any preordained notions or attitudes (which might be termed conventional or traditional) which might prevent the discourse of self with its other, was implicit in Joyce. In fact, he never passed off the opportunity of parodying himself. His letters to Nora shows his central ambivalence towards himself in his refusal to accept himself as a conventional lover while at the same time assuring her of his love. This finds expression in his ambiguity as an exile when he feels alienated from his fellow countryman but at the same time he cannot repudiate his origins, which is seen in his focus on Dublin and Irish questions. Then again, his ambivalence in politics is noted in his love and hate relationship with England and the English language, while simultaneously reserving his own opinion on the fate of Parnell in Irish politics.

As his personality is threatened by the "irruption of the totally other" which makes him impossible to align himself to any single logic or viewpoint, Joyce makes creative use of doubt (Derrida 1978: 94). In *Exiles,* he subjects himself, his own desires and motivations to a searching critique on the stage through his Other, Richard Rowan. Like Stephen, Richard does not resolve his doubts and is uncertain of the centrality of his motives as well as being critical of accepting any watertight solution, which even encompasses the truth of his own self. By wounding himself, he transgresses the ontological limits of his own self and comes to question his own identity. The Joycean discourse, therefore, might be said to be neither centrifugal not centripetal but a continuous flux which is primarily "acentric", consuming in the process of writing its own fictive centrality, forcing the narrator to come to terms with his Other.

Roland Barthes in his *Theory of the Text* (1973) has drawn attention to the plurality of the subject in discourse. According to him, the text issues from the debate of the subject with the other wherein as Barthes indicates, "lies the epistemological mutation" as the subject has lost the wholeness of the Cartesian "cogito" (Young 1987: 36). This plurality of the subject, according to Barthes, has been accounted for only by psycho-analysis. In fact, as he notes in the essay, "the plural is directly at the heart of signifying practice, in the form of contradiction; signifying practices, even if it be provisionally permitted to isolate one of them, always belong to a dialectic, not to a classification" (Young 1987: 36).

Post-structuralist reading of texts focus on the loss of authorship in the infinite play of the signifier by either the scriptor or the reader. These incessant "word-plays" or invention of "ludic meanings" even if overlooked by the author are made possible "even if it was historically impossible for him to foresee them" (Young 1987: 37). In this way the 'signifier belongs to everybody' and it is indeed the text which produces meaning tirelessly, and not merely the artist or the consumer. Barthes comments on the notion of the text as "polysemic space", which is intersected by several possible meanings in the following passage:

> A fortiori, when the text is read (or written) as a mobile play of signifiers, with no possible reference to one or several fixed signifieds, it becomes necessary to distinguish carefully between signification, which belongs to the level of the product, of the statement, of communication, and the signifying work, which belongs to the level of production, enunciation, symbolisation, it is this work that we call the "significance". "Significance" is a process, in the course of which the "subject" of the text, escaping the logic of the ego-cogito and engaging other logics (that of the signifier and that of contradiction), struggles with meaning and is deconstructed ("is lost"). "Significance"—and this is what immediately distinguishes it from signification—is thus work, not the work by which the subject (intact and external) might try to master the language (for example the work of style), but that radical work (which leaves nothing intact) through which the subject explores how language works him and undoes him as soon as he stops observing it and enters it. (Young 1987: 37-38)

Post-structuralist criticism therefore describes the text as a "tissue, something woven", in which the subject like the spider "comes to dissolve itself into his own web", and is undone (Young 1987: 39). In this sense, the text not only redistributes language but also destroys the attempt to arrive at some ultimate truth. The deconstruction-reconstruction process leads to the permutation and combination of texts where they become a tissue of citations, codes, formulae, rhythmic models, cultural patterns, and becomes a field of anonymous formulae, making it impossible to trace its original authorship. This loss of authorship or the fatherhood of the text is due to the epistemological orientation of the intertext, where the entire "volume of sociality: the whole of language, anterior or contemporary, comes to the text", following the path of a "dissemination" and not the path of recognisable filiation or a purposive mimetic process (Young 1987: 39). Finally, as Young in his "Preface to Barthes" essay explains that the French term *jouissance* which in English would be "enjoyment" and which contains the connotation of pleasure in all senses of the term especially sexual climax, may be employed to illustrate "the sense of an ecstatic loss of the subject in a sexual or textual coming—a textasy" (Young 1987: 32).

Letters of James Joyce 3

A true estimate of Joyce can never remain complete merely by a perusal of his major fictions and short stories. For that, it is imperative to take into account his letters, poems, drama as well as his prose essays. The first section which deals with his correspondence gives us a clue to his real identity lying concealed behind his pose of the detached artist who, "like the God of creation, remains within or behind or beyond or above his handiwork, invisible, refined out of existence, indifferent, paring his fingernails" (*P* 215). In these letters, we find an intensity and a range of emotion, coupled with a variety of responses especially where he speaks about his love to Nora or in those where he enunciates his artist's mission amidst profound crises in life. The formative periods of an artist has been laid bare. These reveal the teething moments of his career when he verged on the brink of despair and harboured thoughts of violence. On the other hand, they remain interesting evidence of the cool, practical and calculating temperament which was to form the distinguishing feature of his art. His correspondence help us to understand the mature Joyce, who like Stephen develops his weapons of "silence, exile, and cunning" in his dealings with the world and in the process creates a mystique about himself (*P* 247).

The relevance of Joyce's correspondence in the context of his artistry has been adjudged in the following terms by Stuart Gilbert in his *Introduction* to the letters:

> In the case of James Joyce the Letters have all the more importance and interest for those who wish to arrive at the inside of things as regards a singular and sometimes

> baffling personality because in his published writing he practiced a deliberate detachment, in keeping with the conception of the artist set forth in *A Portrait*. (*Letters* I: 30)

Gilbert reminds us how for Joyce "Art became a jealous god, like the Jehovah of the Ten Commandants, and as her priest he, like Modigliani, demanded for himself special rights and privileges" (*Letters* I: 31). To this extent, we find Joyce coaxing and importuning his publishers, benefactors and friends like Miss Harriet Shaw Weaver, Mrs. Harold McCormick, Miss Sylvia Beach, Grant Richards, Ezra Pound and others. In this context, Gilbert makes an important observation:

> He claimed assistance and allegiance from his friends, publishers, agents and fellow-artists as a right, and in the majority of cases they endorsed the claim. It must not be thought, however, that Joyce was in any sense a megalomaniac or a solipsist; on the contrary, he studied the foibles of those with whom he came in contact with a sympathetic if slightly ironical eye, and thus could enter into their feelings and foresee their responses. There was little of young Stephen Dedalus, arrogant and introverted, in the Joyce I knew—the artist as a mature man. Time and again I was struck by his shrewd estimates of the reactions of others, his social tact, his diplomatic handling of prickly situations. (*Letters* I: 31)

We should guard against any facile and complacent reading of Joyce's personality from a cursory examination of his letters. For the mature artist's mind had many aspects and readers might be tempted to draw very different conclusions as to his true identity. This complexity and ambivalence lies rooted in the artist's struggle to master "the reality of experience" in his effort to "forge" in the smithy of his soul "the uncreated conscience" of his race (*P* 253). For Joyce there was a deep psychological need behind his constant stratagems and simulated poses because he often felt betrayed by his countrymen, fellow litterateurs and enemies, masking as friends as also the constant persecution which he faced in his struggle to publish his works. Often we find him consciously trying to foist upon the recipient of his letters a certain impression, carefully playing upon her responses. On other occasions, and this is quite true of most of his letters, Joyce remains aware of his mission as an artist with an unflinching refusal to compromise himself in the very depth of his privation.

His letters present an unique portrait of a strikingly original artist beset by a host of problematic issues brought on by the exigencies of his art. In his letter to Nora on 22 August 1912 he expresses his self-conscious approach: "I am one of the writers of this generation who are perhaps creating at last a conscience in the soul of his wretched race" (*Letters* I: 311). As an artist, he was on the other hand deeply in need of Nora's love and comfort and the myth of his being detached and impersonal in his private life does not ring true although he preferred to adopt such poses in public. Gilbert cautions us against such a superficial estimate:

> Those who, partly on the strength of the ideas put forward in *A Portrait* and partly on account of the aloofness of manner he affected in public and his indifference to the social problems which obsessed the younger generation, may have formed the opinion that he was heartless like the 'god of creation' to whom in his early work he likened the artist, will find in many of these letters a refutation of this view. Joyce had a heart, though he did not wear it on his sleeve, indeed I have never met anyone else with such a strong sense of the family affections like those of the Jews (vide the 'Scylla and Charybdis' episode of *Ulysses*) were "bound with loops of steel". (*Letters* I: 32)

Impersonality, besides being an artist's creed was also a deep personal need on Joyce's part. He was a man with a multifaceted personality. He constantly recreated himself in different personalities and in an infinite number of ways. He loved to hide behind his art as well as indulge in introspection. Often we find him holding silent enquiry into his inner self. Here, as elsewhere, we are ensured of his point of view as an artist.

What needs to be underlined is Joyce's urge to create and rediscover himself in different attitudes and poses. In this sense, he employed the notion of artistic detachment to his own advantage. Along with this he displays an extraordinary virtuosity of style. Stylistic variations have been used to harp on the different play of emotions and also to unearth essential moments of the subliminal self as seen especially in his letters to Nora during the period 1904-15. Joyce's employment of his affection for Nora to serve artistic purposes must also be noted. He uses his love for Nora not only to achieve a deeper realisation of his inner self but also turns his love to artistic advantage, using his understanding of the female psyche to create characters like Bertha (*Exiles*), Molly Bloom (*Ulysses*), Anna Liva Plurabelle (*Finnegans Wake*) and so on. Behind the inscrutability and ambiguity of the authorial self lies the mystique of the Joycean self.

Referring to his struggle in getting the publishers to put *Dubliners* in print he seems to be almost at the end of his tether in his confession to Nora but we find no trace of self-pity or commiseration. Even in moments of despair, he refuses to compromise. In his letter to Nora on August 23, 1912, he tells her:

> For a long time today I thought of spending the last money I have on a revolver and using it on the scoundrels who have tortured my mind with false hopes for so many years. I will say no more.... Tomorrow I must pawn my watch and chain in order to remain on a little longer. Everything seems to have melted away from me, money, hope and youth. (*Letters* II: 311)

His love for Nora is transferred to another plane when Joyce explains his relationship with his work of art. In this instance he uses the image of parturition to explain his intimacy with his art. He reminds Nora of the child which he has carried over the years in the "womb of the imagination" just as she herself has borne the burden of her children in her womb out of love. The sense of joy and success consequent upon the production of *Dubliners* has been likened to parturition and childbirth. Any discussion of the theory of artistic impersonality must, therefore, take into account the notion of artistic process which, as Stephen reminds us in *A Portrait* concerns "the phenomena of artistic conception, artistic gestation and artistic reproduction requiring a new terminology and a new personal experience" (*P* 209). The letters reveal that there is a vital interconnection between his love of art and love of life, including his passion for Nora and here all interpenetrate. The theory of artistic impersonality must be understood not as a desiccated doctrine but as a final product of Joyce's attitude and conception of love and life. In this respect Schlegel's commentary in *Prosaiche Jugendschriften* on the tales of Boccaccio in 1801 throws light on the problematic nature of artistic objectivity:

> I maintain that the novella is very well adopted to represent a subjective mood and point of view—even of the deepest and most peculiar sort—indirectly and symbolically (sinnbildich), as it were.... But by what magic do (some tales of Cervantes) agitate our inmost soul, and seize it with divine beauty, except by virtue, of the fact that everywhere the feeling of the author—even the innermost depths of his most intimate individuality—gleams through, visibly invisible; or else because, as in the Curioso Impertinente, he has expressed views which because of their very peculiarity and depth, had earlier to be expressed in this way or not at all.... Precisely that which is indirect and veiled in this mode of communication may lend it a higher charm than anything which is immediately lyrical. In a similar way the novella itself is, perhaps, particularly adopted to this indirect and secret subjectivity, because in other respects it tends very much to the objective. (quoted in Abrams 240-41)

The complex nature of artistic objectivity has been employed to its fullest advantage by Joyce. He constantly experiments with his relationship to his material and this equally reflects his portrayal of self. Joyce never shied away from either self-abasement or self-exfoliation but at the same time he was always the master craftsman controlling and playing whatever tune he wanted. In this, however, he was a born egoist. He was a very self-conscious artist even in extreme cases of acknowledging defeat especially to Nora. His letters to Nora are extremely important for the valuable light they throw on the manifold aspects of the Joycean artist. They record the depth of his love for Nora as well as the need for self-exposure to her in terms of variety of roles and postures. He was adept in his usurpation of different identities and this creative urge is manifested in his posture as a lover, thus betraying the desire for possession. There are also those letters which enunciate his sense of the artist's mission and those reflecting his attitude of an exile and a rebel.

His letter to Henrik Ibsen in March 1901 contains a hint as to the complex nature of his personality. Initially, his egoism is reflected in the nature of his praise for the dramatist. He reminds Ibsen of the fact that it was himself who wrote an appreciation of his drama *When We Dead Awaken* in *The Fortnightly* on April 1, 1900. He insists that he has proclaimed his name through the corridors of the college and has claimed for his rightful place in the history of drama by pointing out his "lofty impersonal power". This pose subtly draws attention on himself. But this is not all. Joyce affirms his kinship with Ibsen by a deeper grasp of the artist's mission. Here he unveils his own ambiguity by explaining that he is tempted to adopt a certain façade for the public whereas in the core of his heart he might be actuated by hidden motives and impulses:

> But we always keep the dearest things to ourselves. I did not tell them what bound me closest to you. I did not say how what I could discern dimly of your life was my price to see, how your battles inspired me—not the obvious material battles but those that were fought and won behind your forehead, how your willful resolution to wrest the secret from life give me heart and how in your absolute indifference to public canons of art, friends and shibboleths you walked in the light of inward heroism. (*Letters* I: 52)

Much of Joyce's admission underlines that Ibsen's impersonality was part of his technique behind which the man and the artist took shelter. The audience was belied knowledge of his deepest conflicts and of his firm belief in himself. Henceforth, Joyce was to take shelter behind his innumerable character-fictions and ironical portraiture of himself. The artist must develop firm faith in him, only then will he attain a true insight into the proper nature of his mission. These are secrets, which are to be jealously guarded.

This confidence in his own powers became the distinctive feature of Joyce's artistry, remaining till the very close of his life. Even here, we detect a note of self-exaltation as seen in his letter to Lady Gregory on November 1902:

> I am not despondent however because I know that even if I fail to make my way such failure proves very little. I shall try myself against the powers of the world. All things are inconstant except the faith of the soul, which changes all things and fills their inconstancy with light. And though I seem to have been driven out of my own country here as a misbeliever I have found no man yet with a faith like mine. (*Letters* I: 53)

A deliberate desire to set himself apart from the herd and a keen sense of exile was deeply embedded in him even before he left the shores of England for Zurich in 1904. However, a note of ambivalence is to be found in all his actions. The role of an exile is fraught with various implications. It would not be too much to say that Joyce used his keen sense of isolation to probe deep into his subliminal self and also to gain a profound insight into life. Again, Joyce was never a true exile in the true sense of the term. Unlike Beckett, he never surrendered his Irish inheritance, neither did he forgave his enemies, rather he made capital out of his most bitter experiences by satirizing them under various fictitious names. That is to say Joyce was incessantly critical about his own responses. This was later developed and worked into the texture of his drama *Exiles*.

One of the many facades that he was very fond of adopting was an impish desire to shock the public by exhibiting his antagonism to conventions. He created a flurry among his friends and Nora's relatives by eloping with her without assuring himself of a livelihood on the continent. This was characteristic of Joyce's bohemianism. He risked everything for his art. Although he had much of the gambler in him, like Jimmy in "After the Race" in *Dubliners*, he had firm faith in himself. His letter to Mrs. William Murray from Pola, Austria, on the New Year's Eve of 1904 provides an illustration:

> I shall be glad to hear from you any news you may have—that is if my lax manners have not displeased you too much. I have nothing to relate about myself except that though I am quickly disillusioned I have not been able to discover any falsehood in this nature, which had the courage to trust me. It was this night three months ago that we left the North Wall. Strange to say I have not yet left her on the street, as many wise men said I would. In conclusion—I spit upon the image of the Tenth Pius. (*Letters* I: 58)

Joyce had flexibility and business sense to ingratiate himself with his publishers but when it came to a question of artistic purpose he stuck to his guns. His dealing with Grant Richards evince a certain degree of politeness but underneath he seemed subtle enough to draw attention to his own interests. There is a slight condescending note in his reply to Richards on 20 February 1906:

> I am glad that you are pleased with *Dubliners*. As for the terms you offer me I may say that perhaps it would be best for me to put myself in your hands. I am sure that you will deal with me as generously as you can. As a matter of fact my future work in which you seem to be interested is largely dependent on an improvement of my financial state. (*Letters* I: 60)

In his next letter to Richards on April 26, 1906 he declares his reluctance to suppress or modify his story "Two Gallants" on artistic grounds even if it spelled his financial loss. He shrewdly pointed out to Richards in his letter on 20 May 1906 that any adverse criticism would be in the way of publicity:

> Moreover, from the point of view of financial success it seems to me more than probable that (sic) an attack, even a fierce and organized attack, on the book by press

> would have the effect of interesting the public in it to much better purpose than the tired chorus of imprimatures with which the critical body greets the appearance of every book which is not dangerous to faith or words. (*Letters* I: 62)

Joyce keenly felt the agonised experience consequent upon his not being a popular author. But he was never one to sacrifice anything which he thought was essential for self-expression. He felt betrayed and badly let down by his publishers and printers. This comes out well in his letter to John Quinn on 10 July 1917:

> Ten years of my life have been consumed in correspondence and litigation about my book *Dubliners*. It was rejected by 40 publishers; three times set up, and once burnt. It cost me about 3,000 francs in postage, fees, train and boat fare, for I was in correspondence with 110 newspapers, 7 solicitors, 3 societies, 40 publishers and several men of letters about it. All refused to aid me, except Mr. Ezra Pound. In the end it was published in 1914, word for word as I wrote it in 1905. (*Letters* I: 105)

On his part, Joyce was undaunted by his heroic struggle to get his works published. He never allowed his personal problems or financial worries to influence his art. Referring to his book *Dubliners* he reminds Grant Richards in his letter dated May 13, 1906 that although he would be glad if the book is printed and that he did not mind making money by it, yet he would be the last person to prostitute his talent to the general public by condescending to write according to their taste and need. He could even detachedly speak about his own discomfiture with an equanimity and a sense of humour.

During the last years of his life, that is the period of his stay in Zurich between 1939-41, he increasingly felt the disintegrating effect of his family affairs. With Lucia being schizophrenic and his son's marriage on the rocks, there might have been cause for despair. He himself had undergone seventeen eye-operations, and with the outbreak of World War II existence on the continent was rendered highly unstable. In spite of being in the midst of such crises he writes to Enmund Branchbar on 30 July 1940 from France:

> We are here, my wife and I with our son, and our grandson and following the 'events' I find myself entirely isolated, cut off from my resources in London by British authorities and from my banked resources here by the French authorities, a double blockade.
>
> If you have read my biography you have certainly laughed to read that Mr. Gorman...writes, that the astronomer of the Urania term was named...Siegmund Feilbogenl.
>
> I do not know what has happened to my flat in Paris, to my books and pictures.
>
> I hope that our 'tale of woe' is not too tiresome....' (*Letters* III: 479)

In the same letter, we find Joyce providing the rationale behind his rebellious attitude. He categorically repudiates the social framework including that of religion: "home, the recognised virtues, classes of life, and religious doctrines" (*Letters* II: 48). As for his home he bitterly recalls having to do with a mundane middle-class affair destroyed financially by spend-thrift habits which he had the misfortune to inherit. His mother's death was hastened by his father's indifference, years of affliction and his own "cynical frankness of conduct" (*Letters* II: 48). And when he gazed on her grey face ruined by cancer it seemed to him that her plight was due to the nonchalance and uncompromising nature of a social system. It led him to bring down curses on that very system. Joyce confesses:

> Six years ago I left the Catholic Church, hating it most fervently. I found it impossible for me to remain in it on account of the impulses of my nature. I made secret war upon it when I was a student and declined to accept the positions it offered me. By doing this I made myself a beggar but I retained my pride. Now I make open war upon it by what I write and say and do. I cannot enter the social order except as a vagabond...the

> actual difficulties of my life are incredible but I despise them. (*Letters* II: 48)

Joyce uses his antipathy to social norms in order to perfect his art as a weapon. He was disinclined to allow himself to be labelled in any way. Zealously hiding behind his art, he took up the posture of a parrying fencer, thrusting at his opponent. Brancusi's symbol of Joyce on the title page of *Tales Told of Shem and Shaun* aptly symbolises this aspect of his personality. The two oblique strokes on both sides of the spiral conveyed the "sens duposseur or" the feeling of thrusting, while the coiling whorls of spiral symbolise the artist's desire to recoil behind his innumerable facades and fictive roles (*Letters* III: 169 note).

Joyce loved to mislead people by fostering false notions about himself in them. In reality, his intention lay in offering a sort of challenge to the other person to guess his true identity. He attempted to envelop himself in mystery so as to enable himself to hide behind his creations like God. In his letter to Nora on 10 September 1904, he admits that the idea of him being malicious to his contemporaries was, however, a much propagated one. Stanislaus wrote to Joyce on 31 July 1905 that his friend Ellwood "admires" his satire but adds that he can hardly think him not being malicious on occasions. Often when Joyce was at the end of his endurance he was likely to explode as he once did in his letter to Stanislaus on September 24, 1905:

> For the love of the Lord Christ my curse—O'-God state of affairs. Give me for Christ's sake a pen and an ink-bottle and some peace of mind and then, by the crucified Jaysus, if I don't sharpen that little pen and dip it into fermented ink and write tiny little sentences about the people who betrayed me and send me to hell. After all, there are many ways of betraying people. It was not only the Galilean suffered that. (*Letters* II: 110)

But above everything he was as he himself admitted, "an artist by temperament".

Joyce uses his love for Nora to gain deeper insight into himself. His letter to her on September 2, 1909 shows the artist in a variety of poses, commanding, berating, questing, doubting; touched by jealously and containing shades of masochism:

> Nora, my 'true love', you must really take me in hand. Why have you allowed me to get into this state? Will you, dearest, take me as I am with my sins and follies and shelter me from misery. If you do not I feel my life will go to pieces. To night I have an idea madder than usual. I feel I would like to be flogged by you, I would like to see your eyes blazing with anger. (*Letters* II: 243)

It is through his love for Nora that he became conscious of his greatness and conversely of his own weakness. His egoism was the source of his pride and joy through which others usually saw him. But his honesty and frankness to himself was reserved solely in his intimacy with Nora. Rather than idealise his love like other writers and confer encomiums on his mistress, Joyce has a tendency to degrade Nora's image in the flesh. This is his originality in love which permits a look into his true self. Thus, he says: "I gave others my pride and joy. To you I give my sin, my folly, my weakness and sadness" (*Letters* II: 243). For in Joyce's idiom both the sacred and the profane in love were at par with each other.

Joyce's deep intimacy with Nora comes alive in:

> Her soul: Her name: Her eyes: They seem to me like strange beautiful blue wild-flowers growing in some tangled, rain-drenched hedge. And I have felt her soul tremble beside mine, and have spoken her name softly to the night, and have wept to see the beauty of the world, passing like a dream behind her eyes. (*Letters* II: 267)

The images used by Joyce are quite akin to those employed in his poems which confirm his adherence to Imagism at one point of his career. The tendency towards concretisation and the use of tactile images strongly attest to Joyce's dislike of abstractions. These images culminate in an epiphanic moment, when the poet seems to have caught the essence of Nora's beauty and is again used to describe Bertha in the drama called *Exiles*.

Joyce needs to traverse through an entire gamut of passion to make himself sure of his possession. And in this Joyce was more interested in the light it threw on his own personality. In his letter to her on September 7, 1909 we find an exfoliation of the Joycean self:

> Now, my darling Nora, I want you to read over and over all I have written to you. Some of it is ugly, obscene and bestial, some of it is pure and holy and spiritual: all of it is myself and I think you see now what I feel towards you. (*Letters* II: 249)

The artist's search for true love has led him on to a rediscovery of his true self, which is to say that he becomes conscious of his multi-dimensionality. The possibility of manifold emotions and attitudes within himself precludes any simplistic reduction of the authorial self.

Joyce's letter to Nora on September 5, 1909 posits the connective tissue between love and art. His profound need to love and be loved is part of the artist's penchant to come to terms with his subliminal self. Love and art interpenetrate each other in Joyce's recurrent employment of the image of parturition:

> *Everything* that is noble and exalted and deep and true and moving in what I write comes, I believe, from you. O take me into your soul of souls and then I will become indeed the poet of my race. I feel this, Nora, as I write it. My body soon will penetrate into yours, O that my soul could too! O that I could nestle in your womb like a child born of your flesh and blood, be fed by your blood, sleep in the warm secret gloom of your body. (*Letters* II: 248)

The love which the mother feels for its child may be compared with love which the artist nourishes for his creation.

Joyce also illustrates his desire for possession in his letter to Nora on August 22, 1909. This sense of possession precludes any dissolution of self:

> I see you in a hundred poses, grotesque, shameful, virginal, languorous. Give yourself to me, dearest, all, all when we meet all that is holy, hidden from others, you must give to me freely. I wish to be lord of your body and soul. (*Letters* II: 239)

Any suffering can open up the understanding to a deeper notion of the hidden self. For that even jealousy is welcome for it will give expression to the dormant springs of violence in his nature. Such violence is creative in terms of inspiration because it will bring about a fusion in love. Joyce writes:

> My jealousy is still smouldering in my heart. Your love for me must be fierce and violent to make me forget *utterly*. (*Letters* II: 239)

Joyce explains this theme of interpretation in love by using the image of the opal which he says is qualitatively different from that of the pearl.

The above images clarify in Imagist terms the fusion of art and life. Two types of beauty are described here. First there is the beauty of art divorced from life. This is the stage of Joyce the artist as he was composing *Chamber Music*, when his mind is likened to the "pale, passionless beauty of a pearl". The second stage is that of the mature artist whose mind is like an opal, full of mesmeric hues and colours. The mystery and radiance of life breaks upon Joyce as he becomes absorbed in the uniqueness of a love experience. His love for Nora opens up deeper avalanches of feeling and emotion through which he is able to perceive the beauty of love and life. Joyce's later art is a testimony of jealousy which threatened to take him towards despair as he confesses in the above letter to Nora:

> One cruelty at least I have not been guilty of. I have not killed the warm impulsive life-giving love of your rich nature. (*Letters* II: 237)

It is true that he needed Nora's love to enable him to fight his battles against Ireland. But he also wanted her to side with him in his enmity against all sorts of conversions and systems which bespoke of hypocrisy and dissimulation. In his letter to her on October 27, 1909, he expresses his antipathy to the Irish:

> I loathe Ireland and the Irish.... A few days before I left Trieste I was walking with you in the Station...a priest passed us and I said to you "Do you not find a kind of repulsion or disgust at the sight of one of those men?" You answered a little shortly and dryly. "No, I don't."

> You see, I remember all these small things. Your reply hurt me and silenced me. It and other similar things you have said to me linger a long time in my mind. Are you with me, Nora, or are you secretly against me? (*Letters* II: 255)

Joyce once had misgivings about her fidelity. Earlier in his letter to her in August 6, 1909 he suspected her of infidelity owing to Cosgrave's scandalous suggestion that she was having an affair with him during her courtship with Joyce. Although Cosgrave's imputation was false and he was to follow it with a letter of remorse and supplication on August 7, 1909, the entire period of Joyce's jealousy as a lover gives rise to a number of suggestions. In public, he maintained an air of nonchalance and alertness, but he had a keen sensitivity which bordered on paranoia and was liable to be overwhelmed emotionally. For instance, he was not a man who forgave his enemies.

He also had an ingrained sense of possessiveness, which brooked no rival where his loved object was concerned. Along with this, he had an air of confidence and a sense of self-exaltation which made him think very early in his career that he was destined for fame and success. Joyce was aware of the conflicting forces within himself and he developed the pose of detachment to gain better control over himself. He subtly distances himself from Stephen Dedalus and Richard Rowan (*Exiles*), as instances of self-projection, where he is dealing with his point of view as an artist.

As an exile and a rebel he wanted Nora to be always beside him. Intellectually, she was not his equal and Joyce constantly berates her as he does in his letter to her on 27 October 1909:

> I am a little disappointed in you. Then another night I came home to your bedroom from the café and I began to tell you of all I hoped to do, and to write, in the future and of those boundless ambitions which are really the leading forces in my life. You would not listen to me. It was very late I know and of course you were tired out after the day. But a man whose brain is on fire with hope and trust in himself *must* tell someone of what he feels. Whom should I tell but you?... In spite of these things

> which blacken my mind against you I think of you always at your best.... (*Letters* II: 256)

The quest for a total involvement through love is part of Joyce's deeper need to possess and be possessed. His art on the other hand portrays characters like Stephen Dedalus and Richard Rowan, whose attitude to love is complex and marks a sense of detachment and which is in turn critical of the possessive instinct.

Art and life interpenetrate each other in Joyce's brief affair with Martha Fleishmann in Zurich in 1918-19. It is rather epistolary in nature since he hardly met her save having occasional glimpses of her on the streets or from his flat. Professor Heinrich Straumann, who questioned her on her relationship with Joyce and finally brought his correspondence from her, has thrown an important light on the nature of this affair. During his conversation with Martha, Prof. Straumann

> came to the conclusion that with the exception of one point the episode had meant much less to her than to James Joyce, and that she remembered little of the few meetings she had with the poet. The beginning of their acquaintance however, was significant enough. According to her account she first met him in the autumn of the year 1918. Joyce and his family was then living at Universitatsstrasse and she at Culmannstrasse not much more than a stone's throw from each other. One evening at dusk when she was about to enter her house, Joyce happened to pass by the door. He stopped abruptly and looked at her with an expression of such wonder in his face that she hesitated for just a moment before entering the house. Joyce then apologised in German and said that she very strongly reminded him of a girl he once had seen standing on the beach in his home country. (*Letters* II: 428)

Here the relevance of Chapter IV of the *Portrait* where Stephen has an epiphany of the girl on the beach is too striking to be overlooked. It is all the more so when we remember Prof. Straumann's note that Martha confessed total ignorance of *Portrait* since she did not understand English. Along with this we should also bear in mind a postcard sent to Martha by Joyce which contained greetings sent to Nausikaa by Odysseus and in which there was "no proper signature of James Joyce" (*Letters* II: 428).

Unfortunately, the letter was lost. Hence, Prof. Straumann's testimony is crucial to an understanding of Joyce's motives in this affair. He comments:

> There is a Martha in *Ulysses*, and it is significant that she is both the recipient and the sender of letters. Connected with her are references to the opera. *Martha* and its famous theme, "Come, thou lost one". Even more striking is the use of the Greek in both the letters Joyce wrote and in the one sent by Bloom to Martha. Beyond that however I do not venture to establish a direct connection. After all, Joyce had also addressed Martha as "Nausikaa", and yet it would be difficult to find any similarity between her and Gerty Macdowell. (*Letters* II: 431)

Joyce in this case was engaged in his quest for finding a proper correlative for the image of the lady celebrated in *Chamber Music*. His dedication of a copy of volume of poems duly signed in his name to Martha is itself a pointer in this direction. In many ways, she embodied in flesh the delicate beauty and upbringing which Joyce spoke of in his poems and in connection with the virgin in *Portrait*. His letter to Nora on 21 August 1909 contains a description of the ideal woman: "she was perhaps (as I saw her in my imagination) a girl fashioned into a curious grave beauty by the culture of generations before her, the woman, for whom I wrote poems like 'Gentle Lady' or 'thou leavest to the shell of night'" (*Letters* II: 237).

The affair was largely a product of Joyce's imagination and an enactment of another of his innumerable poses. Something of this kind may be found in Joyce's self-conscious attitude. He confesses to being 35 years of age and adds that Shakespeare "conceived his dolorous passion for the dark lady" and Dante "entered the night of his being" at a similar age. In this letter to her in December 1918, he reveals his vagueness of approach:

> I do not know what I want.
>
> I would like to talk to you.
>
> I imagine a misty evening to myself, I am waiting—and I see you coming towards me dressed in black, young, strange, and gentle. I look into your eyes, and my eyes tell you that I am a poor seeker in this world, that I understand nothing of my destiny, nor of the destinies of others, that I have lived and sinned and created, and that one day I shall leave, having understood nothing in the darkness which gave birth to both of us. Perhaps you understand the mystery of your body when you look at myself in the mirror, where the wild light in your eyes comes from the colour of your hair? (*Letters* II: 433)

Sometimes he even indulges in hyperbole as for instance in his letters to her on 9 December 1918, where he writes: "It seemed that the sole ray of light which in all these last years has pierced the darkness of my life had been put out. I was even out of my mind" (*Letters* II: 435). The very attempt at an actualisation of a fictive representation has an effect of blurring the contours of art and life. In this case, his fondness for the eternal and strange beauty of a woman may be thought of as an affair conducted not merely in the imagination but as being extended into real life, Nora representing the other violent aspect of passion while Martha symbolises the sophistication and refinement consequent upon an idealised portraiture.

Richard Ellmann in his *James Joyce* has discussed Joyce's brief flirtation and correspondence with Martha Fleischmann in Zurich in 1918 to 1919:

> In *Ulysses* Martha Fleishmann is one of the prototypes of the limping Gerty Mac Dowell whom Bloom ogles from a distance, and in part the prototype of Bloom's Penpal Martha Clifford, to whom, as Joyce emphasises, Bloom is always careful to write with Greekre's. (Ellmann 463)

Actually Phillip F. Herring in his essay on "Lotuseaters" points out that in Joyce's work feminine identities coalesce into each other, producing a polyphony of voices, "but the most interesting ones have their basis in Nora" (Hart and Hayman 78).

Finally, no account of Joyce can be complete without a consideration of Frank Budgen's unique portrait of him during his stay at Zurich. G. Stuart comments in his *Introduction*:

> These letters throw light on an aspect of Joyce's personality that rarely comes to view elsewhere and might be called his "Bloom personality". Indeed their Rabelaisian verve tends to show that Joyce was emotionally affected by his material and entered into the lives of the characters who filled his thoughts during the Zurich period: not only Bloom but "the Citizen", "Skin-the-goat", "the unnamed narrator of the Cyclops episode and that, to my mind, singularly attractive old spendthrift Simon Dedalus". This is a far cry from the god like detachment of the artist recognised by the young aesthete of *A Portrait*. (*Letters* I: 37)

Budgen notes that from the time of his meeting with Joyce to the period of the completion of the Cyclops episode, Europe became the scenario of great events. Following the Ludendorf offensive the allies had taken the initiative upon themselves to direct their assault against the Germans. Repercussions were felt on the continent but Joyce seemed supremely indifferent to the turn of tide in the realm of politics and even on one occasion asked Budgen as to who had won the war (Budgen 171). Meeting often at their rendezvous at the Pfauen on the Spanish wine-shops of Niederdorf, Budgen was fond of following Joyce's thinking as he struggled on with the composition of *Ulysses*.

Joyce was often in tireless pursuit of "the solution to some problem of Homeric correspondence or technical expression or trait of character in Bloom or in another personage of *Ulysses*; or some physiological fact was necessary to give him the key to some part of his epic of the human body" (Budgen 175). "There was no end to the variety of material that went to its building", as Budgen recollects:

> I have seen him collect in the space of a few hours the oddest assortment of material: a parody on the "House that Jack Built", the name and action of a poison, the method of caning boys on training ships, the wobbly

> cessation of a tired unfinished sentence, the nervous trick of a convive turning his glass in inward-turning circles, a Swiss music-hall joke turning on a pun in Swiss dialect, a description of the Fitzsimmons shift. (176)

He attempted to extract from his words their own essence and life. Budgen remembers how he used to hear Joyce reciting fragments of *Anna Livia Plurabelle*, which seemed to be typical of his voice and method. "The lower pitch of his speaking voice is darkly metallic, and he slows down the tempo of the verse to the last reasonable degree of extract from each syllable its full essence of sound" (182).

Joyce spent eight years writing *Ulysses*. For half of this period Europe was engaged in war and apart from the tension prevalent, everything seemed to be subjected to the forces of flux and instability. But he had a mind with "an extraordinary toughness of fibre and tenacity of purpose, but neither toughness nor tenacity would have helped him if he had not possessed the faculty of shutting out at will all noises in the street, if he had not been able not to be unduly distressed about what he could not utter" (Budgen 196). But when he was "in impish moods" he was like the magpie, "gloating gravely with bright eyes over the efforts of clumsy humans to find the hidden orange-peel" (Budgen 193).

Joyce's creation "Dooleysprudence" (1916) expresses in a different view "the point of view of the badgered yet optimistic individualist living through war, revolution and commercial depression" (Budgen 206). In this comic fragment the artist is referred to as the common man as in *Ulysses*:

> Who is the funny fellow who declines to go to church
>
> Since pope and priest and parson left the poor man in lurch
>
> And taught their flocks the only way to save all human souls
>
> Was piercing human bodies through with dumdum bullet holes?
>
> It's Mr. Dooley,

Mr. Dooley,
The Mildest man our country ever knew.
'Who will release us
From Jingo Jesus'
Prays Mr. Dooley-ooley-ooley-oo. (*Critical Writings* 246-47)

Budgen's account, therefore, gives us an insight into Joyce's Bloomisms. Stephen Dedalus, being a "self-portrait" was bound to be "one-sided" whereas Bloom "is seen from all angles, as no self-portrait can be seen. He is as plastic as Stephen is pictorial" (Budgen 60). Bloom has been drawn with an "infinite number of contours" and from all conceivable angles (Budgen 65-66). Moreover, as Budgen argues:

> The multiplicity of technical devices in *Ulysses* is proof that Joyce subscribed to no limiting aesthetic creed, and proof also that he was willing to use any available instrument that might serve his purpose. It was hardly likely that, having denied all religious dogma, and having carefully avoided all political doctrine, he would submit to artistic limitations. There are hints of all practices in *Ulysses*—cubism, futurism, simultanism, dadaism and the rest—and this is the clearest proof that he was attached to none of the schools that followed them. (Budgen 198)

Barbara Reich Gluck in her illuminating study, *Beckett and Joyce* investigates the problematic issue of the author's relationship with his fictions in these two avant-garde writers who came together in 1930s. She opines that although Joyce lives up to his reputation as the detached artist, almost resembling God in *Portrait*, this is not singularly "true of his own relationship to his works. On the contrary, Joyce is everywhere in his books always writing about himself, his family, his country. Joyce used both character and plot for self-expression" (Gluck 117). In this context, she quotes John Grass's comment:

> His books derive their power from the intensity of his obsessions and the energy with which he tried to master

> them. They are acts of concealment and exposure, of revenge and reconciliation, of self-purgation and self-definition. (Gluck 117)

Just as *Dubliners* presents "a series of possible selves" of the author, Bloom embodies some aspects of his multi-dimensionality. This self-revelation and self-expression continues till we come to *Finnegans Wake*, where the author and his creations merge and become identical (Gluck 117). In this respect Gluck makes an important distinction between Joyce and Beckett:

> Beckett the author also merges with his fictions; however, there is an important difference. Joyce is capable of distancing himself through irony from even such an autobiographical character as Stephen. Beckett, on the other hand, seems always to be losing identity in that of his characters, and, indeed, as author, *despairs* of ever being able to decisively separate himself from them. (Gluck 117)

This is to say that Beckett was moving away from his master to develop his own distinctive style and perspective.

In spite of his self-expression and revelation in his works, therefore, Joyce was able to develop a technique of distancing himself from his own fictions. Joycean ambiguity becomes inexplicable as he is alternately present "within or behind or beyond or above his hand work", all-encompassing but remaining, "invisible" and inscrutable as God (*P* 216). The term "de-centred self" aptly describes this desire for concealment, irony and role-playing in Joyce. In passing, we may note S. Gilbert's affectionate recollection of one of Joyce's many poses in public. Often he was likely to display during the innumerable tea parties given by Nora:

> Stephen Dedalus' mannerisms and *fin de siēcle* 'weariness' in public. (*Letters* I: 35)

And this was noted by Nora with delicate irony and indulgence.

Poems of James Joyce

4

In his later life, Joyce was once attempting to explain to Louis Gillet the problems of the autobiographical novelist. He said, "When your work and life make one, when they are interwoven in the same fabric..." (Ellmann 154) and then hesitated as if overcome by the strenuous efforts demanded by the writer's profession. Joyce was performing two tasks simultaneously here; he was going through a difficult period of his life and also he was attempting to transubstantiate the raw materials of his life into fiction. This was, as Ellmann notes, during the year 1904 when Joyce was going through the teething period of a writer full of misgivings and uncertainties (Ellmann 154). This same year also witnessed his completion of the first draft of *Stephen Hero* which was later to be published posthumously (as a revised version) in 1944. "A certain degree of detachment" was necessary to put the events of his life in their proper perspective as he was sure to use it for the purposes of his novel (Ellmann 154). It is curious to note that "on the struggling discoloured thread of his jobless days and dissipated nights he strung his verses" since his poetry does not reflect his crisis at all (Ellmann 155). As Joyce confessed later to Herbet Gorman: "I wrote *Chamber Music* as a protest against myself." (155).

Joyce's statement gives us a key to the puzzling nature of his self. If the dates of 1902/04, during which the Pola and the Paris notebook were written are to provide any indication, it was in this period that Joyce formed his own ideas of impersonality in art including his interest in Thomist esthetic. It is quite natural, therefore, for us to suppose that his poems would reflect his preoccupation with theories of artistic detachment. His poems reveal a nascent artist's concern with the beauty and joy in life in an art-form which is at the same time musical, perfect as regards execution and instinct with concrete image-patterns. Indeed they were so far divorced from his actual state of mind and temperament that we find Joyce suddenly having misgivings over them even after having corrected the page proofs of *Chamber Music* at Rome. He informed Stanislaus one evening that he would soon cable Matthews not to publish the book. His brother of course successfully dissuaded him but it is Joyce's confession which forms an important document, illustrative of his attitude to art:

> James said: "All that kind of thing is false." He was no love 'poet'; he had never known any love except the love of God. He did not wish to stand behind his own insincerity and fakery. It was true that some of the 'poems' had introduced an ironic note into the 'feudal terminology' so as to make them modern, but this was not keen or sustained enough; essentially the poems were for lovers, and "he was no lover". (Ellmann 270)

Joyce's expostulations against his sentiments of a lover must have been expressed in 1907, the year in which *Chamber Music* was published. The date of publication and his confession give rise to a number of conjectures. Joyce's love-relationship with Nora began around 1904 and it is quite evident from his letters that he considered his love-making an art in itself. As a lover he is alternately sardonic, ironic, passionate, importunate, lyrical, melancholy, fetishistic and so on. So what he means to say is that his inspiration with regard to *Chamber Music* has been primarily literary, untouched by crisis of emotion. Thomas Kettle in his review in *Freeman's Journal* on 1 June 1907 touched upon similar aspects of the poem:

> There is but one theme behind the music, a love, gracious, and, in its way, strangely intense, but fashioned by temperamental and literary moulds, too strict to permit it to pass over into the great tumult of passion. The inspiration of the book is almost entirely literary. There is no trace of the folklore, folk dialect, or even the

> national feeling that have coloured the work of practically every writer in contemporary Ireland. Neither is there any sense of that modern point of view which consumes all life in the language of problems. It is clear, delicate, distinguished playing with harps, with wood birds, with Paul Verlaine. (*CH* I: 37)

What Kettle overlooks in his criticism of *Chamber Music* is that modern sensibility and especially modern poetry was undergoing a subtle change during the period 1908-14. T.E. Hulme's "A Lecture on Modern Poetry" was composed for delivery in 1908 or 1909, and revised in 1914. His "Notes on Language and Style" belong, according to Sam Hynes to the same period (*Further Speculations* Introduction: XVIII). Also of note is the year 1908 when "Pound arrived in London; Ford began to edit the *English Review*; and T.E. Hulme joined the short-lived Poets' club" (Levenson, Preface: vii).

If Joyce's poems are placed against the context of the Imagist movement in poetry which began around 1908/09, then a clear picture begins to emerge. It is that Joyce with all his precariousness had scored an important landmark with his formulation of esthetic theory in 1902/04 because it helped him to usher in a theory of formal excellence in the arts, which was about to sweep Europe and other countries during the first decades of the twentieth century. Joyce's esthetic was not merely a personal necessity but also part of his literary creed, which was used to define anew the artist's personality. For artistic subjectivity was being subjected to a process of redefinition in the continental arts; a movement which tended towards increased economy of expression and greater control over form. *Chamber Music* was unique in both aspects. It revealed an aspect of Joyce which would never be seen in his novels and prose where he uses his inscrutability as a mask to conceal himself. Secondly, it reflected the shift in sensibility, which was sweeping Europe in the form of Imagism.

None other than a symbolist like Arthur Symons has indicated the underlying excellence of *Chamber Music* in his review on 22 June 1907 in *The Nation* (1, 639). He selects two poems (XXVII and XXVIII) for discussion and comment. Pointing to the verses beginning with "Gentle lady, do not sing", Symons comments: "no one who has not tried can realise how difficult it is to do such tiny, evanescent things as that; for it is to evoke, not only roses in mid-winter, but the very dew on the roses" (*Critical Heritage* I: 38). The theme of the passing of love is of the very commonplace. Yet the music plays on the emotions with a subdued note until the final line which imitates the exhaustion, a tiredness descending through the ages in language which subtly enacts as it were the feeling of eyelids, heavy with sleep. The beginning of the poem introduces the subject almost casually:

> Gentle lady, do not sing
> Sad songs about the end of life;
> Lay aside sadness and sing
> How love that passes is enough.
> Sing about the long deep sleep
> Of lovers that are dead and how
> In the grave all over shall sleep:
> Love is a weary now. (*PJJ*, 643-44)

There is no individualism of emotions, that is to say, the emotions expressed in abstraction escape localisation. But the warmth and sadness is present. This playing down of passion in its bare essentials is made possible by the stringent economy of expression.

Joyce varies his mode of expression as seen in his poem (XXVII) beginning with "Though I thy Mithridates were". He modifies his lyricism with prose touches. In the first stanza, the entire poem comes alive in the poet's subtle evocation of the uncertain and mysterious nature of love. The enigma of love is expressed in:

> Yet must thou fold me unaware
> To know the rapture of thy heart,
> And I but render and confess
> The malice of thy tenderness. (*PJJ* 643)

The fatal attraction has been underlined but then the poet absolves himself of the power of describing this love by mere convention:

> For elegant and antique phrase
>   Dearest my lips wax all too wise;
> Not have I known a love whose praise
>   Our piping poets solemnise....

He, of course, does not fail to end with a rejoinder

> Neither a love where may not be
> Ever so little falsity. (*PJJ* 643)

Joyce's subtle critique of the sentiment of love has been noted by Symons. "Sometimes we are reminded of Elizabethan, more often of Jacobean, lyrics; there is more than sweetness, there is now and then the sharp prose touch, as in Rochester, which gives a kind of malice to sentiment" (*Critical Heritage* I: 38).

In his letter to Nora on 21 August 1909 Joyce explains to her how he was inspired by an imaginative ideal:

> When I wrote them I was a strange, lovely boy, walking about by myself at night and thinking that some day a girl would love me. But I never could speak to the girls I used to meet at houses. Their false manners checked me at once. Then you come to me. You were not in a sense the girl for whom I had dreamed and written the verses you find so enchanting. She was perhaps (as I saw her in my imagination) a girl fashioned into a curious grave beauty by the culture of generations before her, the woman for whom I wrote poems like 'Gentle lady' or "Thou leanest to the shell of night." (*Letters* II: 237)

The refinement and lyrical tone recalls the courtly grace of the Elizabethan sonneteers and of Crashaw, Thompson and Lionel Johnson. Poem XXVI for instance, which begins with the startling image of the beloved leaning against the "shell of night" listening to the "mad tale" of her lover at an unearthly hour, has an insubstantial theme. Yet, as Symons points out, Joyce has excelled himself in making poetry of a "rare kind" out "of the kind of unkind insinuations of lovers" who might not always be under the state of rapture, even when the mood comes for singing, and may, like this love-poet, be turned to a new harmony... (*Critical Heritage* 39). In the poem, the clarity of the image projects the concern of the beloved in unmistakable terms.

Joyce had a flair for bringing out the unique properties of his subject in a concrete image. The laments of the lover in poem under XXIX are shown to be overwhelmed by the beauty of the lady which is itself a form of self-surrender, a pregnant phrase at the close of stanza one aptly summarises his defeat:

Dear heart, why will you use me so?
  Dear eyes that gently me upbraid,
Still are you beautiful—but O,
  Now is your beauty raimented!

(*PJJ* 644)

The poet can underscore the tenderness of lover's kiss by an off-hand comparison with the summer wind in 'O', it was out by Donnycarney (No. XXXI):

Along with us the summer wind
  Went murmuring—O, happily:—
But softer than the breath of summer
  Was the kiss she gave to me. (*PJJ* 645)

Even the rhythm of kisses can crystallise the happiness of lovers as in poem No. XXIII:

This heart that flutters near my heart
  My hope and all my riches is,
Unhappy when we draw apart
  And happy between kiss and kiss;
My hope and all my riches—yes:—
  And all my happiness. (*PJJ* 641)

The very action of combing the hair can go a long way towards suggesting sexual attraction. The poem (XXIV) beginning with "Silently she's combing/ Combing her long hair" exploits this image throughout but Joyce as always drops a dark note of misgiving in the lover's mind. The poem ends with the uncertainties of love:

I pray you, cease to comb out,
  Comb out your long hair,
For I have heard of witchery
  Under a pretty air.
That makes as one thing to the lover
  Staying and going hence,
All fair, with many a pretty air
  And many a negligence. (*PJJ* 641-42)

The above was probably composed on April 8, 1904. Two other lyrics, namely, "What counsel has the hooded moon" (No. XII) and "Lightly come or lightly go" (No. XXI) belong to this period (Ellmann 155). These two poems:

> were written after an excursion with Mary Sheehy, Francis Skeffington, and others into the Dublin hills. Joyce, swaggering a little in his yachting cap and canvas shoes and sporting an ashplant, spent most of his time watching Mary.... He did not give himself away now or at any other time, but they exchanged a few words on the way back from the hills. Mary, gazing at the moon, thought it looked tearful, while Joyce, with mild daring, contended that it was 'like the chubby hooded face of some jolly fat capuchin'. 'I think you are very wicked', said Mary, and he replied, 'No, but I do my best. (Ellmann 155)

The point of the anecdotes is that Joyce loved to wrap himself in ambiguities by coming up with (*PJJ* 629) unexpected attitudes and comic poses. His detachment, all the while tacitly acknowledging Mary's beauty speaks volumes for itself, and so, in his poems, especially in these two lyrics, personal reference has been pruned to the point of abstraction. Only the comic image of the "hooded moon" likened to the "comedian Capuchin" lives on in our minds, while the vehemence of passion seems to be absent in:

...mine, O mine!
No more be tears in moon or mist
For thee, sweet sentimentalist. (*PJJ* 635)

"Lightly come or lightly go" is characteristic of the poet since it is based on antimonies. "Love and laughter" which is "song-confessed" has been placed in a sad context, by being occasioned only "when the heart is heaviest" (*PJJ* 642).

Most of the poems in the collection owe their beauty to the presentation of a particular motif. The entire poem builds up to a climax through the centrality of the image. The simple idea of a lover playing love songs from theme of "Strings in the earth and air" (No. 1) but the poem gains its concentration in the second stanza with the image of the lover with "Pale followers on his mantle" and "Dark leaves on his hair" (*PJJ* 629). The focus of the next poem is on the image of the amethyst turning deeper shades of blue while "The lamp fills with a pale green glow/ The trees of the avenue" and all the time we note that the occasion is very slight and tenuous, namely that of the falling of evening. The third poem in the collection has for its theme the break of dawn but its beauty depends on the pregnant image of love opening "the pale gates of sunrise" with its connotations of the surfeit of love (*PJJ* 630).

The entire beauty of the lyric, "Lean out of the window" (No. 5) is dependent on the image of the "golden hair". The ballad-like repetition of the central image arrests the beauty of the girl merely by emphasising the golden colour of her hair. In a different vein, the comparison of the sky with "a pale blue cup" gives to the poem "My love is in a light attire" (No. VII) a serenity and tenderness which could not be there otherwise. The very fragility and delicate beauty of a cup is juxtaposed with the lady skipping lightly along the grass, holding her dress in her "dainty hand". The blue colour of the sky has a spiritual intensity and depth which suggests the suavity of Crashaw. In "Bid adieu, adieu, adieu" (No. XI) the action of the girl in softly unzoning her bosom in the arms of the beloved has an undercurrent of sexuality. The poem, however, attains its beauty in the image of the "snood" lying on her "yellow hair" and in the final lines the girl is visualised as quietly undoing the "snood" which "is the sign of maidenhood" (*PJJ* 635).

Joyce can make a very simple poem like "O Sweetheart, hear you/ Your lover's tale come alive by exploiting the potentialities of an image". The lines "His hand is under/ Her smooth round breast" not only has sexual connotations but actually enacts the possession of the lady by her lover. The lover's touch conflates the rotundity of her curves along with a gentle assurance of mutual faith in a world where friends are found to be untrue. The lovers encircled by the great canopy of the pine-forest in "In the dark pine-wood/ I would we lay" (No. XX) is another beautiful lyric. The vitality of the poem lies in the word "enaisled" that epitomises the lovemaking of the lovers. The term "enaisled" has a smaller microcosmic parallel in the beloved being enveloped by the soft, tumultuous fall of hair.

If assessed in terms of Joyce's achievement, contemporary reviews sometimes praised the obvious or were depreciatory in tone, but mostly they missed the mark and failed to perceive and isolate the terms of his genius. They praise the "artless, but full of subtly gained effects" in these lyrics, along with Joyce's deliberate manipulation of "the shifting stress, the naively lengthened line, the half-rhyme". In the same review, the critic disparages Joyce's imagist stance:

> and beyond that fact, which is indicative in itself, there are many other indications within the thirty-four lyrics that he is not essentially a poet. There is little of the dreamer in them, nothing of the enthusiast. They make their fragile points by turns of evanescent thought, or rhetoric thrice defined. If we may judge his personality by the zest and spontaneity of his plays and novels it is fair to say that he was in verse a shadow of himself and others, a dilettante playing a safe and pleasant game. (*CH* I: 43-44)

Even Symons missed the mark in his critique of *Chamber Music*:

> If poetry is a thing to be overheard, these songs, certainly, will justify the definition. They are so slight, as a drawing of Whistler is slight that their entire beauty will not be discovered by those who go to poetry for anything but its perfume.... There is only just enough life in them to come into existence, but these instants are, in Browning's phrase, "made eternity". (*CH* I: 39)

Due recognition of Joyce's merit had to wait until the publication of Pound's article in *The Future* (London) II May 1918: 6. During the winter of 1913 Ezra Pound was with Yeats in Sussex and had almost completed his anthology of Imagist poetry. At this point Yeats reminded him of a poem of Joyce, "I Hear an Army Charging upon the Land" and Pound wrote to Joyce, asking his permission to include it in his collection. Thus, began Joyce's relationship with Pound. During 1914 and 1920 there was a constant stream of correspondence between London and Trieste, London and Zurich. In his essay in 1918 Pound was the first to lay the critical premise for a proper evaluation of his poems within the Joyce canon. He indicated that just as Joyce's novels and prose revealed a certain aspect of his personality, his poetry was instrumental in disclosing the other aspect of his temperament. Both poems and novels must be taken together in a proper estimation of Joyce as an artist. His critical statement deserves to be quoted in full:

> The book is an excellent antidote for those who find Mr. Joyce's prose "disagreeable" and who at once fly (a la Mr. Wells, for example) to conclusions about Mr. Joyce's "cloacal obsessions", etc. I have yet to find in Joyce's published works a violent or malodorous phrase which does not justify itself not only by its verity, but by its heightening of some opposite effect, by the poignancy which it imparts to some emotion or to some thwarted desire for beauty. Disgust with the sordid is but another expression of a sensitiveness to the finer thing. There is no perception of beauty without a corresponding disgust. If the price for such artists as James Joyce is exceeding heavy, it is the artist himself who pays.

> If Armageddon has taught us anything it should have taught us to abominate the half-truth, and the tellers of the half-truth, in literature. (Pound/Joyce 139)

Pound's critique of Joyce give us valuable insight into Joyce's art by pointing out that he always saw objects and emotions in their totality. He did not shirk from the presentation of the dark side of things and if he did portray the profanation of sentiment, it did not imply that he was interested in a biased portrayal of things. The joy and happiness of life as revealed in his worship of colour, sound, perfume in his poetry, trembling to points of ecstasy shows that Joyce had something positive to say about life. This vitality in his portrayal of life was later to be seen in *Portrait* and in *Ulysses.* No study of Joyce can, therefore, be complete without an account of his poems. *Pomes Penyeach* and the later poems display a maturity and a deepening vision of life which only comes with a consciousness of the artist's mission.

What makes the reading of *Chamber Music* an unique experience is its "clean-cut ivory finish" and "the cross run of the beat and the word, as of a staff wind cutting the rippletops of bright water" (Pound/Joyce 137). Even though "the wording is Elizabethan" and the metre sometimes suggests Herrick but Pound admits: "in no case have I been able to find a poem which is not in some way Joyce's own, even though he would seem, and that most markedly, to shun apparent originality" (Pound/Joyce 137). Joyce's originality stems from a personal way of looking at things. The succession of images in *Chamber Music* gain their solidity from moments of visionary experience in the poet. They anticipate Joyce's epiphanic mode of vision in their ability to posit the uniqueness of each thing in their own context.

Surprisingly, Hulme's "A Lecture on Modern Poetry" and his "Notes on Language and Style", which were composed around 1908/09 clarify to some extent Joyce's concern with language and rhythm in poetry. From an Imagist point of view Hulme argues in his lecture that modern poetry "has become definitely and finally introspective and deals with expression and communication of momentary phases in the poet's mind", whereas "old poetry dealt essentially with big things, the expression of epic subjects leads naturally to the anatomical matter and regular verse" (*Further Speculations* 72). For the poet "all emotion depends on real solid vision or sound. It is physical" (*Further Speculations* 78).

Hulme stresses the concreteness of imagery in his "Notes on Language and Style". He states that "each *word* must be an image *seen*, not a counter", and as to style he directs that "with perfect style, the solid leather for reading, each sentence should be a lump, a piece of clay, a vision seen, rather, a wall touched with soft fingers" (*Further Speculations* 79). Hulme not only argues for the uniqueness of poetic experience crystallised into something concrete; the solidity of an image but also that style and music of poem should provide the orientation and mark the drift of thought. Dispensing with the erstwhile metric system, he thinks that "modern conception of poetic spirit" entails a much more relaxed rhythm to give free play to thought and "this tentative and half-shy manner of looking at this, into regular metre is like putting a child into armour" (*Further Speculations* 73).

Apart from bringing before his readers the cold, hard lineaments of the image, Joyce had a keen sense of music and his poems reveal his mastery in handling rhythmical expression. The sense of rhythm directs our attention to the image and does not negatively betray a desire for embellishment. Most of the motifs of *Chamber Music* are set to music. Joyce was fond of referring to his lyrics as "book of songs" in his letters. In his letter to Stanislaus in March 1907, he writes that "some of them are pretty enough to be put to music" (*Letters* II: 219). Joyce was quite delighted when G. Molyneux Palmer set five of the lyrics to music. The poem "O, it was out by Donnycarney" (No. XXXI) was published, with Adolph Mann's setting in Cincinnati by John Church on January 19, 1910. In his letter to Mann on June 24, 1910 Joyce appreciates the setting and adds that he would also like the poem "Lean out of the window" (No. V) set to music in the "same vein" (*Letters* II: 287).

Some of the lyrics in *Chamber Music* deserved Pound's special attention for their rhythmic excellence. Selecting "Who goes amid the green wood" (No. VIII) for its delicate artistry, he comments:

> Here, as in nearly every poem, the motif is so slight that the poem scarcely exists until one thinks of it as set to music; and the workmanship is so delicate that out of twenty readers scarce one will notice its fineness. Would that Henry Liawes were alive again to make the suitable music, for the cadence is here worthy of his cunning.... (Pound/Joyce 137)

But Pound lavishes praise especially on the last two poems in the collection. These "emotional poems", that is, "all day I hear the noise of waters" and "I hear an army charging upon the land" are "quite different in tonality and in rhythm-quality from the lyrics in the first part of the book" (Pound/Joyce 138). Noting Joyce's lengthening of the line in the third and fifth lines of "All day I hear", Pound advises that these "should not be read with an end stop. I think the rush of the words will escape the notice of scarcely any one" (Pound/Joyce 138). The poem reaches a crescendo at the end of the first stanza:

> All day I hear the noise of waters
>   making moan,
> Sad as the sea-bird is, when going
>   Forth alone,
> He hears the wind cry to the waters
>   Monotone. (*PJJ* 647)

The hypnotic spell of the penultimate work "monotone" brings before the mind the desolation, the loneliness and the monotony of the movement of waters, thus focusing on their eternal and changeless beauty.

The last poem in the collection has been praised by both Yeats and Pound. In his letter to Edmund Gosse on July 8, 1915 Yeats tells him:

> Joyce had written a book of verse *Chamber Music* and a most remarkable book of stories called *Dubliners* which I thought of for our Academic Committee prize. I would be inclined however to base his claim on a most lovely

> poem in Katherine Tynan Hinkson's Irish Anthology, *The Wild Harp*. It is to the end of that book. (*Letters* II: 351)

Apart from the technical perfection of the poem "I hear an army" its excellence depends on a "phantom vision" and (in Pound's terms) "to a robustezza of expression" (Pound/Joyce 138). The vision of a host of warriors charging through the land has a vitality perceived phantasmally by the poet in the midst of his dream:

> They cry unto the night their battle-name
> I moan in sleep when I hear after their whirling laughter;
> They cleave the gloom of dreams, a blinding flame,
> Clanging, clanging upon the heart as upon an anvil.
> (*PJJ* 642)

The "flame", the sound of "laughter" climaxes in the sound of the iron clanging on the "anvil". Its effect on the mind has been presented in a violent physical image.

> They come shaking in triumph their long green hair;
> They come out of the sea and run shouting by the shore.... (*PJJ* 643)

By its suggestion of virility and malevolence, the image offsets the conclusion of the poem, which is set against the loneliness and fragile marooning of the lover by the beloved:

> My heart, have you no wisdom thus to despair?
> My love, my love, my love, why have you left me alone.
> (*PJJ* 643)

Pound comments:

> There are then two things to distinguish, first the particular faculty of mind to see things as they really are, and apart from the conventional ways in which you have been trained to see them.... Second, the concentrated state of mind, the grip over oneself which is necessary in the actual expression of what one sees. To prevent one falling into the conventional curves of ingrained technique, to hold on through infinite detail and trouble to the exact curve you want.

The point is that the poet can convey a precise esthetic emotion only when he focuses on the exact term. It is by means of the concreteness of the image that the artist is able to arrest the mind and produce the condition of stasis which is necessary for the apprehension of art. Joyce's *Paris Notebook* written on 13 February 1903 describes his esthetic theory and which is instrumental in helping us to understand his quest for the apposite word and the precise emotion in his poetry. Art, according to Joyce must not arouse feelings of "desire" since it produces unrest, the mind constantly moving towards the object of possession. On the other hand, the feeling of joy ushers in a sensation of fulfilment and leaves no scope for distraction. This point of rest is provided by the image. "For desire urges from rest that we may possess something but joy holds us in rest so long as we possess something" (*Critical Writings* 144). Through the state of rest the reader is able to establish a relationship with the image. This is only plausible if Joyce is objective in his portrayal of beauty. The anonymous reviewer in *New Republic* has remarked that "A mere disembodied third person, aloof, detached, is the author of Chamber Music" (*Critical Heritage* I: 45). In his *Paris Notebook*, Joyce explains: "it will be seen afterwards how this rest is necessary for the apprehension of the beautiful—the end of all art, tragic or comic—for this rest is the only condition under which the images, which are to excite in us terror or pity or joy, can be properly presented to us and properly seen by us" (*Critical Writings* 144-45).

Pomes Penyeach, a collection of 13 poems published by Sylvia Beach in the summer of 1927 belongs to the period when Joyce was preoccupied by *Finnegans Wake*. Nearly a quarter of a century separates the publication of these poems from *Chamber Music* but the time gap is rather illusory since Joyce had been busy composing some of these poems and publishing them in the intervening years. The difference between the early and late poems lie in the absence of the lyrical effusion and freshness of imagery which were noted earlier. In contrast, the late lyrics are more complex, more sensitive, and poignant, and there might be instances where the personal element makes itself apparent. Irene Hendry remarks:

> *Poems Penyeach*, while their subject-matter is similarly circumscribed, show a greater individuality and a greater subtlety in their rhythms; one can find here and there a suggestion of the Joyce of unforgettable prose. In such poems, particularly, as "On the Beach at Fontana", and "A Flower Given to My Daughter", there is the same simplicity and dignity of feeling that places the stories of the *Dubliners* collection beside the best of Chekhov and Thomas Mann. (*CW* II: 651)

The continuity between the early and late poems are definitely to be found in the poet's search for exactitude and concrete imagery, along with his use of rhythm and variation of music. "Tilly", for instance, was written after his mother's death. A couple of days following her decease Joyce found a packet of love letters from his father to his mother and when Stanislaus asked for his reaction, he replied "Nothing". Ellmann notes that Joyce had changed from "son to literary critic". He records Joyce telling Stanislaus that "when the Bard writes he intellectualizes himself". Joyce later spoke of her mother's secrets in *Ulysses* but for the time being he composed a poem "Tilly" (1903), which was not published until later. He describes the cattle being driven along a lonely road under the winter sun above Cabra by a man with a "flowering branch" in his hand. The last stanza or the poem, however, suddenly rushes to a crescendo of feeling:

> Boor, bond of the herd,
> Tonight stretch full by the fire!
> I bleed by the black stream
> For my torn bough! (*PJJ* 649)

The next poem, "Watching the Needleboats at San Sabba" (September 7, 1913) mourns the past vivacity of youth.

> This poem was conceived as he watched Stanislaus, who preferred to take part in sports, in a race of needleboats (racing shells) at San Sabba, near Trieste, as the scullers pulled towards the shore began to sing an aria from Puccini's La Fanciulla del West. (Ellmann 358)

The beauty of poem depends on Joyce's variation of the refrain which gives a doleful and sad impression. The end of the first stanza with "No more, return no more!" is balanced by the final refrain "Return, no more return", thus ushering a note of finality (*PJJ* 649-50).

"The poems which Joyce composed between 1912 and 1916 reflect his relationship with Signorina Popper. It was she who gave Lucia a flower, as he noted in the *Giacomo Joyce* notebook: 'A flower given by her to my daughter. Frail gift, frail giver, frail blue-veined child'" (Ellmann 356). This was transubstantiated in verse as:

> Frail the white rose and frail are
> Her hands that gave
> Whose soul is sere and paler
> Than time's wan wave.
> Rosefrail and fair—yet frailest
> A wonder wild
> In gentle eyes thou veilest
> My blueveined child. (*PJJ* 650)

The delicate appeal of the poem lies in its Swinburnian echoes and archaic phrasing of "sere" and the "wan wave". The impression of frail beauty is stressed in the last line where the epithet "blueveined" continues the suggestion of pale colours of the "white rose" of the first line. "Nightpiece" (1915) is composed against the dream image of Signorina Popper standing beside him at Notre-Dame in Paris:

> In the raw veiled spring morning faint occurs float of morning Paris: aniseed, damp sawdust, not dough of broad: and as I cross the Pout Saint Michel the steel blue waking waters child my heart.... Tawny gloom in the vast gargoyled church. It is cold as on that morning.... The voice of the unseen reader rises.... She stands beside me, pale and chill, clothed with the shadows of the sindark nave, her thin elbow at my arm. Her flesh recalls the thrill of that raw mist-veiled morning, hurrying torches, and eyes. Her soul is sorrowful, trembles and

would weep. Weep not for me O daughter of Jerusalem. (Ellmann 357)

In the poem "Nightpiece" the personal reference to Signorina Popper has been deleted, while the image of the worshippers praying in the gloom has been intensified by a select use of epithets like "Night's sindark nave", "starknell tolls" and the incense surging upward, the depth and solidity of the gloom is evoked by a comparison of the darkness of night's "nave". The climax of the poem, however, depends on the implicit connection between the "sindark nave" of night and the suggestion of Lucifer and the fallen angels in the second stanza. The image of the Seraphim is brilliant in its intensity:

Seraphim
The lost hosts awaken
To service till
In moonless gloom each lapses muted, dim,
Raised when she has and shaken
Her thurible. (*PJJ* 653)

Another poem, which bewails the passing of his youthful days, is "Tutto é Sciolto" (13 July 1914). The title, which means "all in unloosed" has a touch of sadness about it. The lyrical tone is slight, bemoaning "the clear young eyes" soft look, the "candid brow" and the "fragrant hair" but a poignancy is achieved by the reproving tone in the last stanza:

Why then, remembering those sky
Sweet lures, repine
When the dear love she yielded with a sigh
Was all but thine? (*PJJ* 651)

In these poems Joyce shows his mastery in singling out the proper image which reflects the tragic awareness that beauty fades with the passing of time. "She weeps Over Rahoon" softly portrays the falling rain over Rahoon whose voice is heard, calling softly and sadly to his lady at "grey moonrise". The poet sums up the mood in a significant image in the last stanza:

Dark too over hearts, O love, shall lie and cold
As his sad heart has lain

Under the mongrey nettles, the black mould
And muttering rain. (*PJJ* 651)

A similar melancholy is felt in the embrace of lovers in "On the Beach at Fontana". Whereas the first stanza focuses on the wind groaning and whining among the shingles while "A senile sea numbers each single/ Slimesilvered stone", the last stanza revolves around the comfort and warmth of the lovers in each others' arms:

Around us, fear descending
Darkness of fear above
And in my heart how deep wounding
Ache of love! (*PJJ* 652)

The unmistakable sombre note is found in the sense of brooding darkness and fear. Even when the poet is about to languish on the colourful image of the vine, "Goldbrown upon the stated flood" in *Flood*, he finds no permanent symbol of happiness in the "waste of waters" which "ruthlessly/ Sways and uplifts its weedy mane". It can only express uncertainty of life:

Uplift and sway, O golden vine,
Your clustered fruits to love's full flood,
Lambent and vast ruthless as is thine
Incertitude! (*PJJ* 653)

Irene Hendry in her article (1938) notes:

> "Tilly", "Nightpiece", and "A memory of the Players in a Mirror at Midnight" are Sensitive tapestry patterns, worked with the precision in the choice of the exact word that is one of the characteristics of Joyce's meticulous craftsmanship and that is probably responsible for the metamorphosis of Molly Bloom's vernacular into the strange dream-language of *Work in Progress*. "A Memory of the Players in a Mirror at Midnight" is the most graphic with sharp, flesh-and-blood imagery and a dramatic blending of realism and symbolism....
>
> There is music in these poems—music and depth of feeling and a perfection of phrasing.... But they are

> ephemeral, comprising only the mood of the moment and rooted only in a limited personal emotion. (*Critical Heritage* II: 651)

These poems reflect a change of mood but the poet's technical dexterity remains the same. The anguish in the late poems is, however, undeniable. In a small poem "Alone" (1916) written at Zurich the romance of the night shines effulgent as "the moon's greygolden meshes make/ All night a veil" whole "The shorelamps in the sleeping lake/ Laburnum tendrils trail" (*PJJ* 654). But the mesmerism of the moon is never complete without the assurance of the beloved's name which the "sly reeds whisper to the night" and to the poet: "all my soul is a delight/ A swoon of shame" (*PJJ* 654).

The mood intensifies in the crude and brutal picture of lust in "A Memory of the Players in a Mirror at Midnight" where the lovers are whipped by the "nude greed of the flesh". The breath of the lovers are found to be "as sour as cat's breath" and as "Harsh of tongue" (*PJJ* 654). The poet reminds the lovers that nobody who possesses a refinement will care to choose her what you see to mouth upon:

> Dire anger holds his hour,
> Pluck forth your heart, saltblood, a fruit of tears,
> Pluck and devour. (*PJJ* 655)

The poet is incomparable in portraying the impatient greed of the turgid flesh by epithets "itch and qualing", "sour", "stark skin and bone" and "saltblood", finally terminated by a cannibalistic plucking and devouring.

The Bahnhofstrasses is a small poem lamenting the fleeting years and of "highhearted youth" that comes not again. The slight mocking tone is evident. Finally, a *Prayer* shows an urgency in its insistent and anguished desire for the possession of a much-needed love:

Again:

> Come, give, yield all your strength to me!
> From far a low word breathes on the breaking brain
> Its cruel calm, submission's misery,

Gentling her awe as to a soul predestined,
Cease, silent love: My doom:
Blind me with your dark nearness, O have mercy,
beloved enemy of my will:
I dare not withstand the cold touch that I dread.

(*PJJ* 655)

The poet grovels pityingly before his lady, entreating her not to leave him and claims to be soothed by her touch:

Come! I yield. Bend deeper upon me: I am here.
Subduer, do not leave me: Only joy, only anguish,
Take me, save me, soothe me, O spare me!

(*PJJ* 656)

Shades of masochism is here apparent in the poet's willing submission to the lady. Both this poem and the "Villanelle of the Temptress" in the *Portrait*:

> ambiguously entertain the idea of supplication addressed to a woman who is both temptation and doom. Joyce, in many ways so controlled, relished the notion of being overcome. (Ellmann 86)

George Russell finds *Pomes Penyeach* informed by a "greater psychological than poetic interest" though he admits that he would be "the last to deny the charm and precise beauty of some of the lyrics in *Pomes Penyeach*" (*Critical Heritage* I: 349). In his review (1927) Russell states that the poem "She Weeps Over Rahoon" has

> a psychological interest suggesting that somewhere in the realist a submerged sentimentalist was sighing and that also in other lyrics there are traces of this submerged mentality. The strongest poems are those in which he is further from the old mood, poems like "A Memory of the Players" or "A Player", in which he seems to have deserted "his old ideal of a carved", exquisite beauty and to have expressed a personal feeling or experience with passion and intensity. (*CW* I: 349)

What Joyce was attempting in *Pomes Penyeach* was far more difficult than what he had earlier tried in *Chamber Music*. He has made an effort to strike a balance between his search for formal excellence and his poignant emotion. It is his consciousness that he has set out on a difficult task is what gives these later poems much of their maturity. In his poems, passionate favour does not transcend the lineaments of the artistic form. Wilson praises Joyce's achievement in *Pomes Penyeach*:

> a success in this field, where the short lyric, with something of the completeness of epigram, must border on the vagueness of music and carry some poignant feeling, always has somewhat the air of a miracle. Only the Shelleys and the Yeatses can do it—and they not often. In these thirteen poems, Joyce has outgrown the limitation of his early masters and caused the influences to contribute to a kind of lyric unmistakably original and with far more colour and complexity than the songs in *Chamber Music*. (*CH* 351)

Joyce's multidimensional nature is, therefore, found in his violence, his self-surrender, his tenderness, his pathos and love of laughter and life, above all in his impishness, which made him want to hide the real man within him. Sometimes we perceive the agony of the artist torn between two conflicting emotions and Joyce's life was an incessant reminder of the struggle he had to go through in order to satisfy the demands of his art.

"Gas from a Burner" (1922) was composed while he was on the train between Flushing and Salzburg. The speaker is George Roberts, the manager of the Dublin firm, Maunsel and Company and Falconer. Joyce had been to Dublin with the hope of solving the issue with Roberts who had refused the publication of *Dubliners*. In the poem, the publisher is supposed to be speaking of an imaginary audience. After subjecting *Dubliners* to an intense scrutiny, he discovers the writer's "foul intent" and becomes inwardly troubled. Speaking of Ireland, Roberts states that the country found pleasure in banishing writers and artists and even cites the betrayal of Parnell by his disciples as an instance of Irish humour. Ireland is dominated by the intrigues of both the English King and the Pope. Paradoxically, Roberts is made to portray the degradation of Ireland even in the midst of his praise. Using both invective and slang, he ends the poem with the image of Maunsel doing penance:

> This very next lent I will unbare
> My penitent buttocks to the air
> And sobbing beside my printing press
> My awful sin I will confess. (*CW* 245)

It may be noted that the poems Joyce exploits the human anatomy as part of his satiric intent. Commenting on *The Holly Office* Ellmann notes: "This splendid attack, in which the scatology only enhances the pride, was a foretaste of vengeance; the main attack would come in his novel and stories" (208). In his letter to Stanislaus about 24 September 1905 Joyce venomously declared to his brother:

> For the love of the Lord Christ change my curse-O'-God state of affairs. Give me for Christ' sake a pen and an ink—bottle and some peace of mind and then, by the crucified Jaysus, if I don't sharpen that little pen and lip it into fermented ink and write tiny little sentences about the people who betrayed me send me to hell. After all, there are many ways of betraying people. It wasn't only the Galilean suffered that. (*Letters* II: 110)

This shows that Joyce often regarded his art as a weapon. His contemporaries were sometimes scared of him, and although he was twice invited to Ireland by W.B. Yeats in connection with the Tailteann Games and the occasion of the foundation of the Irish Academy of Letters, he preferred to decline them.

At the very inception of our discussion, we had noted how Joyce wrote *Chamber Music* in the form of a "protest" against himself and his troublesome state of affairs. We have also noted his evolution as an Imagist in both this volume and in *Pomes Penyeach*. In all these, we have been struck by his quest for the opposite word, which could arrest and highlight the precise temper of an esthetic emotion. Finally, we come across two virulent lampoons which satirise his contemporaries, defining his status as an artist, who is portrayed as one constantly betrayed by friends, detractors and publishers. This enmity which he developed was nourished right till the end of his life and was to find its way in his novels and stories. As Joyce always liked to think of himself as an exile this anchored his sense of detachment from contemporary politics and the tide of nationalism in Ireland. Yet the emotional aspect of his nature is revealed in his poems although, as has been stressed, he effects a fine balance between his feelings and art. This of course is due to his control over the materials of his art and it is this, which prevents the man in him from being too assertive. The uniqueness of Joyce lies in this fine tension between the man and the artist.

Critical Essays

5

> The criticism of writers like Henry James or Thomas Mann attracts us mainly because of what they reveal about other writers. Joyce's criticism is important because of what it reveals about Joyce. All writers are egocentric by necessity, but Joyce is more so than most. These writings are best understood as part of the dramatised autobiography which he spent his life in piecing perfectly together. (Mason and Ellmann *CW*: 12)

Mason and Ellmann in their introduction to Joyce's *Critical Writings* have put their finger on the pulse of Joyce's criticism. Joyce's critique of other writers and artists are less interesting from the point of view of literary criticism than from what they reveal about his own person and his art. He himself disliked the appellation of a critic. Through his reviews and criticism he formulated his theories of arts and promulgated the person of the artist-hero by justifying his role in ideological context, praising their agency in the bringing about of a new era of thought and culture. Joyce made his own impressions the base of his criticism in the arts. In this sense, when we go through Joyce's criticism of Ibsen or Shaw or Yeats, we are more concerned with the evolution of his aesthetic theories than a comparative evaluation of their literary merits.

Mason and Ellmann also score another significant point of interest by drawing our attention to the fact that Joyce

> ...did not depreciate the critical faculty; on the contrary, he widened the borders of his novels to make them include criticism. *A Portrait of the Artist as a Young Man* contains an aesthetic system, *Ulysses* contains a

> new and elaborate theory of Shakespeare's life and works in one chapter, and in another a group of parodies—themselves a form of criticism—of English prose styles; *Finnegans Wake* continues the parodies, and brings them up to date with examples from Yeats, Synge, Eliot, Wyndham Lewis and others. (*CW* Introduction: 9)

Of course, it is true that some of his essays foreshadow his preoccupations with subjects of a similar kind in later years. His essays on "Aesthetics" in the Paris and Pola notebooks (1903/1904) are later developed into a mature form by Stephen in *Portrait* (1916). His essay "Shakespeare Explained" (1903) shows Joyce's interest in the dramatist, which was to be taken up later in *Ulysses* (1922). He was a prolific writer of reviews but most of them were written very early in his career. Joyce was only fourteen when he wrote his first essay "Trust not Appearances" (1896) and reached fifty-five when he wrote his last essay "Communication de M. James Joyce sur le Droit Moral des Ecrivains" (1937). However, most of his reviews and essays were composed during 1903, 1907 and the period of 1910-12:

> After 1912 Joyce resisted Ezra Pound's efforts to persuade him to turn a quick penny by writing literary articles. He excused himself on the ground that he had no subjects, but he had probably discovered that his criticism was effective only when it had some powerful instigation from his experience. He wrote no more articles, but he occasionally expressed his critical opinions. (*CW* Introduction: 11)

The first few essays are tentative and exploratory in nature. Nevertheless, the sudden twists of ideas and change of style shows, although in embryonic pose, the penetration of the author. At Belvedere College Joyce's proficiency in composing the weekly essay was widely recognised (*CW* 15). He "received national recognition by winning, in 1897 and 1898, the prize for the best English composition in his grade in the Intermediate Examination" (*CW* 15). His first essay "Trust not Appearances" (1896?) was written when he was only 14 and is the only example of his weekly assignments which have survived. It harps on the common theme of how appearances can often prove to be deceptive. It begins with the sudden changes of mood in nature and emphasises the treachery of man in "The cringing, servile look; the high and haughty mien" which often "conceal the worthlessness of the character" (*CW* 15). Thus, the "hypocrite is the worst kind of villain yet under the appearance of virtue he conceals the worst of voices. The friend who is but the fane of fortune, fawns and grovels at the feet of wealth" (*CW* 16). In later life the truth of this proverb was to be felt by Joyce in the long history of betrayal by friends and enemies so that he came to develop through Stephen the weapons of "silence, exile, and cunning" (*P* 247). He also became reluctant to bare himself in public, adopting Dedalus's isolated posture, which was not only an artistic equivalence but also an innate wish for nonchalance.

Joyce's next essay, "Force" (1898) was written when he was pursuing his matriculation course at University College, Dublin. The paradox that force ought to be employed to bring about a reign of kindness and love is the focus of the essay. There are forms and varieties of subjugation, all with the aid of force either for malevolent or beneficial purposes, proving that force is not in itself evil but may be corruptible due to impure motives. This intention on the part of the author to go behind a particular object or situation to perceive it from all sorts of angles becomes a Joycean characteristic. The revelation of the multidimensional character of human existence, personality and objects in nature issues from Joyce's profound study of human life and the universe. The essence of this revelation lies in the microcosmic parallel of the artist who, like God expresses himself in a thousand ways and means, underlining his infinite malleability of self, the roots of which lie embedded in experience. This is why Joyce, unlike Blake did not kill "the dragon of experience and natural wisdom" (*CW* 22). And yet he, very much like Blake reveals "an innate sense of form of a coordinating force of the intellect in his principal essays and reviews" (*CW* 221).

His essay on "Force" for instance illustrates Joyce's control over his material and his ability to expand his subject by underlining its relevance in natural, political and artistic spheres. The ploughman tilling the ground, the gardener pruning his hedges and wild vines, the sailor mastering the squalls of wind and using it to his own advantage, the miller's wheel utilizing water for domestic purposes—all these illustrate the merits of using force to one's own advantage. Thus, the White man lords it over the Negroes and Red Indians, proclaiming himself conqueror. But the most remarkable use of force is seen when a writer struggles with his own imagination to give expression to his own sense of beauty. Often he is overwhelmed by a "too prolific imagination", which sweeps his away, landing him "in regions of loveliness unutterable" and thereby beyond the grasp of his senses, defying speech and expression till everything resembles a vision (*CW* 21). Such is the case with Shelley.

> When however the gift—great and wonderful—of a poetic sense, in sight and speech and feeling, has been subdued by vigilance and care and has been prevented from running to extremes, the true and superior spirit, penetrates more watchfully into sublime and noble places, treading them with greater fear and greater wonder and greater reverence, and in humbleness looks up into the dim regions, now full of light, and interprets, without mysticism, for men the great things that are hidden from their eyes, in the leaves of the trees and in the flowers, to console them, to add to their worship, and to elevate their awe. This result proceeds from the subjugation of a great gift, and indeed it is so in all our possession. (*CW* 21-22)

In this way, the subtle balance between expression and feeling, between form and content becomes the essence of all true art, painting, scripture and music without which everything will be steeped in chaos. The artist like God holds a balance between chaos and cosmos because he learns to develop an impartiality towards all created things in nature and also with respect to his own passions. Herein lies the importance of force. Early in his career, therefore, Joyce was well on his way towards forming his own idea of the detached artist. He felt that artistic control was an important requisite for the expression of the multifarious personality within him. This is only possible through experience. Hence, Joyce came to nourish a deep antipathy for everything, which seemed to be touched with mysticism or had anything to do with idealism. In 1899, however, the tone of his essays change suddenly:

> ...the young man finds a subject, and the subject is drama. He is so full of his discovery that he can talk of little else. He finds drama in a painting of the Crucifixion, he writes an article on Ibsen's *When We Dead Awaken*, and he brings together his ideas and enthusiasm in a culminating pronouncement, his paper on "Drama and Life". (*CW* Introduction: 9)

Joyce's essay "Royal Hibernian Academy Ecce Homo" was written a year after the essay on "force" on June 1899 when he enrolled himself at University College, Dublin. In this essay, we find Joyce eager to adumbrate his own artistic standpoint:

> While his remarks on painting and sculpture sound naïve, his conception of drama does not. It liberates him and enables him to approach the subject of a religious painting from a purely aesthetic point of view. The separation anticipates his irreverent later development of Thomistic ideas to suit his literacy purposes, Munkacsy has succeeded as dramatist because he has treated Christ as a human being. (*CW* 31)

That is to say, the painter's grasp of "the sense of life" is unique in itself (*CW* 32). "Ecce Homo" has the potentialities of drama for that very reason. It portrays "instantaneous passion" and hence it is dramatic (*CW* 32-33). The scene shows the denunciation of Christ by the mob while Pilate looks on. Underneath the two main figures of Christ and Pilate are displayed the moods and expressions of the populace through various facial expressions and gestures. Even patterns of dress and shapes of arms, the actions of the Jewish rabble are all portrayed faithfully. The amazed expression of the rabbi. The "self-possessed contempt" of the soldiers who "look on Christ as an exhibition and the rabble as a pack of unkennelled animals" (*CW* 35). Pilate is portrayed with distinction but this distinction is evident in the feverish expression of his eyes.

From all this it appears that the entire scene is pregnant with drama:

> waiting but the touch of the wizard wand to break out into reality, life and conflict...it is a frightfully real presentment of all the baser passions of humanity, in both sexes, in every gradation, raised and lashed into a demoniac carnival. So far praise must be given, but it is plain through all this, that the aspect of the artist is human, intensely, powerfully human. (*CW* 35)

Munkacsy's supreme merit is that he has probed under the skin of humanity. He has found Pilate to be self-seeking, Mary maternal and motherly, the weeping woman remorseful, while the conflict within John is portrayed in no uncertain terms (*CW* 35). He has shorn his picture of all religious connotations, scaling down the cosmic to human terms. Munkacsy does not portray Mary as a Madonna or John as the evangelist. Even with regard to Christ the painter is careful not to emphasise his divinity and his super-human qualities. But this is not the painter's defect. Since his "view of the event is humanistic", it has rendered his portrayal of Christ's denunciation as pure "drama" (*CW* 36). Joyce comments:

> It is this treatment of the theme that has led me to appraise it as a drama. It is grand, noble, tragic but it makes the founder of Christianity, no more than a great social and religious reformer, a personality of mingled majesty and power, a protagonist of a world-drama. (*CW* 37)

In "Ecce Homo" Joyce's purpose is to show how Munkacsy remains in control over his material, never yielding to any impulse of passion. The very fact of his dealing with Christ's denunciation shows that he has taken up a volatile subject. But his manner of presentation is enough to proclaim his impartiality. Just as a dramatist detachedly portrays both good and evil, as well as the opposite ends of a spectrum, similarly Munkacsy has been successful in dramatising through his painting the variegated emotions of different characters. This totality is productive of a subtle balance between the form and matter in his painting. It is also due to the fact that the painter has tried to depict fully the paradox within humanity itself.

Joyce's paper on "Drama and Life" was delivered before the Literary and Historical Society at University College, Dublin, on January 20, 1900. It contained "one of his most important artistic pronouncements" (*CW* 38). He explores the "vital" relationship between drama and life in the Attic and Shakespearean Theatre. He finds Greek drama to be restricted by conventions. Not only is it true that "its rise dominated its form" but that "the conditions of the Attic stage suggested a syllabus of greenroom properties and cautions to authors, which in after ages were foolishly set up as the canons of dramatic art, in all lands" (*CW* 39). Joyce opines that "Greek drama is played out" and its revival is more of a "pedagogic significance" than a dramatic one (*CW* 39). A reaction ensued on the Elizabethan stage when the "Shakespearean clique" dealt a "deathblow to the already dying drama" (*CW* 39). This was possible because the Shakespearean drama "arose out of a movement in literature" and Shakespeare himself was a "literary artist" blessed with "humour, eloquence, a gift of seraphic music, theatrical instincts" (*CW* 39). The difference between literature and drama lies in the fact that the former reflects the uncertain fashions and mannerisms of an age, limited by time whereas the latter concern itself with the fundamentals of human emotions as it embodies the permanent and unchanging laws in every society. Literature is bound to reflect the evolution of human beings as they change in each period. Drama according to Joyce concerns itself with:

> The interplay of passion to portray truth, drama is strife, evolution, movement in whatever way unfolded; it exists, before it takes form, independently; it is conditioned but not controlled by its scene. However subdued the tone of passions may be, however ordered the action or commonplace the diction, if a play or a work of music or a picture presents the everlasting hopes, desires, and

> hates of us, or deals with a symbolic presentment of our widely related nature, albeit a phase of that nature, then it is drama. (*CW* 41)

In this essay, Joyce categorises literature as a low form of art compared to drama. It is circumscribed by conventions. But in the case of drama the very wish for something new or a change of taste is fatal to its spirit. "Drama is essentially a communal art and of widespread domain. The drama—its fittest vehicle almost presupposes an audience, drawn from all classes" (*CW* 42). Moreover it "transcends criticism" since it reflects the total human situation. Ibsen's *The Wild Duck* reveals a profound personal sorrow. On the other hand every other form of art focuses upon the personality of the author, "mannerism of touch, local sense" and the fashions of time (*CW* 42). But on the stage itself, every dramatist "foregoes his very self and stands a mediator in awful truth before the veiled face of God" (*CW* 42).

In this entire essay, Joyce is preoccupied with the theme of objectivity in art. The artist must never be swayed by passions, nor must he surrender his freedom by attaching himself to the conventional artistic practice of his time. Yet he must record faithfully the primal human emotions and present the conflict of passions. Joyce calls drama a mass-based art. In this, it is never obligated to religion or politics, which are no more than passing aberrations:

> I believe that drama arises spontaneously out of life and is coeval with it. Every age has made its own myths and it is these that early drama finds an outlet. The author of Parsifal has recognised this and hence his work is solid as a rock. When the mythus passes over the borderline and invades the temple of worship, the possibilities of its drama have lessened considerably. Even then it struggles back to its rightful place, much to the discomfort of the stodgy congregation. (*CW* 43)

Any effort to subdue the essence of drama, to any "special ethical claims" in the form of instruction or elevation of the mind destroys its pristine appeal. Even when it is elevated to serve religious purposes it is likely to sink in the mire of a "stagnant quietism" (*CW* 43). But a further peril for the dramatist lies in the temptation of pure form:

> A yet more insidious claim is the claim for beauty. As conceived by the claimants beauty is as often anaemic spirituality as hardy animalism. Then, chiefly because beauty is to men an arbitrary quality and often lies no deeper than form, to pin drama to dealing with it, would be hazardous. Beauty is the swerga of the aesthete, but truth has a more ascertainable and more real dominion. Art is true to itself when it deals with truth. Should such an untoward event as a universal reformation take place on earth, truth would be the very threshold of the house beautiful. (*CW* 43-44)

This essay is an important landmark in the Joycean canon because it promulgates very early in his career his theory of art and its close relation to truth by which he does not imply the Aristotelian concept of "mimesis". By truth Joyce refers to the eternal laws and the fundamentals of life in all ages. His thesis on drama affirms its close proximity with life, and any mistaken adherence to any religious, moral and aesthetic or idealising tendencies is apt to falsify its true purpose. The artist should appreciate the truth and complexity of life whether it is ugly or beautiful because he is not bound by any moral or aesthetic standards. The dramatic form envisages a perfect synthesis between form and matter and any emphasis on either tends towards the destruction of balance.

Joyce's stance towards the world of experience has none of the escapism of Wilde, but in some respects it is closer to that of Pater. At the same time, however, it should be noted that Joyce adjures the Wildean insistence on form at the expense of matter. Whereas Wilde emphasises that nature as such has no beauty of its own and is often uncouth and wild, the artist being the sole agent of beauty, Joyce affirms a close relation between art and natural processes of life. According to him, there is nothing either so humble or ugly that cannot be transubstantiated into art. All of nature and human life pertains to the subject-matter of art.

In his "Conclusion" to *The Renaissance,* Pater had advocated the pristine nature of experience unfettered from any constructing moral or philosophical obligations:

> Every moment some form grows perfect in hand or face; some tone on the hills or the sea is choicer than the rest; some mood of passion or insight or intellectual excitement is irresistibly real and attractive for us, for that moment only. Not the fruit of experience, but experience itself, is the end. A counted number of pulses only is given to us of a variegated, dramatic life. How may we see in them all that is to be seen in them by the finest senses? How shall we pass most swiftly from point to point, and be present always at the focus where the greatest number of vital forces unite in their purest energy. (*Renaissance* 222)

This positioning of the artist in terms of the concreteness of experience is echoed by Joyce in "Drama and Life". He states: "Life we must accept as we see it before our eyes, man and women as we meet them in the real world, not as we apprehend them in the world of faery" (*CW* 45). Something of a similar motive is revealed in Pater's pronouncement: "the theory or idea or system which requires of us the sacrifice of any part of this experience, in consideration of some interest into which we cannot enter, or some abstract theory we have not identified with ourselves, or what is only conventional, has no real claim upon us" (*Renaissance* 223).

At the same time, Joyce's attitude to man and the world has more of a timeless quality about it, something that tends towards the archetypal, the primal, defying the changing, relative character of existence:

> The great human comedy in which each has share, gives limitless scope to the true artist, today as yesterday and as in years gone. The forms of things, as the earth's crust, are changed.... But the deathless passions, the human verities which so found expression then, are indeed deathless, in the heroic cycle, or in the scientific age. Hohjengrin, the drama of which unfolds itself in a scene of seclusion, amid half-lights, is not an Antwerp legend but a world drama.

> Ghosts, the actions of which passes in a common parlour, is of universal import.... (*CW* 45)

In the dramatist's presentation of the absolute and changeless quality of human passions and their conflict there is the suggestion of mind triumphing over matter. Although Joyce insists on the artist's grasp of facts like his precursor Defoe, yet "he also insists on the mind's supremacy over all it surveyed" (*CW* 214). Mason and Ellmann in their introductory note to Joyce's essay on "William Blake" (1912) explain his standpoint in the following manner:

> Joyce's resemblance to Defoe is clear enough, and he is closer to Blake than may at first appear. While he took pride in grounding his art on brute, honest fact, he insisted on the mind's supremacy over all it surveyed. Beyond these general resemblances, his lectures suggest two specific affinities. Defoe and Blake, in their different ways, were working with the conception of an archetypal man. Robinson Crusoe summarises a people and a time as Bloom does. Blake's Albion, the universal man who symbolises eternity, is related to that other giant form, Finnegan, in whose life, death and awakening Joyce finds all human enterprise and aspiration. (*CW* 214).

Joyce's essay on Blake highlights the danger of being a visionary. Through the vision of agonised innocence in the chimney sweep and other little children, Blake had a penchant for indulging in the abstract and the unknown. These visitations of imagination told upon his sense of fact. Referring to his idealism, Joyce indicates Blake's attachment to the literary-revolutionary school of Mary Wollstonecraft and Thomas Paine and points out that "the same idealism that possessed and sustained Blake when he hurled his lighting against human evil and misery prevented him from being cruel to the body even of a sinner, the *frail* curtain of flesh, as he calls it in the mystical book of *Thel*, that lies on the bed of our desire" (*CW* 216). But then, Joyce astutely points out that Blake was not a "great mystic" (*CW* 220). Any thought of mysticism must include the orient, which is its "paternal home", and it is inescapable that "Blake is probably less inspired by Indian mysticism than

Paracelsus, Jacob Behmen, or *Swedenborg*" (*CW* 220). Joyce's observation focuses on the unique "visionary faculty" in Blake, which is "directly connected with the artistic faculty" (*CW* 221). Blake is primarily an artist and in this category he is unique because "he unites keenness of intellect with mystical feeling" (*CW* 221). Compared to St. John of the Cross, Blake is entirely of a different class. Whereas Blake evinces "an innate sense of form or a coordinating force of the intellect, St. John is a profound idealist and his *The Dark Night of the Soul* is instinct with ecstatic passion" (*CW* 221).

Joyce explains the contradiction in Blake by indicating that the poet served two masters in Michelangelo Buonarotti and Emmanuel Swedenborg, who share the same predilection for "formal precision". The influence of Michelangelo may be seen in Blake's insistence "on the importance of the pure, clean line that evokes and creates the figure on the background of the uncreated void" (*CW* 221). On the other hand, the effect of Swedenborg may be seen in Blake's "vision of glorified humanity" (*CW* 221):

> Swedenborg, who frequented all of the invisible worlds for several years, sees in the image of man, heaven itself and Michael, Raphael, and Gabriel, who, according to him, are not three angels, but three angelic choirs. Eternity, which had appeared to the beloved disciple and to St. Augustine as a heavenly city, and to Alighieri as a heavenly rose, appeared to the Swedish mystic in the likeness of a heavenly man, animated in all his limbs by a fluid angelic life that forever leaves and re-enters, systole and diastole of love and wisdom. (*CW* 222)

Blake has the singular distinction of undermining the authority of the senses:

> Armed with this two-edged sword, the art of Michelangelo and the revelations of Swedenborg, Blake killed the dragon of experience and natural wisdom, and, by minimizing space and time and denying the existence of memory and the senses, he tried to paint his works on the divine wisdom. (*CW* 222)

To perceive the secret of earthly existence the power of human senses have been denigrated in favour of the guidance of the spirit. The mental process by which Blake reaches God is by ascending from the infinitesmal to the gigantic from a "drop of blood to the universe of stars" (*CW* 222). The process is paralleled by Dionysus, the pseudo-Aeropagite, in his book *De Divinis Nominibus*, who reaches Godhead "by denying and overcoming every moral and metaphysical attribute" (*CW* 222).

Joyce himself is warned against the dangers of consorting with the visionary company of Blake, Swedenborg and Shelley, but he is never reluctant to admit that Blake is primarily an artist. Being in that category, he had an instinct for form under the command of his intellect. Explaining the relationship of the artist with his material Joyce often argues in favour of greater control. He never permits his imagination to run riot. He argues for a perfect coordination between matter and form in art. This cohesion was highlighted in late nineteenth century aesthetics especially in his essay on "Style" in *Appreciations* which praised the master's perfect artistic blending of style and matter (20). Art being a perfect blending of such forces, it was the vocation of the artist-hero to be present at the confluence of such forces. A remarkable point of affinity lies in Joyce's perception that Blake had followed Dionysius in arriving at Godhead by transcending all moral and metaphysical concern (*CW* 222). Joyce himself went so far as to describe the artist's holy office as transcending all philosophical, moral and political strictures. In both Pater and Joyce, the world of senses remains a primary criterion of aesthetic apprehension. Both of them are alike in sharing a deep distrust for the erratic flights of romantic fancy, which verges on the irrational.

Defining the context of the artist's isolation in the "Day of the Rabblement" (1901) Joyce is careful to note that any form of compromise is apt to injure the artist's search for truth. "No man", said the Nolan, "can be a lover of the true or the good unless he abhors the multitude; and the artist, though he may employ the crowd, is very careful to isolate himself" (*CW* 69). Quoting Giordano Bruno, Joyce illustrates that although the artist deals primarily with life, he must be sufficiently detached from the polluting multitude in order to perceive its beauty and truth:

> If an artist courts the favour of the multitude he cannot escape the contagion of its fetishism and deliberate self-deception, and if he joins in a popular movement he does so at his own risk. Therefore, the Irish Literary Theatre by its surrender to the trolls has cut itself adrift from the line of advancement. Until he has freed himself from the mean influences about him—sodden enthusiasm and clever insinuation and every flattering influence of vanity and low ambition—no man is an artist at all. (*CW* 71-72)

This is to say that although drama is mass-based and appeals to heterogeneous audience, the dramatist must retain his impartiality by being uninfluenced by any movement, which is likely to prejudice his study of human life and passions. Joyce was initially absorbed in the Irish Literary Theatre, which changed into the Abbey Theatre and even attended the performance of Yeats' *The Countless Cathleen* and Edward Martyr's *The Blending of the Bough*. But when the Theatre began to stage plays like Douglas Hyde's *Casud-an-Sugán* and an unrealistic play taken from Irish heroic legend like *Diarmaid and Grania*, Joyce wrote against its parochialism.

In his essay, Joyce notes that at first the Irish Literary Theatre promised to be a champion of progress and to wage war against forms of vulgarity and commercialism. "It had partly made good its word and was expelling the old devil, when after the first encounter it surrendered to the popular will" (*CW* 70). The final nail in the coffin, according to Joyce, was hammered in by the Theatre's reluctance to experiment with European models. Joyce rationalises that the Theatre was left with no model for artistic guidance. "A nation which never advanced so far as a miracle-play affords no literary model to the artist, and he must look abroad" (*CW* 70). Consequently the theatre and its literary assumptions in its greed to satisfy the poor tastes of the rabble.

Joyce's affinities with the classical idea of art may be observed in his essay on "James Clarence Mangan" (1902). In this essay, he emphasises that "the laws of his art" must never "be forgotten in the judgement of a man of letters by the supreme laws of poetry" (*CW* 75). Here Joyce reiterates his belief in two sets of laws: one for poetry since often "poetry in art transcends the mode of its expression" and another for literature, which occupies a wide expanse between "ephemeral writing and poetry" (*CW* 75). Thus, "much of Wordsworth" and "almost all of Baudelaire" is merely literature in verse and must be judged by the laws of literature (*CW* 75).

In the highest category of poetry there is often to be found a perfect synthesis between thought and expression, between its signification and execution:

> A song by Shakespeare or Verlaine, which seems so free and living and as remote from any conscious purpose as rain that falls in a garden of the lights of evening, is discovered to be the rhythmic speech of an emotion otherwise incommunicable, at least so fitly. But to approach the temper which has made art is an act of reverence and many conventions must be first put off, for certainly the inmost region will never yield to one who is enmeshed with profanities. (*CW* 75)

The artist shows his creativity nor merely by means of an original conception of feeling but by selecting the proper medium for its expression. A particular emotion on thought may be conveyed through a certain form and no other. To take it further, the conception or feeling determines its expression. But the reader approaches it through a sensible medium. Hence, he ought to discard all presuppositions when assessing the work of a particular author. Appreciation of art is a difficult proposition for the critic for this particular reason. A work of art must be judged on its own merit, and not on *a priori* standards. We should take into account the organic nature of art.

In his second essay on "James Clarence Mangan" (1907), Joyce elucidates Mangan's role by pointing out his social relevance:

> There are certain poets who, in addition to the virtue of revealing to us some phase of the human conscience unknown until their time, also have the more doubtful virtue of summing up in themselves the thousand contrasting tendencies of their era, of being, so to speak, the storage batteries of new forces. For the most part it is in the latter role rather than the former that they come to be appreciated by the masses, who are by nature unable to evaluate any work of true self-revelation, and so hasten to recognise by some act of grace the incalculable aid that the individual affirmation of a poet gives to a popular movement. (*CW* 176)

Mangan represents the spirit of the times and in "his poetry" a narrow and hysterical nationality receives a last justification (*CW* 82). His work reflects the deep anguish and suffering as well as the aspiration of someone who tries to transubstantiate his sorrow on to a lyrical plane. The theme of his songs originates from his "noble misery, as his favourite Swedenborg would say, out of the vastation of soul" (*CW* 80). But he has his limitations. He fails to find within himself 'the faith of the solitarity, or the faith, which in the middle age, sent the spires signing up to heaven, and he waits for the final scene to end the penance since unlike Leopardi he does not possess "the courage of his own despair" (*CW* 80). It is in poetry that the "human mind, as it looks backward or forward, attains to an eternal state. The philosophic mind inclines always to an elaborate life" (*CW* 82). On the other hand, the poet's life has an intensity, comparable to the life of Blake or of Dante, "taking into its centre the life that surrounds it and flinging it abroad again and planetary music" (*CW* 82).

According to Joyce, the poet, however, must also be conscious of the corrupting influence of the marketplace as well as the debilitating effects of solipsism:

> poetry considers many of the idols of the marketplace unimportant—the succession of the ages, the spirit of the age, the mission of the race. The poet's central effort is to free himself from the unfortunate influence of these idols that corrupt him from without and within, and certainly

> it would be false to assert that Mangan has always made this effort.... He cries out in his life and in his mournful verses against the injustice of despoilers, but almost never laments a loss greater than that of buckles and banners. He inherits the latest and worst part of a tradition upon which no divine hand has ever traced a boundary...and precisely because this tradition has become an obsession with him, he has accepted it with all its regrets and failures and would pass it on just as it is. (*CW* 185)

The poet being the nucleus of his own age, is bound to echo the spirit of his own race and the temper of his people. But he must develop his own critique of his times and not simply be a spokesman of contemporary belief and ideas. Although he accepts life, he must be on guard against the vulgar appeal of popularity. It is true that Mangan is successful in summing up both the "soul of a country" and that of "an era"; and was reluctant to prostitute himself to the rabble or to make himself the loudspeaker of politicians (*CW* 184). His belief in his inner life led him to shun the populace but he has relatively little control over his own feelings.

The radical principle of artistic economy requires the artist's isolation by which no physical alienation is implied but discipline where the passions become subject for poetic material. Mangan's own countrymen lament the combination of his poetic faculty with "so little rectitude of conduct" and are "surprised to find this faculty in a man whose vices were exotic and who was little of a patriot" (*CW* 76).

> Surely life, which Novalis has called a malady of the spirit, is a heavy penance for him, who has, perhaps, forgotten the sin that laid it upon him, a sorrowful portion, too, because of that fine artist in him which reads so truly the lines of brutality and weakness in the faces of men that are thrust in upon his path. (*CW* 76)

Mangan's failing is in his inability to master his own emotions.

Joyce is fond of equating beauty and truth in his theory of art. He draws close to aesthetics in his conception of the unique nature of the poetic personality, who epitomises within himself the intense emotional life as well as the conflicting currents of the thought of his age. He shows his kinship with the classical artist when he harps on the precise balance between matter and form in art; an ideology that also influenced nineteenth century aesthetes like Walter Pater. Joyce shows his own brand of realism by forcing on the poet an acceptance of life and a deep mistrust of idealism in art. But his equation of beauty and truth give a new orientation to his theory of art:

> Beauty, the splendour of truth, is a gracious presence when the imagination contemplates intensely the truth of its own being or the visible world, and the spirit which proceeds out of truth and beauty is the holy spirit of joy. These are realities and these alone give and sustain life.... In those vast courses which enfold us and in that great memory which is greater and more generous than our memory, no life, no moment of exaltation is ever lost; and all those who have written nobly have not written in vain, though the desperate and weary have never heard the silver laughter of wisdom. (*CW* 83)

Art being the "continual affirmation of the spirit" it is the artist's duty to present life in all its manifold phenomenon and this is only possible if he develops a certain degree of detachment with respect to both the materials of his art and to his own emotions.

Joyce's most elaborate statement on art figure in his essay on "Aesthetics" in his "Paris" (1903) and "Pola" (1904) notebooks. The Paris notebook primarily deals with the relationship of the artist to his material and the Pola notebook centres round the act of artistic apprehension. In their introductory note to Joyce's essay, Mason and Ellmann note that in the Paris notebook:

> ...Joyce grandly follows the manner as well as the topics of Aristotle. Unleashing, like Stephen Dedalus later, his "dagger definitions", he elaborates in pat contrast the differences between tragedy and comedy. He argues for the superiority of comedy over tragedy on the grounds that comedy makes for joy and tragedy for sorrow, and

> that the sense of deprivation is imperfect, and therefore, he implies, inferior to the sense of possession. With more originality he expertly redefines pity and terror and finds in the arrest of these emotions, as in that of joy, the stasis necessary to art. He then distinguishes between the lyrical, epical, and dramatic modes, covertly awarding the palm of drama as the most impersonal. Finally he insists that art moves towards an aesthetic, and not a moral end. (*CW* 142)

Expatiating on the degree of the artist's involvement Joyce states that both desire and loathing are improper emotions since they either consume his total attention or provoke his rejection. Feelings confirm an artist's preoccupations with an object but must not assume such proportion as to divert his intellect from a proper appraisal of its inherent beauty. This is seen in the of tragedy. The feeling of terror establishes a connection between a norm or what is constant in human fortunes and an unknown element in nature. The feeling of pity posits a relationship between a stable component in human fortunes and the human sufferer (*CW* 143). In tragedy, catharsis or stasis brings about an equilibrium of emotions when pity and terror are qualified in a final act. The mind is asserted and not agitated.

But more than tragedy, the feeling of joy in comedy provides a perfect instance of the possession of something good. Desire in this sense indicates partial possession because the mind is moved to possess some object outside it. The motive of aesthetics is to focus on this sense of self-possession for only then can the artist present the conflict of emotions from a detached perspective:

> Desire, the feeling which an improper art seeks to excite in the way of comedy, differs, it will be seen from joy. For desire urges us from rest that we may possess something but joy holds us in rest so long as we possess something. Desire, therefore, can only be excited in us by a comedy (a work of comic art) which is not sufficient in itself inasmuch as it urges us to seek something beyond

> itself; but a comedy (a work of comic art) which does not urge us to seek anything beyond itself excites in us the feeling of joy. (*CW* 144)

Joyce's use to terms like "arrest" or "rest" is only intelligible if associated with his notion of "clarities"; or radiance in connection with Thomist aesthetics, later adumbrated in *Portrait.* The mind in the final act of aesthetic apprehension is compared to the state of a fading coal, to borrow Shelley's phrase or to use a term from medical science, it resembles the enchantment of the heart. The "luminous silent stasis of aesthetic pleasure", of which he speaks about in *Portrait* has some affinities with the notion of rest in the feeling of joy proper to a comic art (*P* 213). Joyce states in his Paris notebook:

> All art, again, is static for the feelings of terror and pity on the one hand and of joy on the other hand are feeling which arrest us. It will be seen afterwards how this rest is necessary for the apprehension of the beautiful—the end of all art, tragic or comic—for this rest is the only condition under which the images, which are to excite in us terror or pity or joy, can be properly presented to us and properly seen by us. For beauty is a quality of something seen but terror and pity and joy are states of mind. (*CW* 144-45)

Aesthetic pleasure is consequent upon a sense of proportion and on the coherence between form and matter. For art appeals to our sense of sight, our mind and to out feelings. Invoking the Hellenic ideal of harmony, Joyce stresses that unless the mind attains an equanimity, no perception of beauty is possible. Hence, the romantic search for the infinite is to be adjured since it urges the heart towards an insatiable pursuit of the unattainable, bordering on the irrational. Thus, art is defined by Joyce as "the human disposition of sensible or intelligible matter for an aesthetic end" (*CW* 145).

Joyce tones down the emotive connotations in aesthetics in favour of cognitive activity and this stresses greater artistic control over the materials of art. By emphasising the "aesthetic end" of art Joyce affirms his kinship with Aristotle as a teleological philosopher. He is primarily concerned with the end of art. As such his insistence that art should be a "human disposition of sensible or intelligible matter", focus on the role of the human component in the production of art (*CW* 145). The Paris notebook also initiates Joyce's preference for speaking of art in connection with natural processes like parturition, a favourite analogy which finds later expression in Stephen's theory that the creation of artefact necessitates the phases of "artistic conception, artistic gestation, and artistic reproduction" (*P* 209). Mason and Ellmann are of the opinion that when Joyce, quoting Aristotle, liken "artistic process" to that of "natural process" he anticipates his later analogy with the idea of parturition (*CW* 145).

In his Pola notebook dated November 15, 1904 Joyce describes two necessary phases in the act of aesthetic apprehension, namely the "activity of cognition or simple perception" and the "activity of recognition" (*CW* 147). In itself the phenomenon of simple perception is unable to determine the beauty of an object. We depend upon the activity of recognition to decide whether a sensible object satisfies the requirements of beauty. According to Joyce:

> Sensible objects; however, are said conventionally to be beautiful or not for neither of the foregoing reasons but rather by reason of the nature, degree and duration of the satisfaction resulting from the apprehension of them and it is in accordance with these latter merely that the words "beautiful" and "ugly" are used in practical aesthetic philosophy. (*CW* 148)

When he talks about the "nature, degree and duration of the satisfaction" provided by an object he actually refers to the third stage of aesthetic apprehension and that is "the activity of satisfaction" (*CW* 148). His observations on November 16, 1904 confirms that Joyce goes beyond Aquinas, who speaks of "pleasing": and not "satisfying" (*CW* 148). Further, Mason and Ellmann point out that here Joyce seems to be bridging from his theory of *stasis* in drama to his theory of *claritas* as both the final quality of a work of art and the highest aspect of response to it. Satisfaction, which implies rest and calm, is therefore essential to his theory of apprehension (*CW* 148).

There is a world of differences between the terms "pleasing" and "satisfying". The first denotes a sense of conforming to certain principle or standard of beauty which is itself derived from a mode of comparison. It is, therefore, relative, implying the notion that standards of beauty are apt to fluctuate. But "pleasing" itself restricts the notion of beauty to a sensuous medium, referring to the senses and the intellect. Joyce introduces a further terminology of "satisfaction" in order to indicate that there is a third psychological dimension of art ensuing from a condition of "rest" or calm of mind. This condition of "rest" is comparable to the "luminous silent stasis of aesthetic pleasure" when the mind is arrested by the object. This certainty of possession on the part of the artist has been confirmed on all accounts, sensuous, intellectual and psychological. Knowledge implies a sense of possession from which clarity of perception ensues. There is no total affinity as in the case of Keats's "negative capability" where the poet surrenders his identity to the object of perception in an act of empathy.

In much of romantic aesthetic especially that of Keats, the poet is taken up with the notion of "the holiness of the heart's affections and the truth of imagination" (*Letters* 36-37). In his letter to Benjamin Bailey on November 22, 1817, Keats speaks of the sovereignty of imagination "what the imagination seizes as Beauty must be truth—whether it existed before or not—or I have the same Idea of all our passions as of Love they are all in their sublime, creative of essential Beauty" (*Letters* 37). Romantic ethos is primarily focused on the sublimation of life. Hence, everything, however little or ugly or sinful is sublimated through the alchemy of the imagination. The romantic poet is taken up with the intensity of his vision. Thus, Keats is displeased with the picture entitled "Death on the Pale Horse" because "there is nothing to be intense upon; no women one feels mad to kiss; no face swelling into the reality. The excellence of every art is its intensity, capable of making all disagreeables evaporate, from their being in close relationship with Beauty and Truth" (*Letters* 42).

Romantic ideology is based upon a profound awareness of the existential tragedy of man. Often in Keats' letters we find him complaining as he does in his letter to Bailey on November 3, 1817: "The thought that we are mortal makes us groan" (*Letters* 33). His critique of Wordsworth bears on this important aspect of his thought. In his letter to J.H. Reynolds on May 3, 1818, Keats compares human life to a huge mansion with many rooms of which two are only accessible to the poet. The first symbolises "the infant or thoughtless chamber" while the second is described as "the Chamber of Maiden-Thought" (*Letters* 95).

Keats himself shies away from an inordinate preoccupation with the world of thoughts. In his letter to Bailey in 1817 he cries out:

> O for a life of sensations rather than of
> Thoughts: It is "a Vision in the form of
> Youth" a Shadow of reality to come—
>
> And this consideration has further convinced me for it has come as auxiliary to another favourite Speculation of mine, that we shall enjoy ourselves here after by having what we called happiness on Earth repeated in a finer tone and so repeated. (*Letters* 37)

It is remarkable that Keats' theory of the selfless or chameleon poet is itself a critique of the romantic ethos; its melancholy stress on the sufferings of the individual which is consequent on a solipsistic alienation of the self from the world. This abstraction of the self into the realm of thoughts rival that of the real world. The agency is imagination, which brings about a sublimation of the harsh, stark world of experience. Keats himself adumbrates an end to this solipsistic isolation. In his letter to Richard Woodhouse on October 27, 1818, he states:

> As to the poetical character itself, (I mean that sort of which, if I am any thing, I am a Member; that sort distinguished from the Wordsworthian or egotistical sublime; which is a thing *per se* and stands alone) it is not itself—it has no self—it is every thing and nothing—it has no character—it enjoys light and shade; it lives in gusto, be it foul or fair, high or low, rich or poor, mean

> or elevated—It has as much delight in conceiving an ego as an Imogen.... A poet is the most unpoetical of any thing in existence; because he has no Identity—he is continually in for—and filling some other Body.... (*Letters* 157)

In the same letter he presses for the annihilation of personality on the part of the poet:

> When I am in a room with people if I ever am free from speculating on creations of my own brain, then not myself goes home to myself; but the identity of every one in the room begins to (for so) to press upon me that I am in a very little time an(ni)hilated.... (*Letters* 158)

Here the dialogue between the romantic poet and the other is sublimated and fused into a singular oneness.

Joyce's approach to life is qualitatively different from that of the romantics in that he is content to present both the ugliness and beauty of life without any attempt at idealisation. This acceptance of both the modest and the sublime aspects of life is a distinctive note and this determines Joyce's choice of the average man, Bloom, who has no touch of heroism about him. Joyce's humanism is evident when he talks about the simple pleasures, the trivialities and the small things of life. He stresses more on the truth rather than the beauty of life. And over everything we note the enveloping spirit of joy. In a certain sense he shares the romantic notion of epiphanic vision when he reveals the uniqueness of an object or experience in his theory of "claritas" or radiance, which provides the third dimension of the act of apprehension according to Aquinas. The revelation brought about through this imaginative activity, however, is not philosophical in nature.

In spite of Joyce's insistence on the act of imagination through the epiphanic mode of vision, there is none of the romantic note of empathy in his act of aesthetic apprehension. He never identifies himself with the object of perception or with his creations. Maintaining a distance with respect to his characters, Joyce liked to criticise them, make fun of them, pointing out their absurdities and failings without any attempt at idealisation. Joyce's critique of his own creations helps us to understand the note of self-appraisal, which runs through all his works. This extreme instance of objectivity with respect to one's own person provides the occasion for drama in all his creations, and through this way led the route of self-discovery. The sense of drama, however, is concomitant to the dramatist's impartial standpoint, arguing for a greater artistic control over the materials of creation. Therefore, we often find Joyce expatiating on this sense of certainty and possession, which determines his distinctive approach to aesthetics.

Within the image of parturition, Joyce professes that the artist is both mother and father, giving birth to the artefact. It is true that the artefact as child is bound to have an existence of its own in its post-natal condition. Nevertheless, it remains true that the artefact inherits some essential traits and characteristics of its Creator. The artist in the moment of creation has brought a new creature in the world but he has projected an essential part of his personality in his art. Without the agency of human intervention art is never possible and hence any creation is bound to reflect the idiosyncrasies or biologically termed, the generic characteristics of the parent author. This insistence on the genetic code is apparent in Joyce's description of the artistic process as one of "artistic conception, artistic gestation and artistic reproduction" (*P* 209).

From a religious point of view, the artistic process may also be seen as an act of transubstantiation wherein the artist-God is metamorphosed into the artefact or the bread and wine in the Mass of the Eucharist. The celebration of the Host in the sacrament does not merely indicate a symbolic presence but also animates the actual presence of the Lord Christ. The Roman Catholic Mass promulgates with the sacrament both the symbolic and the mystical presence of Christ (Fairweather 318). This was one of the messages of the Oxford Movement which had a far-reaching effect on the aesthetics of Newman, Keble and Hopkins. Thus Robert Isaac Wilberforce, quoting from an oblation from Mede explains how the sacrament mystically represents in the "creatures of bread and wide not only the idea of sacrifice but also our union with Christ in terms of our prayer and thanksgiving" (Fairweather 318). This analogy extended into the metaphor of artistic creation has an important signification. It ensures the presence of the artist within the artefact whether he may be hidden, within, beyond or above his handiwork.

Joyce's adumbration of the impersonal theory of art includes both the idea of transubstantiation of the artist's personality and the legacy of the parent-artist in the artefact. This indicates a significant departure from Eliot's impersonal theory of art. In his "Tradition and the Individual Talent" Eliot expatiates on the "continual surrender" of the artist:

> The progress of an artist is a continual, self-sacrifice, a continual extinction of personality.
>
> There remains to define this process of depersonalisation and its relation to the sense of tradition. It is in this depersonalisation that art may be said to approach the condition of science. I therefore invite you to consider, as a suggestive analogy. The action which takes place when a bit of finely foliated platinum is introduced into a chamber containing oxygen and sulphur dioxide. (*Selected Prose* 40)

The polarisation of Joyce and Eliot is evident in their theory of the artist's relationship to his material. Of course, Joyce was to a certain extent classicist in his insistence on the detachedness of the artist and in his highlighting the principles of artistic composition. We have seen in the section on poetry how his thoughts on the artistry of the poet ran parallel to that of Hulme in the section on Joyce's poetry. We have also taken note of his focus on the concrete particularity of the image but alongside we have also remarked upon the complexity of his later poems, where the presence of the author was felt both, directly and indirectly.

Throughout the Joycean canon it is evident how the author argues for a subtle coordination between matter and form in art; a Hellenic ideal of which he was a champion all throughout his life. Yet in all of his works, we come to note the artist's ambiguous presence in his conscious absence. In other words, Joyce's impersonality is itself a dramatic pose, an attitude touched with irony—ironies also connected with self-portrayal in his art. Hence, the author reserves for himself the prerogatives of criticising his very creations even though they embody and illustrate an essential part of his own self. This is his mask by means of which he confounds the attempt to reach his inner self—a mask, which both hides and reveals. Hence, his adumbration of the theory of artistic isolation through which he tries to ensure the inviolability of his sovereign self. This idea of the disappearing self has its origin in his fear of the pollution of the masses. Joyce desired to escape the contagion of being a popular writer and refused to cater for people or as he himself would put it, to prostitute his art to every whim and caprice of the public. He would escape vulgarisation by retiring like the artist in Ibsen's dramas, to the dizzy but rapturous heights of a mountain. Further, his own experiences show his ingrained fear of betrayal by his friends, detractors and countrymen, to which his letters bear ample testimony.

The theme of the betrayed artist runs right through his works and is often harped upon in essays as diverse as "Ireland, Island of Saints and Sages" (1907), "Oscar Wilde: The Poet of 'Salome'" (1909), "The Shade of Parnell" (1912) and so on. In his essay on Ireland Joyce felt:

> compelled to point out that his country had its history or betrayals, of eloquent inactivity, of absurd and narrow belief. His attitude, though he calls its objective, wavers between affectionate fascination with Ireland and distrust of her. (*CW* 153)

Mason and Ellmann's introductory note reveals the central ambiguity in Joyce's thought. This is especially evident in his essay on "Oscar Wilde" where he represents the aesthetic as a type of betrayed artist. The paradox may be seen in Wilde's fame as the "spokesman of the aesthetic school" around whom "was forming the fantastic legend of the Apostle of Beauty" (*CW* 202). Joyce delineates how "the cult of the sunflower, his favourite flower spread among the leisured class, and the little people heard tell of his famous white ivory walking stick glittering with turquoise stones, and of his Neronian hair-dress" (*CW* 202). And yet he finds the "subject of this shining picture" to be more "miserable than bourgeois thought" since often his medals and "trophies of his academic youth" were pawned and his wife had to borrow money for a decent pair of shoes (*CW* 202). Only in his later years did he become rich with his fame as a dramatist only to squander away his hard-earned fortune. The irony lies in the fact that the artist who thought he was bringing back a "Golden Age and the joy of the world's youth" by his insistence on a theory of beauty (which threatened to become a way of life) was actually howled down by a crowd of people who celebrated his condemnation by dancing outside the court.

> Like the other Oscar, he was to meet his public death in the flower of his years as he sat at table, crowned with false vine leaves and discussing Plato. Like that savage tribe he was to break the lance of his fluent paradoxes against the body of practical conventions, and to hear, as a dishonoured exile, the choir of the just recite his name together with that of the unclean. (*CW* 201)

A similar fate was reserved for Parnell by his countrymen. Parnell's strategy as Joyce outlines in his essay. "The Shade of Parnell" was to utilise any English party either Liberal or Conservative to secure his country's emancipation. To this end, he rallied behind him "every element of Irish life" and forced the Liberal Government in England to restore autonomy to Ireland (*CW* 227). In 1886, Gladstone was forced to "read the first Home Rule Bill at Westminster" (*CW* 227). Suddenly Parnell was discredited owing to his love-affair with a married woman and the Liberals used this situation to their own advantage, negotiating the autonomy of Ireland against Parnell's conviction. At this moment he was betrayed by his own people who castigated him. Joyce comments on this act of treachery by his countrymen:

> The melancholy which invaded his mind was perhaps the profound conviction that, in his hour of need, one of the disciples who dipped his hand in the same bowl with him would betray him....
>
> In his final desperate appeal to his countrymen, he begged them not to throw him as a sop to the English

> wolves howling around them. It redounds to their honour that they did not fail this appeal. They did not throw him to the English wolves; they tore him to pieces themselves. (*CW* 228)

Yet, in spite of his fear of betrayal Joyce was not in the true sense of the term an expatriate. His frequent visits to Ireland testify to this fact. What is most interesting in his own ambivalence towards the Irish question? It would not be true to say that he did not love Ireland. But it is also a fact that Joyce exhibited a deep antipathy towards the very attitude which may be termed insular or parochial. The regeneration of Ireland must be put in the hands of the avant-garde who will not yield to the demands of popular nationalism but make themselves amenable to literary currents and innovations from the continent.

Much of the same ambivalence may be noted in his attitude to art and the poetic personality. Making much of the concept of artistic detachment, he could never escape a subtle ironic attitude towards both; his characters and to himself. The mystery of the Joycean artist lies precisely in this role-playing, an incessant making, unmaking and remaking process, which defies any attempt to reach a stable consensus on the true identity of the artist. In spite of noting, therefore, certain points of similarity between Joyce's theory of impersonality and that of Eliot, there is a fundamental difference in their approach to the theory of art and the personality of the artist.

Exiles (1918)

6

Around November 1913, Joyce had started his work on *Exiles* and completed it by April 1915. In his letter to James B. Pinaker on April 1, 1915 he states: "I have written a play in three acts, *Exiles* but should prefer to hold it over till my novel *A Portrait of the Artist as a Young Man* has been published in book form" (*Letters* II: 338). In his artistic career, this was an important period for Joyce. He had finished *Dubliners* (1914) and *Portrait* (1916) and following his completion of *Exiles*, was to start writing his epic *Ulysses* in March 1914. The Dedalus spell hangs like a pall over the play, overwhelming the protagonist Richard Rowan who is an introvert and a dedicated artist. He has almost succeeded in transmuting his life into art but not quite since the presence of other characters like Robert Hand and Bertha qualify his impersonal approach and introduce warmth and vitality into the play. The presence of Beatrice Justice and Robert are instrumental in ruffling the intellectual tone of the play as well as affect the apparent stability in the conjugal relationship of Bertha and Richard. The play is full of psychological interest. The complex situation produced by the extra-marital affairs between Richard and Beatrice and between Bertha and Robert raises a few fundamental queries on man-woman relationship in this play. The drama also subjects Richard's theories on art and life to intense scrutiny.

Ibsen's influence over the play has been recognised by critics like Desmond MacCarthy and Francis Ferguson. In the *review* in *New Statesman* (xi) on 21 September 1918, MacCarthy writes:

> To be made to wonder and to think about characters in a play is a rare experience—outside the drama of Ibsen.

> It is a pleasure far excelling the simple pleasure of delighted recognition, which is all that the character-drawing in the ordinary respect-worthy play provides.... Exiles excited me for the same reason that the plays of Ibsen excite me—the people in it were so interesting. Ibsen's character has roots, which tempt one to pull at them again and again. (*CH* I: 140)

The remarkable nature of the play is seen in the way it has puzzled a generation of critics. Even MacCarthy admits to being puzzled. Granting that *Exiles* focuses on the subconscious, the conflict being between will and instinct in Richard, John Rodker in *Little Review* (Vol. 9) on January 1919 indicates that the analysis is so profoundly executed that "at a certain moment" we lose track and "mind will go no further". Thus, "interaction of thought and will is carried so close to this borderline that the reader fears continually lest he miss any implication" (*CH* I: 148).

The tension between Richard's theories and the warm current of passion and life flowing between Bertha and Robert defy the comprehension of the audience. Francis Hackett in New Republic (xvi, No. 206) on October 12, 1918 objects to the dramatist's tendency "to force human beings to do and say unlikely things, and to jumble up the true perspective of their lives" (*CH* I: 146). Elaborating on this perspective, he claims:

> There is an unreality around certain passages in *Exiles* that suggests the literary alchemist vaguely striving to transmute pretty theories into honest flesh and blood. The flesh and blood Exiles, so far as it is honest, does not fit the theories. They are imposed by their author on subjects unwilling and rebellious. The result is a disharmony that almost defies literary analysis. (*CH* I: 146)

Pound in his essay on "Mr. James Joyce and the modern stage" in the Drama, Chicago (IV, 2) on February 1916 comments that *Exiles* is "absolutely unfit for the stage, as we know it" (Pound/Joyce 50). Of course, he grants the play has "inner form". It is dramatic in the sense that the dialogues have "dramatic-edge" and interpenetrate thoughts and actions of the characters, making the play an integral whole. It also preserves the unities of time and place and forcefully deals with the problem of adultery. But, he adds:

> The trouble with Mr. Joyce's play is precisely that he is at peace with reality. It is a "dangerous" play precisely because the author is portraying an intellectual—emotional, struggle, because he is dealing with actual thought, actual questioning not with clichés of thought and emotion.
>
> It is untheatrical, or unstageable, precisely because the closeness and cogency of the process is, as I think, too great for an audience to be able to follow.... (Pound/Joyce 52)

And yet it is Joyce's achievement to construct a drama out of this pure cerebration. *Exiles* is a product of the modern psyche and its struggle with deep-seated problems of twentieth century life. Like *A Portrait* it reflects the artist's struggle with his material and his integrity in relation to his environment. But whereas *Portrait* deals with the artist's vision of life and art, *Exiles* undertakes to probe much deeper within the artist's psyche, making inroads into his subconscious. The play dramatises the Joycean ego, the implications of which will be apparent to the reader who has undertaken a study of both Stephen Hero and Portrait and has carefully noted the artist's titanic struggle with his own inner self. Jane Heap in the *Little Review* symposium on January 1919 has the following comment to offer on the play:

> Propagandists declare it is a play on the freedom of the individual. Other reviewers talk of triangles and Ibsen and neurotics. All these are easy and semi-intelligent things to say. But when it is unanimously agreed that Joyce hasn't "put over his idea clearly" or that he hasn't known just what he was trying to put over, I grow a bit nervous and wonder why it doesn't appear to them that perhaps Joyce couldn't reach their darkness. I also wonder why not read *Exiles* with Joyce in mind. The man who wrote *A Portrait of the Artist as a Young Man* and *Ulysses*, a highly conscious, over-sensitised artist

> living at the vortex of modern psychology, would scarcely go back to dealing with material in a Pre-Nietzsche-manner. (*CH* I: 153)

Exiles is a complex play because it presents a number of psychological issues simultaneously. Not only is it about adultery, it also focuses on the themes of betrayal, of exile and on Richard's theories of freedom with respect to conjugal relationship. The dramatic conflict is between will and instinct in the protagonist, Richard. There is also a struggle for supremacy between Bertha's lovers; the uniqueness and elusiveness of Richard as against Robert's earthiness, vitality and passion. The conflict is portrayed both externally and internally. Although critics have stressed the character of Richard as occupying the centre of the stage, yet the importance of Bertha can never be minimised. She herself forms the emotional epicentre of the drama since she is loved by both men. There is tension between her love for Richard and her lover for Robert. This tension holds the play together, shifting the point of emphasis until her surrender to Richard at the close of the play.

The structure of the drama forms a sort of counterpointing as it were between Richard's guilt and Bertha's innocence, between Richard's faithfulness and Bertha's fidelity, between Richard's faith in Robert and Robert's betrayal of his friend, between Richard's betrayal of wife and Robert's betrayal of friend, between the versions of amorality as typified by Richard and Robert. The introduction of Beatrice as a lover of Richard further complicates relationships since she excites Bertha's jealousy who in turn uses her liaison with Robert to excite her husband's jealousy and possessive instinct.

The play is instilled with a feminist message as it argues cogently for the emancipation of women. The two women play vital roles in the play but their prominence is somewhat overshadowed by the towering personality of Richard. There is something remarkable in the championing of the cause of women by the two leading male characters. Very surprisingly, they seem to arrive at the same conclusion from the opposite ends of the scale. The male possessive instinct has been thoroughly castigated in the avant-garde theories of Richard and in Robert's much-advertised promiscuity.

Exiles has been composed in an avant-garde spirit because it raises fundamental questions about the freedom of man from plethora of viewpoints like conjugal, existential and metaphysical. It asks whether man can be really free from social conventions. Here Richard's iconoclasm nearly parallels that of Joyce who consistently argued for the emancipation of man from the hypocrisy of religion, hackneyed customs and ancient taboos prevalent on conjugal relationship. This Stephen-Richard-Joyce equation is something which needs careful investigation because it imparts to the play much of its psychological interest.

Joyce's letter to Nora on August 29, 1904, in which he explains the logic behind much of his non-conformism forms a necessary document which illuminates his motive in creating such characters like Stephen and Richard. In that letter Joyce shows why he rejects orthodox religion and conventional patterns of behaviour, thereby developing within himself a resistance which crystallises into rebellion. The germ of revolt may be found in the kind of alienation, which engulfed him as he looked upon the stream of life around him:

> While I was repeating this to myself I knew that life was still waiting for me if I chose to enter it. It could give me perhaps the intoxication it had once given but it was still there and now that I am wiser and more controllable it was safe. It would ask no questions, expect nothing from me but a few moments of my life, leaving the rest free, and would promise me pleasure in return. I thought of all this and without regret I rejected it. It was useless for me: it could give me what I wanted. (*Letters* II: 49)

Stephen in *Portrait* shies away from involvements in life through love, religion and politics. He denies any surrender of his own life to any thing outside him. This absorption in self-knowledge has both merits and demerits. It might lead to the liberation of self from all ties of attachment. Alternately, it might lead to self-love or megalomania. It can make one a recluse or might foster promiscuity. In other words, it is a dangerous state of mind which has both positive and negative implications. Joyce was aware of his central ambiguity in his thinking and was careful in watching his step. This is to say that he did not completely fall under the Dedalus spell. If by any chance the hapless reader is tempted to identify Joyce with Stephen he will be making a mistake. *Ulysses* confirms our suspicions when we realise that Joyce balances his ethos through the binary perspective of Stephen and Bloom. He was already on his way towards the dissociation of an extreme Joycean perspective in the figure of Stephen.

In this drama, Rowan's consciousness has been turned inside out. An extreme absorption in self leads Rowan to an abyss of doubt which assumes metaphysical dimensions. He is almost cut off from the main current for his experiment, he has suffered the negation of his humanity. An excessive reliance on theories in life brings about its own reversal and in Rowan, it is finally instinct which becomes victorious. Thus, if the Rowan-Joyce equation be made, the Dedalus connection is minimised because it is through Rowan that Joyce's artistic standpoint undergoes constant evolution and it seems to be an injustice to equate him with any character in his fiction.

True it is that Richard overshadows all the other characters by uniqueness, imagination and daring; a combination, which defies and holds all others spellbound. But more than this it is his power and ability to raise fundamental questions about man's nature and existence which casts over others a hypnotic spell which is only explicable in terms of the author's deep involvement in the conception and creation of his central characters. However, it must also be admitted that the unique personal significance of Richard is found to be contradicted and annulled by the action of wounding himself. This laceration heaped upon himself is found to be necessary and concomitant to his pursuit of freedom—both conjugal and existential. He himself has sought to be free through his involvement in his extra-marital affairs. Consequently, he desires that his wife should also partake of a similar freedom through her liaison with Robert.

The ultimate act of betrayal by which Richard exposes himself is to surprise his wife at the serenade where she is supposed to meet her lover, Robert. Having given his consent and having encouraged the affair right from the inception it is quite out of character on his part to step inside the love nest to surprise Robert. This might be termed an instance of authorial intrusion. Joyce as the lover of Nora subconsciously shows his jealousy towards his supposed rival. Richard's argument that Robert betrayed him and invited his wife like a common, sneaking-thief runs on thin ice because as Robert ensures him and he indeed must have common knowledge of the fact that everything is fair in love and war. Moreover, nobody can predict, as Robert says, the ways which passion can take.

In Act II Robert reminds Richard of the pitfalls of allowing his wife to continue her affair with him. Robert cautions him by telling him that if Richard had not intervened timely, his affair with Bertha might have culminated in a physical relationship:

> It would have been different, would it not? For then it might have been too late while it is not too late now. What could I have said then? I could have said only: You are my friend, my dear good friend. I am very sorry but I love her. (With sudden fervent gesture.) I love her and I will take her from you, however I can, because I love her. (*PJJ* 575-76)

Robert clarifies his stance by explaining to Richard that "no man ever yet lived on this earth who did not long to possess—I mean to possess in the flesh—the woman whom he loves. It is nature's law" (*PJJ* 577). Richard expostulates that the physical longing to possess a woman who does not signify love but Robert is explicit on this account:

> There are moments of sheer madness when we feel an intense passion for a woman. We see nothing. We think of nothing. Only to possess her. Call it brutal, bestial, what you will. (*PJJ* 577)

Robert is always carried along the tide of passion, whereas Richard on the other hand, argues for a total affinity of mind and body in love. A love-relationship is not merely based on nakedness of desire. Richard asks Robert:

> Have you the luminous certitude that yours is the brain in contact with which she must think and understand that yours is the body in contact with which her body must feel? Have you this certitude in yourself? (*PJJ* 577)

He adds that he had once been in possession of such a certitude "as luminous" (*PJJ* 577). If however, he felt that Robert had this certitude in himself he says that he is quite willing to admit his defeat. He would then go away for Robert and not himself would be necessary to her.

Richard's explorations into the ramifications of the love relationship between Bertha and Robert is to a certain extent clinical in nature. Here he is arguing for a detached perspective in love. Like Stephen he wishes to achieve the "luminous silent stasis of aesthetic pleasure" in enacting a perfect synthesis of body and mind in love (*P* 213). There is no annihilation of personality through torrential passion. Emotions are never allowed to run riot but are complementary to psychic activities. Where love degenerates into physicality it will tend towards carnality. Thus Richard admits that he has been guilty of extra-marital sex but not love-relationships. At the same time he is anxious that his wife should know not only the nature of his betrayal but also the psychology of her erring husband. He recollects:

> I remember the first time. I came home. It was night. My house was silent. My little son was sleeping in his cot. She, too, was asleep. I wakened her from sleep and told her. I cried beside her bed; and I pierced her heart. (*PJJ* 580)

Richard confesses to Robert that his wife should be acquainted with his true personality. "Feeding the flame of her innocence" with his guilt, Richard had sullied her pure mind and killed the "virginity of her soul" (*PJJ* 580-81). He declines to hide anything from his wife. The notion of stealth, secrecy and cunning in love is something, which is inimical to his philosophy of life. It is largely because of this that he cannot possibly endure Robert's betrayal, calling him a common liar, a thief and a fool. Richard tells his friend that he could never steal in his house because the door stood open nor achieve anything by violence if not resistance was offered.

Because he has been guilty of infidelity, he desires his wife to be free to choose her own destiny. Granting her full liberty, he advises her to choose her partner in life. She is free to accept Robert as her lover if she so desires. Richard says:

> .... You may be his and mine. I will trust you, Bertha, and him too. I must. I cannot hate him since his arms have been around you. You have drawn us near together. There is something wiser than wisdom in your heart. Who am I that I should call myself master of your heart or of any woman's? Bertha, love him, be his, give yourself to him if you desire—or if you can. (*PJJ* 589)

Beneath his altruism and concern for his wife, however, there is a deep masochistic within Richard to wound himself. This provides the dramatic action of the play as the entire plot revolves around his desire to free Bertha from the rigid social conventions of marriage. His act in attempting to free his wife challenges social norm and revolutionises the concept of fidelity and trust between wife and husband. When Bertha asks him to direct and advise her on her proper course of action, Richard confesses his inability and encourages her to have confidence in herself:

> I have a wild delight in my soul. Bertha, as I look at you. I see you as you are yourself. That I came first in your life or before him then—that may be nothing to you. You may be his more than mine. (*PJJ* 589).

Richard's 'wild delight' consists in his subconscious desire to be betrayed by his best friend and by his wife. He tells Robert:

> ...in the very core of my ignoble heart I longed to be betrayed by you and by her—in the dark, in the night—secretly, meanly, craftily. By you, my best friend, and by her. I longed for that passionately and ignobly, to be dishonoured for ever in love and in lust....
>
> .... To be for ever a shameful creature and to build up my soul again out of the ruins of its shame. (*PJJ* 583-84)

The deep wound which Richard inflicts on himself is not only explicable in terms of his masochism but as a consequence of his pursuit of freedom. His quest for liberty in all senses of the term is fraught with danger. His declaration to Bertha that she is free promises no salvation. It might be a direct consequence of Richard's philosophy of freeing the individual from all kinds of bondage; bond of marriage, friendship, including that of morality. The motive behind Richard's action is explained variously. In one sense, he is troubled inwardly for having taken the benefits of liberty while denying her the taste of freedom. He explains to Robert:

> But that I will reproach myself than for having taken all for myself because I would not suffer her to give to another what was hers and not mine to give, because I accepted from her loyalty and made her life poorer in love. That is my fear. That I stand between her and you, between her and anyone, between her and anything. I will not do it. I cannot and I will not. I dare not. (*PJJ* 582-83)

In another sense, Richard's motive lies in exploring the fundamentals of human love beneath the social façade of marriage; in a sort of primitivistic union of man and woman. It argues for a perfect affinity between two people defying the appellations of wife and husband. The basic primal need of man and woman can never be adequately explained by the conventions of marriage or by the sentiment of love. Love becomes too abstract and theoretical a term to describe the basic sexual impulse. In this argument for total emancipation Richard cuts himself off from the ties of family, society and religion, that is, everything which spells security in modern society. Hence, he feels both the torment and exhilaration of living perpetually on the limbo of doubt. He explains to Bertha at the very close of the play:

> I have wounded my soul for you—a deep wound of doubt which can never be healed. I can never know, never in this world. I do not wish to know or to believe. I do not care. It is not in the darkness of belief that I desire you. But in restless living wounding doubt. To

> hold you by no bonds, even of love, to be united with you in body and soul in utter nakedness—for this I longed. (*PJJ* 626)

Doubt is essential for the liberation of self but it does not promise salvation. The point is that Richard is not in a position to know whether Bertha had actually yielded to Robert physically or not. When Bertha asks him whether he desires to know what exactly transpired the night before, when she was with Robert, Richard answers that he will never know. Bertha is willing to tell her husband but he is disinclined because as he says that he will never be in a position to know the truth: "You will tell me. But I will never know. Never in this world" (*Portable* 616). Knowledge does not bring peace and joy also because in his subconscious Richard is guilty of deserting his wife as a critical moment when she anxiously craved his love and support. Bertha complains to him: "Surely you believe me. I gave you myself—all. I gave up all for you. You took me—and you left me" (*Portable* 624). She also accuses her husband of using her as an instrument for his selfish experiments:

> You urged me to it. Not because you love me. If you loved me or if you knew what love was you would not have left me. For your own sake you urged me to it. (*PJJ* 616)

She points out that Richard's search for freedom has been undertaken with a view to release himself from the bond of marriage so that he might be free to love Beatrice. Richard on the other hand, is reluctant to surrender his self to Beatrice. It had been the same case with respect to his mother also. It is Richard's pride which restrains himself from self-surrender in love. Bertha calls him a "woman-killer" and says that he is responsible for the unhappiness caused to his mother, Beatrice and herself.

The point is that Bertha disregards the rationale behind Richard's desire for liberation. Richard himself does not believe in love, which he thinks is merely a form of bondage deriving from a social convention. Like Stephen, Richard is content to escape from the nets of religion, family, politics and love. Yet, as has been remarked earlier, he can scarcely withhold himself from being present at the serenade of the lovers. Thus, his motivations are suspect. Moreover, the final lines of the play, spoken by Bertha forces upon him the lesson that the human emotion of love defies any rigid analysis or any simplistic reduction to the desire of possession. As the curtain descends Bertha cries out to her husband:

> Forget me, Dick. Forget me and love me again as you did the first time. I want my lover. To meet him, to go to him, to give myself to him. You, Dick. O, my strange wild lover, come back to me again! (*PJJ* 626)

Ellmann in his analysis of the play has an important insight to offer, which sheds light on the complexity of Richard's motivation which he terms "ambiguous". He wants to have it both ways. On the one hand, his wife to participate in his search for liberty and on the other hand he cannot tide over his possessive instinct and allow her freedom to result in infidelity.

> But secretly he wishes also to feel the thrill and horror of being cuckolded. Her infidelity and Robert's will confirm his view of the impossibility of a genuine tie between people; yet in his partial wish for confirmation, he is an accomplice in the infidelity. He is caught in his two conceptions of himself: as a searcher for freedom he cannot try to control another, as a necessary victim he cannot resist for himself. There is also another element, his love for his wife, to keep him from acting. But to his wife, love is not what it is to Richard; rather than the bestowal of freedom, it is the insistence upon bonds. She waits for the sign which he will not give, and encourages Robert less for himself than in the hope of bestirring her husband to express his love. Richard begotten the situation from which he proceeds to suffer. (Ellmann 366)

The assumption that Richard is both agent and patient, the doer as well as the sufferer, which complicates his search for freedom, has its origin in the complex psychology of Joyce as the lover of Nora.

In his letter to Nora on 3 December 1909 Joyce confesses to being sexually excited by the idea of his wife's infidelity. His wild lust for Nora is compounded by the thought that she might have had sexual relations with her lovers like Vincent Cosgrave and Michael Bodkin before her marriage (*Selected Letters* 182-83). He confesses openly:

> Sweet heart, answer me. Even if I learn that you too have sinned perhaps it would bind me even closer to you. In any case I love you. I have written and said things to you that my pride would *never again* allow me to say to any woman. (*Selected Letters* 183)

As has been noted earlier, Joyce had some misgivings about Nora's loyalty to him during the period of his courtship. This was due to Cosgrave's suggestion that Nora had been guilty of paying attention to both himself and Joyce during the period of her courtship with latter. This suggestion of promiscuity came from an enemy masked as a friend. Although subsequently Joyce learnt about the falsity of Cosgrave's accusations and of his plot of discredit him, his reaction is interesting because it had a far-reaching effect on his relations to Nora and on his art. In his earlier letter to her on 6 August 1909 he had accused her of infidelity:

> At the time when I used to meet you at the corner of Merrion Square and walk out with you and feel your hand touch me in the dark and hear your voice...as the time I used to meet you, *every second night* you kept an appointment with a friend of mine outside the Museum....
>
> I have heard this only an hour ago from his lips. My eyes are full of tears, tears of sorrow and mortification.... My faith in that face I loved is broken.... I cannot call you any dear name because tonight I have learnt that the only being I believed in was not loyal to me. (*Letters* II: 232)

It was much later that he could feel assured of Nora's love towards him and came to think of their relationship as something special and unusual. This belief cemented the rift between them. But, even though he was certain of her loyalty "he took pleasure in proving it, trying it, questioning it, allowing himself to have doubts of it" (Ellmann 293). He imaginatively recreates his horrible feelings of doubt in Richard, who cannot answer to himself the question whether his wife was actually unfaithful or not. The question of Bertha's fidelity remains unsolved in the play whereas in his own life Joyce could overcome his doubts about Nora. In the play Joyce seems to be returning to his old difficulty of deciding what to be in love is, but now he resolves it, for Richard at any rate, by urging that his emotion for Bertha, instead of being as he once feared less than love, was more than love, a naked union of body and soul (Ellmann 293).

In his conversation with Arthur Laubenstein, a young American organist, Joyce is reported to have asked him: "Which would you say was the greater power in holding people together, complete faith or doubt?" (Ellmann 567). When Laubenstein opted for faith, Joyce deferred and said:

> No, doubt is the thing. Life is suspended in doubt like the world in the void. You might find this in some sense treated in *Exiles*. (Ellmann 568)

Joyce makes creative use of doubt in his play. Like Richard he had experienced the uncertainties and the horror of doubt but whereas he possessed the certainty of belief and had occasion to dispel his doubts, Richard has been consigned to hellish torments of anguish. Finally, one comes to understand that the centre of the play is not Bertha's lover but her husband. The quest for freedom, therefore, begins and ends with Richard, the erring husband. This is because he has a more mature knowledge of life and love than others. Here he seems to outgrow Stephen's adolescence and flower into the mature personal of Bloom. Ellmann points out:

> His notes for *Exiles* are dated November 1913, and show the conception of the play to be already formed. The themes, of return, friendship, and cuckoldry, are close to those of *Ulysses*. Joyce focuses attention in both books on husband rather than on lover; in the notes he attributes to the newly published pages of Madame

> Bovary (discarded by Flaubert) the current movement in thought which takes more interest in the husband's dilemma than the lover's glamour. But principally the husband-hero was a figure through whom he could keep his own matured personal as the centre. (366)

Robert Hand, Bertha's lover was a complex origin. He is a composite figure in whom we find the attributed of Gogarty, Cosgrave, Kettle and Prezioso.

> From his experience with them Joyce drew the picture of friendship which appears in the play: a friend is someone who wants to possess your mind (since the possession of your body is forbidden by society) and your wife's body, and longs to prove himself your disciple by betraying you. (Ellmann 366)

In Joyce's preliminary notes for *Exiles*, dated 12 November 1913 there is an entry concerning 'N.(B)', or Nora Barnacle:

> Garter; precious, Prezioso, Bodkin, music, palegreen, bracelet, cream sweets, lily of the valley, convent garden (Galway), sea: Bodkin was Nora's young Galway suitor who brought her boxes of cream sweets. In this series the new item is Prezioso, the jaunty, dapper Venetian who had been one of Joyce's best friends in Trieste. (Ellmann 327)

Prezioso was an eminent journalist who had helped Joyce "with references for various positions, and had paid him well for his articles in the Picco della Sera" (Ellmann 327). Ellmann is of the opinion that it was during the period of 1912 that Joyce's rift with Prezioso occurred (327). Prezioso had a habit of visiting Nora in the afternoon and sometimes held back for dinner. Joyce approved of his visits and did not object to the attention lavished on Nora.

> Prezioso's admiration for Nora was combined with an admiration for Joyce, whose musical and literary knowledge he tried to absorb. It was probably this peculiar relationship with Prezioso that Joyce drew upon in the later chapters of *A Portrait*, where, with homosexual implications, Stephen's friend is as interested in Stephen

> as in Stephen's girl. At first Joyce followed Prezioso's activities, of which Nora kept him informed, with detachment, and studied them for secrets of the human spirit. But at some time in 1911 and 1912 Prezioso endeavoured to become Nora's lover rather than her admirer. (Ellmann 327)

In spite of Joyce's objectivity and love for his friend, his jealousy was aroused and subsequently he had a confrontation with him, accusing him of broken faith. When Richard accuses Robert of betrayal of the trust confided on him in *Exiles* we are reminded of Prezioso's betrayal of Joyce. Robert is a variation of Roberto, the first name of Prezioso and much of Robert's overtures to Bertha has been modelled on the latter's infatuation with Nora.

In the play, Robert's sensuality has been highlighted in no uncertain terms. To him the beauty of woman is not the prime criterion of her excellence. He seeks in female pulchritude the essential charm of a woman:

> I mean how her body develops heat when it is pressed, the movement of her blood, how quickly she changes by digestion what she eats into—what shall be nameless, laughing. I am very common today. Perhaps that idea never struck you. (*Portable* 556)

It is, therefore, quite consonant with his character when he expresses his idea of freedom in love. Advocating free sex bordering on libertinism, he says that a woman also has the right to try with many men until she finds love (*Portable* 579). When Bertha meets him in the deserted garden house Robert uses all his powers of persuasion to try to seduce her. He informs her that it is her husband's mission in life to liberate himself from every form of bondage including that of law and morality. For sometime in the past he has been trying to break free from the rigid conventions of society and he has more or less succeeded with the single exception of his marriage bond. This bond is now in danger of being broken. Robert passionately states:

> I am sure that no law made by man is sacred before the impulse of passion. Almost fiercely. Who made us for

> one only? It is a crime against our own being if we are so. There is not law before impulse. Laws are for slaves. (*PJJ* 601)

Throughout the play, he fulfils the role of the seducer who tries to drive Bertha inexorably to the moment of final surrender.

Yet there is some justification in his arraignment of Richard in Act II of the drama. When the latter assures him that he was all the while cognizant of Robert's overtures to his wife, he is taken aback:

> I mean, watching me. And you never spoke: You had only to speak a word—to save me from myself. You were trying me.... It was a terrible trial; now also. Desperately. Well, it is past. It will be a lesson to me for all my life. You hate me now for what I have done and for.... (*PJJ* 574)

When Robert tries to apologise, Richard's reaction is not amazing. He openly encourages the affair because he thinks it will lead to self-discovery and true love. At the same time, he pities Robert's advances towards Bertha, dismissing them as a "great mass of overblown rose" (574). Robert is shocked to find that every move of his has been reported to Richard by Bertha. Richard tells him:

> I told you that when I saw your eyes this afternoon I felt sad. Your humility and confusion, I felt, united you to me in brotherhood.... At that moment I felt our whole life together in the past, and I longed to put my arm around your neck. (*PJJ* 583)

Critics have deduced Richard's "homopsychism" from his attitude and conduct in the play (*Critical Heritage* I: 151). Samuel A. Tannenbaum in the *Little Review* (No. 9: V) symposium on January 1919 has this comment to offer on the play:

> To the psychologist trained in psycho-analysis, on the contrary, the book will be agreeably welcome as an inspired contribution from the depths of an artist's soul to one of the most tabooed and falsified motives of human conduct—we mean homosexuality. It is true that

> the reader unlearned in such matters, and perhaps the author too, may not be aware that this is the theme of the play and may look for it in vain. Of course, this is not all there is to play just as in a dream the main motive is overladen and disguised with other subsidiary and rationalizations, so is it in the drama before us. (*CH* I: 150)

Complicated motives inform Joyce's creation of both the central characters, Richard and Robert. It would be too much to say that Joyce betrayed a physical attraction for his friend Prezioso but the fact remains that

> Joyce was half-responsible for Prezioso's conduct, in an experiment at being author of his own life as well as of his work. No doubt he was taking too much upon himself, but he did not do so for pleasure, except perhaps the pleasure of self-laceration. (Ellmann 328)

The play has a daring, experimental nature, which defies Joyce's conservatism in actual life. The dramatist, however he might wish for Nora's freedom in real life, can never prove to be an accomplice in her act of infidelity in real life. Yet the characters are based on genuine experiences in life. Bertha, for instance, is modelled on Nora. Just as Richard feeds the flame of Bertha's innocence with his guilty admission of his extra-marital affairs, so in a different vein Joyce seemed very keen:

> to wound her image of him by swaggering as a desperado, and also wanted her to break through this second image and detect the vulnerable boy. She was not allowed to ignore her crimes; she must absolve them out of love, out of mercy, out of awareness that his real nature was not in them. (Ellmann 175)

As he declared to Nora on 29 August 1904 that he could never reconcile the artist in his with that of the lover. Nora was not exactly his intellectual companion and she could never partake in his literary ventures. Something of the same kind may be witnessed in the hiatus between Bertha and Richard. The dramatist, however, satisfies himself by presenting the liaison between Beatrice and Richard as much more gratifying on the intellectual plane. Whereas Beatrice can keep track of Richard's mind and confesses her sympathy and love for his artistry, Bertha is much more single-minded like Nora and is at a loss of account for Richard's theoretical approach to life. The lacuna in Bertha-Richard relationship is much more vivid than that of Nora and Joyce in real life. It is largely because Richard's act of wounding himself has existential implications.

The artist as Richard is unafraid and life Stephen does not hesitate to proclaim:

> I do not fear to be alone or to be spurned for another or to leave whatever I have to leave. And I am not afraid to make a mistake, even a great mistake, a life long mistake, and perhaps as long as eternity too. (*P* 247)

For this it is essential that he learn "what the heart is and what it feels" (*P* 253). Like Stephen, the artist learns to live with his doubts and does not "wish to overcome them" (*P* 239). He must be conversant with the nature of his shame, ignoble longings and dark passions, consenting to "be for ever a shameful creature" and "to build up his soul once again on the desecration of his spirit" (*PJJ* 584). He even understands the "humility" and "confusion" of his wife's lover and is in collusion with him in secret. Like Stephen he feels, "the thoughts and desires of the race to which he belonged flitting like bats across the dark country lanes, under trees by the edges of streams and near the pool-mottled bags" (*P* 238).

Francis Ferguson in his article on "*Exiles* and Ibsen's Work" in *Hound and Horn* (V), April-June, 1932 has commented on the shadow of Ibsen looming large over Joyce's play. "This spirit blows through Exiles with a super-Ibsen keenness over a colder-than-Ibsen structure of cut stone" (*CH* I: 155). Moreover, as he says:

> In Ibsen and *Exiles* the newness is the point, and in *Exiles* the point is the finality also.... Joyce, faced with this problem (of presenting characters who debate, self-consciously, their rights and wrongs), manages differently. His characters all come clear in the mere presence of the compelling and inquisitorial Richard. He makes their

> halting apologias more credible, as he makes them more complex, once you grant him Richard, in the light of whose mind and under the influence of whose strenuous ethic everything is presented.... And the characters meet, if at all, on the basis of the barest facts of the inescapable human relations, those of parent to child and of man to woman. There is the lamp of the spirit with a vengeance but with its flame not "practically exposed", but as near to "utterly naked" as Rowan-Joyce can make it. Richard Rowan will not have it that the world and the flesh can make him different from what he chooses to be. And the mind of this Rowan-Joyce being is far less provincial than James's own. (*CH* I: 156)

This is actually the heart of Joyce's thesis in Exiles. He takes the modern intellectual drama, the drama of "individualism" to its extreme limits but "at the same time he attains a static perfection of vision which carries him quite beyond that genre, and even amounts to destroying it" (*CH* I: 156). Joyce was especially influenced by Ibsen's *When We Dead Awaken* and composed an article on it before he was 18 years of age. The essay on "Ibsen's New Drama" appeared on April 1, 1900 issue to *The Fortnightly*. Joyce's concern with the life and preoccupations of the artist in *Exiles* is somewhat foreshadowed by Ibsen's presentation of the central dilemma of the sculptor Rubek in *When We Dead Awaken*. Rubek has the unique distinction of transubstantiating Irene's beauty into stone effigies. He has been successful in animating his models but has denuded Irene of her vitality and life-force. She has served Rubek not only with the seriousness of a model but in frank and stark nakedness, giving everything she possessed to his art, but society has cast her out. Rubek proposes to her that they should live life to its full until death arrives.

In *Exiles*, the note of individualism is carried further in the figure of Richard, whose uniqueness lies in his power of subjugating all the other characters to the force of his own theories. The dilemma of the artist has been internalised, rather, the artist Richard becomes his own critique. Joyce's perception of Richard's dilemma is much deeper. Ferguson comments:

> In the last speech of the play, a speech of extreme beauty, wherein a Joycean character comes very near the Ibsen trick of speaking with the author's voice, Bertha places Rowan-Joyce himself among the exiles: "Forget me, Dick", she says. "Forget me and love me again as you did the first time." Which we see—if we remember that all is shown in the light of Richard's mind—as making the exile-vision absolute, removing it from the relativity of meaningfulness of action. (*CH* I: 157)

If, therefore, we refer to something like dramatic action that imparts to the play a meaning with reference to anything outside the shell of the play, we must concede that the personality of the central character has usurped such action. Ferguson is of the opinion that:

> Nowhere outside *Exiles* will you find human isolation so finely rendered—that obstinate incommensurability of human longings which seems to be the cold little wisdom special to our time—both in its bracing fear and exaltation, and in its pity. Yet even while you mourn and thrill you may begin to feel, as in Ibsen, that the case is too special to be satisfying, and the simplification, however brilliant, somehow arbitrary. This is my experience. The "silent stasis of esthetic pleasure" gives place, for me, at a certain point, to an obsessive circling of the mind around a fixed, compelling thought, which is the Stephen-Rowan-Joyce thought of himself. (*CH* I: 158)

Dubliners (1914)

7

The question of distance between the author and his artefact within the Joycean canon may be seen from various points of view. The classical view as adumbrated by W.K. Wimsatt and Monroe C. Beardsley in "The Intentional Fallacy" necessitates the segregation of an author from his work. According to Patrick Cruttwel, the "separation of the author from the man has been prominent only since late in the eighteenth century—that is, since after the Age of Reason". Against this view, however, there is the Romantic insistence on an expressive theory of art, which assigns a determinate function to the poet himself. This affirmation of the artist's presence in his work initiated "as in the English Platonists, so in the Romantic writers, the favourite analogy for the activity of the perceiving mind" which "is that of a lamp projecting light" (Abrams 1958: 60). Brivic in his study *Joyce the Creator* points out that:

> Joyce admired a series of personalities who played productive roles in their writings. Such as Rabelais, Bruno, Swift, Sterne, Blake, Byron and Yeats. Though he never embodied himself in fiction as a narrator, Joyce was increasingly present in his work because he projected himself in parts that added up to a complex Joycean entity. (Brivic 1985: 16)

This notion of the author as multi-mind is taken up by Brivic. He is of the opinion that Joyce's concept of mind grows more complex and sophisticated with the growth of his canon. This was made plausible by his employment of a number of theories of the mind that work together within the entire mental structure constructed by him:

> The creative writer, however, because he deals in metaphors as such and because he tends to be obliged to assume various points of view, is relatively free from the danger of assuming that his figures for the mind are physically real. As the Joycean mind grows through the canon to include more parts and levels of personality, this developing conception comes to unite with a group of minds in one multimind without a single centre. The value of this conception rests on the fact that such an elaborate, populous model of the mind had never been imagined in action before, with one multitudinous exception—the mind of God. Yet through all of this expansion, the construct remained a projection of Joyce's own personal identity. (Brivic 1985: 4)

It is precisely this self-generated myth, centring round his own personality that has given rise to various interpretations explaining the omnipresence of "patriarchal" of "logocentric" authority for the past twenty years or so without radically changing the notion of Joyce within that frame. Vicki Mahaffey in her study *Reauthorizing Joyce* comments:

> This disjunction of attitudes toward authority that separates the mainstream of criticism of Joyce from the mainstream of post-structuralist theory is one of the most interesting cruxes in literary criticism today, partly because Ulysses in particular and the whole of Joyce's corpus in general constitute a reading of such differences and their relationship to one another. What I've called—respectfully-mainstream criticism of Joyce is firmly rooted in the epistemology of Joyce is as strongly rooted in the epistemology of the Wake. The difficulty, and the challenge, is to engineer a point of contact between critics with such opposite orientations and a model for such a bridge may be found in *Ulysses*. (Mahaffey 1988: 2)

Any talk of Joyce's modernity must insist as Helene Cixous points out in her essay "The Use of Writing" on discrediting the subject as a self-contained unit. The notion of self must be opened up to the forces of solicitation, which Derrida speaks about in his *Writing and Difference* (Derrida 1978: 6). Cixous in her essay initiates:

> a reading of Joyce which will point out by means of certain fragments of *Dubliners*, of *A Portrait*, or of *Ulysses* how Joyce's work has contributed to the discrediting of the subject; how today one can talk about Joyce's modernity by situating him "on that breach of the self" opened up by other writings whose subversive force is now undermining the world of Western discourse; how his writing, which is justly famed for its system of mastering signs, for its control over grammar (including its transgressions and dislocations which cut across a language which is too much a 'mother' tongue, too alienating, a captive language which must be made to stumble), how this writing takes the risk of upsetting the literary institution and the Anglo-Saxon lexicon: by hesitating over the interpretation of sings, by the vitiation of metaphor, by putting a question mark over the subject and the style of the subject. (Attridge and Ferrer 1984: 15)

The notion of identity as process is bound up with the subject's "anxiety about language" (Derrida 1978: 3). This anxiety may express itself in various ways. On the one had the prevalent structures of discourse which are codified within societal norms through the ideologies of literature, art, politics, family, church and state may impose restrictions on the free movements of individuality. In this respect, Calvin Thomas notes in the article "Stephen in Process/Stephen in Trial: The Anxiety of Production in Joyce's *Portrait*":

> The subject's struggle for identity-in-language, the subject's attempt to accede to itself by designating itself in a statement, involves its mediation in a complex dialectic of internalization and externalization for which its body and the bodies of others serve as boundaries—imaginary, symbolic and real. It is, however, upon the phenomenon of externalisation that the burden of anxiety

> most heavily falls. For there always lies in wait for any speaking subject a socially determined systems of "ideal receptacles" pre-mobilized to channel or contain whatever the body produces and externalizes from itself-biologically, libidinally, or linguistically. (Thomas 1990: 282-83)

Dubliners forms a unique illustration of the subject's attempt to emancipate itself from such 'socially determined systems of "ideal receptacles" of thought in political, social, religious institutions which threaten to stifle the discourse of the individual (Thomas 1990: 282-83). "The Sisters" present the appropriation of the boy's discourse by that of the old priest. Actually, the tyranny of logocentric authority which encages the boy's self may be located both within himself as well as outside him. It is part of the narrative strategy of *Dubliners* to focus on the inevitable deconstruction of self which issues from the dispassionate prose that becomes self-reflexive as it move from the paralyzing effects of logocentrism outside the subject to within himself.

This shift through narrative technique enables the character to confront his own ontological limits. The narrator comes to terms with his own contradictions in "An Encounter" and "Araby". The fracture of self is also witnessed in "Eveline" and "Two Gallants" and in stories like "The Boarding House", "A Little Cloud" and in "A Painful Case" where the individual in spite of coming to terms with the deconstruction of his self, is actually helpless and incapable of engaging in any positive action. The subject is finally freed from the tyranny of his own discourse in the figure of Gabriel in "The Dead" where he recognizes his own folly in making his wife, Gretta the object of his own desire. The tale of love narrated by Gretta not only forces Gabriel to perceive the warm humanity of his wife who is never a commodity to be possessed but also signifies the deconstruction of his own self. He encounters the negative impulses within him, which tear apart the centrality of his self.

The authorial standpoint in *Dubliners* is primarily neutral, revealing as well as enacting the fracture of the subject without any involvement on his part. To a large extent, the absence of authorial intervention is not merely due to his ideal of the detached artist but because of the lack of centrality in him, which prevents him from being partial to his creations. Rather the willingness to adopt multiple positions within the text shows the decentring of his self, which is equally effected by the undermining of various discourses in the text. It is interesting to note that nowhere in these stories has the voice of the individual been allowed to dominate the narrative. Indeed, the text itself becomes ambiguous, spelling the dissolving of the subject through the colourless narrative that is almost innocent but acts ironically in exposing its own contradictions in the very moments of self-revelation.

In *Dubliners*, the decentring of the authorial self is made possible by means of the epiphanic mode of style. The use of epiphany enables Joyce to avoid the stereotyped narrative modes in order to capture the essence of a trivial moment in the life of an individual. By this means, the materiality of writing not only unconsciously exposes the subject's inner motivation but also the author's consistent irony in implicitly allowing the narrative to dominate the proceedings. Joycean irony unfolds itself in the absence of any position that equally might imply his intention of subjecting the fixity of his authorial viewpoint to a consistent self-critique. This opening up of the writer's self to the forces of his own contradictions drives Joyce to his ontological limits from where he participates in his own deconstruction. According to Robert Langbaum, in the *Poetry of Experience*, Joyce has adopted this mode of perception to give richness to the short story:

> Joyce has taught us, in connection with the latest form of the short story, to call this way of meaning an epiphany a manifestation in and through the visible world of an invisible life.... For the epiphany, in the literary sense, is a way of apprehending value when value is no longer objective—when it is no longer in nature, which is to say in a publicly accepted order of ideas about nature. (Langbaum 1972: 46)

This view of epiphany as originating in the subjective and unconscious aspect of one's personality was later given a new meaning by Joyce. Primarily used to denote a mode of perception it was deployed as an artistic strategy by him. Stephen Hero charts this change of orientation:

> By an 'epiphany', he meant a sudden spiritual manifestation, whether in the vulgarity of speech or of gesture or in a memorable phase of the mind itself. He believed that it was for the man of letters to record these epiphanies with extreme care, seeing that they themselves are the most delicate and evanescent of moments. (188)

According to Stephen, the moment of epiphany is also the instant wherein the mind in an aesthetic act perceives the "quidditas" or "whatness" of a thing. Here the reference is to the object, not to the perceiving mind. Thus Stephen explains that an "object achieves its epiphany" when "the soul of the commonest object, the structure of which is so adjusted, seems to us radiant" (SH, 190). These epiphanies may be thought of as "psychological slips" which people betray and which they most anxiously conceal. But as Peter K. Garrett explains in his editorial introduction to *Twentieth Century Interpretations of "Dubliners"*, Joyce understood the potentialities of his new method and employed it successfully to give concrete embodiment to the moments of paralysis of "hemiplegia" which grips the city of Dublin (Garrett 1968: 11). Thus, "from the outset, Joyce conceived of his method as the ironic, epiphanic exposure of his central theme" of paralysis of will (Garrett 1968: 11). As Attridge and Ferrer write:

> The notion of irony is vital in understanding the necessity of the strategies of hesitation of Joyce's tests. Gripped in a general paralysis, Joyce's writing is obliged to effect a constant activity of refusal of available meanings, explications, discursive forms, "all the very texture of the paralysis". It is precisely the evasion and baffling of the available, the given, its hesitation, to which the writing of Joyce's early texts is devoted and which defines their negativity. (1984: 34)

In *Dubliners,* Joyce uses the epiphanic mode of writing to develop this negative style, which distances the author from the narrative. This kind of writing usually occupies itself with a fragment of dialogue: "The definition of a climactic moment of paralytic banality by its copying down in writing" (Attridge and Ferrer 1984: 35). An appropriate illustration of this kind of writing may be found in Araby where the narrator, who is a young boy goes to the bazaar to buy some gift which would actualize in concrete terms his feelings for Mangan's Sister. On reaching the bazaar his quest is nullified as the bazaar closes for the night. All the boy can do is to listen to a desultory conversation between a young lady and two gentlemen at a stall.

> "O, I never said such a thing:"
>
> "O, but you did!"
>
> "Didn't she say that?"
>
> "Yes, I heard her."
>
> "O, there's a...fib:". (*D* 32-33)

As the boy listens, he feels a deflation, a loss of identity. This note of humiliation which crushes his self spells the loss also of desire: "Gazing up into the darkness I saw myself as a creature driven and derided by vanity: and eyes burned with anguish and anger" (*D* 33).

The keen alienation, which the boy feels, is partly due to his exclusion from social discourse and also because he is intentionally marginalized by the adult community:

> The tone of her voice was not encouraging: She seemed to have spoken to me out of a sense of duty. I looked humbly at the great jars...and murmured: "No, thank you". (*D* 33)

This exclusion, it may be noted, is not merely due to adult apathy and refusal to recognise his value but also caused by his paralysis of will. His failure to act stems from his realisation of the futility of his quest: "I lingered before her stall, though I knew my stay was useless, to make my interest in her wares seem the more real" (*D* 33).

But it was actually boy's imagination which had assigned a fictitious value to the bazaar, "Araby". He had earlier patterned his feelings on the image of Mangan's Sister; carrying her image "even in places the most hostile to romance" (*D*, 28). Every morning he used to watch her through the blind in the front parlour of the house. And when she used to come about on the doorstep he was in the habit of following her and crossing her path without ever talking to her. Yet he confessed that her name was like a "summons" to all his "fallfish blood" (*D* 28). Even the cacophony of voices in the market place converged in a single sensation of life for him. The point is that he could not escape from the agony of his thralldom:

> All my senses seemed to desire to veil themselves and, feeling that I was about to slip from them, I pressed the palms of my hands together until they trembled, murmuring: "O love: O love:" many times. (*D* 29)

It is one of the climaxes of the story that he is liberated from the thralldom of his other self in the moment of epiphany, when he comes to hear the voices of social discourse. Earlier he could hear only his own selfish voice, his imaginative Other. *Dubliners* have for its theme this liberation of self from its own tyranny a disappearing into the selves of others.

This emancipation of self from the despotic influence of others may be seen in the boy's predicament in "The Sisters". Father Flynn becomes synonymous with the word "paralysis":

> Every night as I gazed up at the window I said softly to myself the word paralysis. It has always sounded strangely in my ears, like the word gnomon in the Euclid and the word simony in the Catechism. But now it sounded to me like the name of some maleficent and sinful being. It filled me with fear, and yet I longed to be nearer to it and to look upon its deadly work. (*D* 7)

The boy is gripped by something "uncanny" about the old priest. He cannot break away from his sinister influence. The parents and old Cotter have reservations on this pernicious effect, which the priest was having on the boy. Even when Cotter reprimands him, he is unable to break away from his obsession:

> "It a bad for children", said old Cotter, "because their minds are so impressionable. When children see things like that, you know, it has an effect...". I crammed my mouth with stir about for fear I might give utterance to my anger. (*D* 9)

The apparition of the priest haunts him even in his sleep. As he pulls the blanket over his head, the grey face of Father Flynn pursues him:

> It murmured; and I understood that it desired to confess something. I felt my soul receding into some present and vicious region; and there again I found it waiting for me. It began to confess to me in a murmuring voice and I wondered why it smiled continually and why the lips were so moist with spittle. But then I remembered that it has died of paralysis and I felt that I too was smiling feebly as if to absolve the simoniac of his sin. (*D* 9)

Here the prose takes a dispassionate view of the entire situation. It follows the boy's thoughts, including his reservations while at the same time it presents a critique of his obsessional ideas through the opinions of other characters, without overtly passing any judgement. The sense of powerlessness is evoked in the mood of resignation, following Father Flynn's death. The banal repetitions underline the colourless prose of the narrator in an inhuman world where the essential self of each person is suppressed and mutilated, only to reveal its negativity in a moment of epiphany:

> "He had a beautiful death, God be praised". "He looks quite resigned," said my aunt. That's what the woman we had in to wash him said. She said he just looked as if he was asleep. He looked that peaceful and resigned. No one would think he'd make such a beautiful corpse. (*D* 13)

The epiphanic moment at the close of the story reveals the actual truth of Father Flynn. His madness is described in the impersonal third person narrative technique:

> Wide-awake and laughing-like to himself.... So then of course, when they saw that, that made them, think that there was something gone wrong with him.... (*D* 16)

The image of the old priest laughing insanely at the confession-box at the odd hours of the night haunts the boy. It is only with his death that he feels liberated from tyranny. It is interesting to note that the prose very ironically portrays this sense of relief:

> I found it strange that neither I nor the day seemed in a mourning mood and I felt even annoyed at discovering in myself a sensation of freedom as if I had been freed from something by his death. I wondered at this for, as my uncle and said the night before, he had taught me a great deal. (*D* 10).

The boy comes to face the inexplicable in him. As he grasps his very ambivalence he comes to terms with his multidimensionality which can never be restricted to a single impression. Primarily, it is a triumph of Joyce's prose which split open the very inviolability of self to what Derrida terms an act of soliciting: "a solicitude and solicitation of Being, a historico-metaphysical threatening of foundations" (Derrida 1978: 6). Thus, a comprehension of self in its totality is due to the production of writing which methodically threatens its illusory completeness. As Stephen Heath in his essay, "Ambivalences" points out that the prose of *Dubliners* like that of *A Portrait* produces "its irony of suspended sense", a "strategy of hesitation" which "provokes a confusion in reading" (Attridge and Ferrer 1984: 37). It is this note of "hesitation, held in the Strategy of style (in Flaubert's sense)" and which "stands against the stupidity of conclusiveness", of the lack of any "fixity", deconstructing the "myth of the absolute centre" which made Pound compare Joyce's style with that of Flaubert (Attridge and Ferrer 1984: 37). In his essay "Past History" which appeared in *The English Journal*, Pound commented that: "In *Dubliners*, English prose catches up with Flaubert" (Pound 1968: 248). Again with reference to *Ulysses* he had earlier commented that Joyce "has done what Flaubert set out to do in *Bouvard and Pecuchet*, done it better, more succinct. An epitome" (Pound 1968: 1389).

Joyce's notion of the God-like artist in *A Portrait* who "remains within or behind or beyond or above his handiwork, invisible, refined out of existence" may be thought of in this context of the production of writing which gives rise to a perpetual displacement of sense and meaning (*P* 215). Stephen Heath explains that this idea of the God-like artist does not refer to:

> the question of the artist as substantial subject dominating everything from the fixity of his position, but of the absence of any position, and indifference which is here an illumination, a perpetual movement of difference (in the very movement of hesitation) in which the subject is no longer visible, is dispersed in the writing. (Attridge and Ferrer 1984: 37)

The absence of any fixed point of view may be seen in the portrayal of the central ambiguity in the character of the pervert in "An Encounter". But first it is necessary to realize that the narrator and Mahony both represent two opposite facets of human personality, those of the super ego and the id respectively and the story dramatizes the complex struggle in human nature between these two impulses. James P. Degnan in his essay "The Encounter in Joyce's *An Encounter*" has noted the implications of this fracture of self within the author who submits to the splitting or cleaving within the process of narrative itself:

> Although there are a few hints of an overt conflict between the two boys—the narrator's mild protest against Mahony's—bullying the smaller children, for instance-essentially the struggle mentioned above takes place in the consciousness of the narrator-protagonist. Within the person of the narrator, the reader sees throughout the story, a struggle the narrator himself is never clearly aware of; the struggle between the narrator's values (those of the super ego) and Mahony's (those of the id). (Degnan 1989: 90)

Whereas Mahony represents the natural impulses, the appetites, instincts and aggressive tendencies of the primitive man, the narrator-protagonist has negated his self by listening to the voices of codified morality and institutionalized his subjective responses within prescribed social norms. Although Degnan's essay draws our attention to Freudian echoes in the story (considering the fact that Joyce had not read Freud during the time of composing *Dubliners*) we are much more interested in the ambivalence of the protagonist-narrator. It is because of his divided sympathies that he secretly participates in the voyeurism and sexual perversions of the stranger as well as alienating himself from his pernicious influence. When the pervert pronounces that every boy has a sweetheart and exposes his liberal views, the protagonist-narrator finds his ideas "reasonable" in themselves (*D* 23). But when he starts describing young girls in a salacious manner the protagonist recognizes the banality of his phrasing:

> At time he spoke as if he were simply alluding to some fact that everybody knew, and at times he lowered his voice and spoke mysteriously, as if he were telling us something secret which he did not wish others to overhear. He repeated his phrases over and over again, varying them and surrounding them with his monotonous voice. (*D* 24)

The idea is that the pervert's discourse is impure and contains a mixture of many secondary narratives, which the protagonist recognizes and rejects. What he can't understand is the stranger's newly-found sadism in his theory that boys like Mahony were wild and they need a dose of punishment. Surprised, he looks at the man's face and finds a pair of bottle-green eyes peering at him. Meanwhile the stranger forgets his liberalism: "He said that if ever he found a boy talking to girls or having a girl for a sweetheart he would whip him and whip him; and that would teach him not to be talking to girls" (*D* 25).

The protagonist-narrator is keen to shun the malevolent reality of the stranger and invents fictional identities for Mahony and himself: "In case he asks for our names" I said, "let you be Murphy and I'll be Smith" (*D* 24).

It is necessary to understand that it is this fictitious identity of Murphy who rescues him from the sinister attraction of the pervert:

> I had to call the name again before Mahony saw me and hallooed in answer. How my heart beat as he came

> running across the field to me: He ran as if to bring me aid. And I was penitent; for in my heart I had always despised him a little. (*D* 25-26)

With this, the narrative ends its equivocation, for throughout the story the same pattern may be noticeable. There are of course levels of equivocation: those of the pervert and that of the protagonist-narrator with reference to the stranger and to himself. With the entry of the stranger, therefore, the narrator's malady of his own self has been exposed and he is brought face to face with the different facets of this persona. The pervert, therefore, stands for the other or the locus from which the subject's question of his existence is presented to him. In this instance the other does not support the existence of the protagonist-narrator. It invades him and tears him apart.

In the special issue on feminist readings of Joyce in Modern Fiction Studies, Garry M. Leonard pursues this concept of the other as "The Woman" by a masculine subject in his article on "Araby". In his essay "The Question and the Quest: the story of Mangan's Sister" Leonard points out that:

> For the narrator, Mangan's Sister is a representation of femininity—that is to say the opposite of masculinity.... She does not exist for him except as the representation of lack that confirms the fullness and authenticity of his masculine subjectivity. "The Woman" represents to the masculine subject The Other.... When a woman is taken to be "The Woman" by a masculine subject, she is perceived as enigmatic and powerful because she appears to have the power to nurture or destroy...to confirm the authenticity of his identity or to undermine it. In fact she has the power to do neither; the enigma of femininity merely reflects back to the masculine subject a division that already exists within him. (Leonard 1989: 461)

Actually, the notion of "The Other" refers back to the masculine subject. The denial of the identity of Mangan's Sister is a must so "that he can believe in the myth of himself and thus bear his chalice safely through a throng of foes" (Leonard 1989: 464). But when he fails, it calls into question the precise terms of his own being. This moment of paralysis, which splits open the male psyche to a searching self-examination, also brings about a critique of male domination in female circles.

The conventional mode of textual analysis restricts "Eveline" to a negative theory, which explains the girl's refusal to accept Frank's offer of a new life at Buenos Ayres as her surrender to a paralysis of will. The claustrophobic life at her house necessitated constant hard work with occasional threats from her father. Frank with his promise of marriage in a far-off city on the other side of the globe offers an escape from her hopeless thraldom. As he calls repeatedly to her to follow her on to the barge, she for the first time feels uncertain: "Their passage had been booked. Could she still draw back after all he had done for her?" (*D* 38).

Later she gets scared because her venture with Frank would spell the negation of her separate selfhood: "All the seas of the world tumbled about her heart. He was drawing her into them: he would drown her" (*D* 38). Finally, she abstains from her departure with him. The prose vividly describes her momentary paralysis: "she set her white face to him, passive, like a helpless animal. Her eyes gave him no sign of love of farewell or recognition" (*D* 39).

This refusal of Eveline to accept Frank as a symbol of escape from her drab life implies a denegation of the signified of which he acts as a dubious signifier. For Eveline, Frank fails to act as the signifier of a life of freedom and happiness. This is clearly obvious in her musings when she balances her life with Frank with that of her home:

> Her father was becoming old lately, she noticed; he would miss her. Sometimes he could be very nice. Not long before, when she had been laid up for a day, he had read her out a ghost story and made toast for her at the fire. (*D* 37)

Again when she thinks of her drudgery at home she actually has second thoughts about leaving it: "It was hard work—a hard life—but now that she was about to leave it she did not find it a wholly undesirable life" (*D* 36). Joyce writes:

> She knew very well that if she goes away with Frank she will be respected in a foreign country as his wife whereas staying back might subject her to her father's violent temper, drinking and erratic behaviour. (*D* 36)

Eveline's inability to accept Frank lies in her ambiguous attitude to her home, which she loves although it is morbid and therefore cannot reject it. On the other hand, she does not accept Frank although he acts as a doubtful signifier of a new life. The difference lies in her idea that her home carries a stable signified, a concrete meaning which she feels it is there in reality whereas Frank's signification is based on uncertainty, a perpetual hesitation. It is remarkable that the colourless prose bears on both sides of the question. Her negation of male domination, signified by Frank is also balanced by a weakening of logocentric authority at home signified by an aging father. If Frank, therefore, is taken to signify an Other, it is his love which forces Eveline to fall back on her love for home as her ultimate refuge. Joyce's pattern of discourse balances the two kinds of love against each other and points to a central irony. It is only when Frank becomes importunate that she rejects his domination and guidance. Thus, the moment of epiphany highlights Eveline as a subject, controlling her own mode of discourse, in contrast to her earlier position as an object or a commodity, being made a victim of logocentric authority. This change of roles points to her multidimensionality and her reluctance to be labelled by any single terminology. It must be noted that this positive reading of Eveline's moment of paralysis differs radically with the traditional interpretation as represented by Brewster Ghiselin in his essay, "The Unity of *Dubliners*". She comments:

> At the end, Eveline is "passive, like a helpless animal", as if soulless, paralysed by fear. Lacking the virtue of fortitude that strengthens the soul for compliance with the dictates of reason, she must turn back from danger and from life. (Garrett 1968: 73)

"Two Gallants" focuses on the sin of avarice. "The two characters Lenehan, who is a social parasite (a 'leech'), and Corley, a philanderer embark on a sexual adventure in which their prime ambition is to hoodwink the girl and part with her money."

As Levin and Shattuck have pointed out in their essay,

> the "fine decent tart" whom Lenehan covets and Corley enjoys is a debased Nausicaa, Princess of a seagoing people and befriender of Odysseus.... She is not wholly a succoring princess, though Corley relies on her for gold pieces; she is no angel of the waters, but a gutter sprite. (Garrett 1968: 73-74)

The two gallants' obsession with money however, is part of a wider theme which is one of shifting identities and the attempt to reduce human persona to the level of a commodity with which it becomes almost interchangeable. The labelization of the woman in the description, a "fine decent tart" and of Corley as a "gay Lothario" are quite deceptive. As the romantic adventures of the girl are narrated we realize that adjectives "fine" and "decent" does not quite fit in with her image of a "tart". As for Corley, he is not merely a coquette but it is his hobby to cheat people and cash in on his feigned identities. He confesses to putting on different roles:

> "I told her I was out of a job", said Corley. "I told her I was in Pinis. She doesn't know my name. I was too hairy to tell her that. But she thinks I'm a bit of class, you know. (*D* 48-49)

In the course of their conversation, Corley leaks out some intimate details of the woman's life. As a male, he takes pride not in duping the prostitute but also in subjecting her to the demands of his ego. Lenehan calls him a "base betrayer". Even more interesting is Lenehan's attitude. On his own he can never pride himself on his success with girls and he can only bask in the glory of Corley's success. His ambition was to "be able to settle down in some snug corner and live happily if he could only come across some good simple-minded girl with a little of the ready" (*D* 55). Corley's triumph with girls becomes a symbol of what he always wishes for but can never get:

> In his imagination he beheld the pair of lovers walking along some dark road; he heard Corley's voice in deep energetic gallantries, and saw again the leer of the young women's mouth. (*D* 55)

In these terms, therefore, Corley becomes his fictional embodiment of the desire within him—a desire which he is powerless to satisfy but which he vicariously fulfils through Corley's success. The gold coin, which shines in Corley's palm, becomes a guarantee not only of his success but also that of Lenehan who has willed it. The epiphanic moment occurs when the gold appears magically in the seducer's palms, thus splitting open the contours of Lenehan's hidden and hopeless desires, here culminated through Corley, an extension of his own personality in the man of action, which he can never hope to be.

"The Boarding House" presents the dilemma of Mr. Doran who is cleverly trapped by Polly into marriage under the able machinations of her mother Mrs. Mooney. The interest of the story lies in the vacillations of Mr. Doran as he is gradually trapped by his conscience in a state of paralysis which robs him of his powers of decision and detains him from action. This lack of perspective and of fixed determination makes him an unworthy contestant to Mrs. Mooney who, as the narrator qualifies, "dealt with moral problems as a cleaver deals with meat: and in this case she had made up her mind" to capitalize on the situation (*D* 61). The irony lies in the situation in which Mr. Doran finds him; a predicament from which there is no escape.

The harm was done. What could he do now but marry her or run away? He could not brazen it out. The affair would be sure to be talked of, and his employer would be certain to hear of it. Dublin is such a small city (*D* 63).

Mr. Doran's keen sense of defeat lies in his vague realization that "he was being had" (*D* 64). Perhaps his friends might ridicule him on his being duped. It was true that Polly "was a little vulgar". And yet as he thinks: "But what would grammar matter if he really loved her?" (*D* 64). However, in the situation he finds himself no form of discourse reigns supreme because he becomes the victim of his own indecision: "He could not make up his mind whether to like her or despise her for what she had done. Of course he had done it too" (*D* 64). The uniqueness of the story lies in the gradual paralysis of will. The narrative has prepared us for the ultimate thraldom of Mr. Doran all throughout in impersonal terms.

The prose penetrates deep into the psyche of Mr. Doran, following the movements of his thoughts but refraining from any comment in an irony of suspended sense:

> On nights when he came in very late it was she who warmed up his dinner. He scarcely knew what he was eating, feeling her beside him alone, at night, in the sleeping house. And her thoughtfulness.... Perhaps they could be happy together.... (*D* 65)

The narrative omits all details of seduction. It only objectively traces the contours of her body visible through her sleeping clothes:

> Then late one night as he was undressing for bed she had tapped at his door, timidly. She wanted to relight her candle at his, for hers had been blown out by a gust. It was her bath night. She wore a loose open combing jacket of printed flannel. Her white instep shone in the opening of her furry slippers and the blood glowed warmly behind her perfumed skin. (*D* 65)

Both Doran and Poly hesitate indecisively over the question: "What am I to do?" (*D* 64). Without ensuring identity none of the characters can offer any positive course of action. Yet none of them is acquainted with their true selves. The question of doing recoils on being. Thus, the same question can be seen from both angles: "What am I to do?" (*D* 64). But none are able to answer the first part of the question. In this sense, identity becomes endlessly deferred and selfhood disappears under the burden of fiction. The final bitter lesson confronting Doran is the submission of his self to the hounding voices of codified, institutionalised morality: ".... A force pushed him downstairs step by step. The implacable faces of his employer and of the Madam stared upon his discomfiture" (*D* 65-66).

Fear also prevents Little Chandler in "A Little Cloud" from realising his true self. As he compromises with social forces his identity is perpetually deferred and finally lost in the process. This denegation of himself is implied in Chandler's frustration as he sees Gallaher returning from the continent as a successful reporter who possesses the magic key to self-realisation. When he hears of his friends' return Chandler imaginatively fulfils his lost ambitions by living in a daydream:

> For the first time in his life he felt himself superior to the people he passed. For the first time his soul revolted against the dull inelegance of Chapel Street. There was no doubt about it: if you wanted to succeed you had to go away.... Every step brought him nearer to London, farther from his own sober inartistic life. (*D* 70-71)

Chandler fancies that he has turned a poet, distinguished by a note of melancholy tempered by resignation, appealing to a group of kindred minds. He creates a fiction of his new identity as a successful poet eulogised by critics:

> "Mr. Chandler has the gift of easy and graceful verse"... "A wistful sadness pervades these poems"... "the Celtic note" (*D* 71). His construction of a new identity clashes with the old. Hence he remains dissatisfied with his name: "It was a pity his name was not more Irish-looking. Perhaps it would be better to insert his mother's name before the surname. He would speak to Gallaher about it." (*D* 71)

Chandler's change of identity will be henceforth confirmed by Gallaher, who represents all that he wished for but can never be. In terms of fiction, therefore, his selfhood will be eternally deferred since the ultimate referentiality which will give meaning to his usurpation of a new identity does not exist. The epiphanic moment highlights Chandler's defeat as he comes to realise that his projection of desire on Gallaher will be of no help to him in transcending his present identity. Angered by the failure of his vision he takes it out on his little child but then he cannot control him once the boy starts sobbing. The mother rushes in to comfort the child and as she softly caresses him, Little Chandler feels humiliated and ashamed. The attempt to replace his self by that of another amount to a negation of his humanity.

Mr. James Duffy in "A Painful Case" is guilty of a similar failing. He consciously suppresses his sexual impulses, the uncertain demands of the id. This denial of the vital springs of life within him makes him "Saturnine". He detests everything "which betokened physical or mental disorder". The narrative focuses on his inhumanity without any comment:

> He lived at a little distance from his body, regarding his own acts with doubtful side-glances. He had an odd autobiographical habit which led him to compose in his mind from time to time a short sentence about himself containing a subject in the third person and a predicate in the past tense. He never gave alms, to beggars, and walked firmly, carrying a stout hazel. (*D* 106)

But Duffy's impersonal attitude is based on negation. He never consorted with friends or relatives, neither belonged to church or creed, visited his relatives only at Christmas and escorted them to the Cemetery on the occasion of their death. This absence from the centre of life's discourse implies also an escape from an essential part of his self. The problem arises when he comes in contact with Mrs. Emily Sinico, the wife of a sea-captain. For Duffy the flirtation was singularly untouched by passion:

> This union exalted him, wore away the rough edges of his character, emotionalised his mental life. Sometimes he caught himself listening to the sound of his own voice. He thought that in her eyes he would ascend to an evangelical stature; and, as he attached the fervent nature of his companion more and more closely to him, he heard the strange impersonal voice which he recognized as his own, insisting on the soul's incurable loneliness. (*D* 109)

This positioning of the conscious self outside the perimeters of desire and yet partaking of the physical proximity of "The Woman" lands both of them in an ambiguous relationship. On one level Duffy is clearly looking for an extension of his male ego in his search for the other in Emily. But does Mrs. Sinico really appear at the locus of the question about the masculine identity?

> Essentially, the other is a concept designating the reference point from which we establish our identity—between consciousness and unconsciousness, between others and language, somewhere between our sense of what is inside and outside. (Leonard 1989: 461)

It is quite evident that Duffy is reluctant to consider Mrs. Sinico as the Other. He is trapped within his ego. But he is determined not to part with his inviolable self. He says, "We cannot give ourselves,... We are our own" (*D* 109).

The result is that when one night she had manifested her passion to him, he gets "disillusioned". Confirming their estrangement on a last encounter Duffy sends her to her death:

> They agreed to break off their intercourse: every bond, he said, is a bond to sorrow. When they came out of the Park they walked in silence towards the tram; but here she began to tremble so violently that, fearing another collapse on her part, he bade her good-bye quickly and left her. (*D* 109)

Four years later, he reads of her death in the Mail. The impersonal narrative of the reporter contains an ironic note because the newspaper account ends conclusively, exonerating everyone from blame, the coroner having pronounced a verdict of suicide. The reportorial detachment describes vividly Mrs. Sinico's suicide as she threw herself against an oncoming steam engine.

But the point is that the indirect narration shocks Duffy very differently at first. He initially has a notion that she has debased herself in giving reins to her uncertain impulses. A conscious attempt on his part to detach himself from his memory of her, however, lands him in trouble. It is a triumph of Joyce's prose that it narrates the predicament of Duffy in an objective manner, showing an absence of any fixed point of view. But the ironic tone underlies Duffy's damnation without ever explicitly uttering it. The last sentence of the reporter reads: "No blame attached to anyone" (*D* 112). Similarly, as he thinks of her suicide Duffy confirms his course of action: "He had no difficulty now in approving of the course he had taken" (*D* 113).

But as he walks the park at night memories of his former tryst with her invade his mind and his self-complacency is blasted. He begins to recognize his guilt:

> At moments he seemed to feel her voice touch his ear, her hand touch his. He stood still to listen. Why had he withheld life from her? Why had he sentenced her to death? He felt his moral nature falling to pieces. (*D* 114)

Duffy's escape from his own instincts has at last led to a fracture of his own inviolable self. He comes to recognize the multiplicity of his desires and failings and learns that his perpetual deferment of his own essential self has brought him to a crisis of identity. It is a moment of defeat for him since he has damned himself by postponing to himself the object of his own desire, which was always present lurking beneath the surface of his fictitious identity which he always believed in. Yet, although he gains knowledge, he cannot return to his origins. He is marginalized from the centre of his true identity, becoming an "outcast from life's feast". In the moment of epiphany when he feels the shadows of the park alive with human forms making "venal and furtive loves" it fills him with "despair". He is forced to gnaw at the "rectitude of his life". He is sickened with the knowledge that "one human being had seemed to love him and he had denied her life and happiness: he had sentenced her to ignominy, a death of shame" (*D* 114). He suffers the fracture of his own self but does not make any attempt at reparation. The knowledge paralyses him. He creeps back, the wretch, to his self-imposed isolation: "He felt that he was alone" (*D* 115).

In a certain sense, Duffy's inability at self-articulation is part of what Trevor L. Williams in his essay "Resistance to Paralysis" calls the individual's loss of control:

> over the production and reproduction of her or her world. Joyce's characters are precisely in this position of loss of control, and consequently as human subjects they are deactivated. However, they are not inactive; they continue to function as human beings, their activity merely displaced into certain kinds of false consciousness. (Williams 1989: 438)

The individual's powerlessness in controlling his world can be seen also as his loss of "linguistic ownership" (Williams 1989: 440). Adopting this term from Feruccio Rossi-Landi, Williams explains that it denotes:

> the tendency (frequent in Joyce) for characters not to be in control of language, indeed for language sometimes to speak the characters, as in the hell-fire sermons of *A Portrait*; and, above all, for characters simply not to possess a language, to be, like Eveline, Voiceless. (Williams 1989: 437-38)

Williams finds both males and females in *Dubliners* "complicit in their own oppression" although it is only in the last story that we find females resisting "the mystification and reification of the male world" (Williams 1989: 438). In "A Painful Case" Mr. Duffy thinks that conventional mode of discourse is insufficient to become a vehicle for his ideas. He considers it preposterous to "compete with phrasemongers" and "submit himself to the criticisms of an obtuse middle class which entrusted its morality to policemen and its fine arts to impresarios" (*D* 108-09). But if he rejects bourgeois narrative he fails to clarify his position in the passionate situation he finds himself in the proximity of Mrs. Sinico. When she shows signs of "unusual excitement" Mr. Duffy is taken aback. "Her interpretation of his words disillusioned him" (*D* 109). This discrepancy between expression and the implied brings into the text an uncertainty and deferment of meaning. Duffy's subjective interpretation of the newspaper report of Mrs. Sinico's death is another instance in point: "The threadbare phrases, the inane expression of sympathy, the cautious words of a reporter won over to conceal the details of a commonplace vulgar death attacked his stomach" (*D* 112).

Duffy's thought that the indifferent and terse report contributes to the degradation of her soul and by reference also brings about his degradation is supremely ironic. Thus as Williams explains:

> ...it is now possible to see that even in Dubliners characters struggle to impose meaning upon their experience, only to be defeated by the slipperiness of

> language and grammar-meaning always appears to be elsewhere. (Williams 1989: 447)

As language suffers from the instability of meaning, the achievement of selfhood is indefinitely deferred.

The same hiatus between what is said and what is meant is apparent in the last story, "The Dead". M. Norris in her essay "Stifled Back Answers: The Gender Politics of Art in Joyce's 'The Dead'", "cautions us" towards the "grandiose" phrases and ideological assumptions of its own aestheticist narrative' which inculcates in us a "Scepticism":

> We must be especially careful, like the woman in "The Dead", not to be seduced by the story's exceptionally beautiful prose, for its lyrical narrative voice is not "innocent". It effectively promotes a cultural ideology that is especially inimical to the female subject and to the female artist, and Joyce nudges us repeatedly to think against the ideological grain of the narration by genderizing ourselves not merely as subjectively female but as politically feminist, as resisting readers, critics, and skeptics of the text. (Norris 1989: 481)

The ambiguity of Joyce's prose may be seen in the description of Gretta through the eyes of her husband, Gabriel Conroy. As he looks up at her through the gloom he is fascinated by her still pose in the shadow.

There was grace and mystery in her attitude as if she were a symbol of something. He asked himself what is a woman standing on the stairs in the shadow, listening to distant music, a symbol of (*D* 207). This denegation of the woman as a persona by a gradual process of social decontextualising into a mere symbol exhibit the male's desire to possess her in the name of romantic love. The narrative underlines this lordship of the male in impersonal terms: "It was his wife" (*D* 207). M. Norris comments:

> In this superb staging of the aestheticising act, Joyce displays his acute awareness that in their genderised form, in the male artist's representation of the female, the politics of representation are expressed in doubly

> brutal gestures of occlusion, oppression, and exploitation; doubly brutal, because these acts are masked as love. (Norris 1989: 482)

The ironical implications of this prose, however, lies deeper. Here the picture of his wife as he would like to draw has been perceived by Gabriel, who assigns a title to her portrait, calling it "Distant Music". Initially, the irony lies in a contradiction between the thoughts of possession which fills Gabriel's mind and the fact that his wife is actually recollecting the tragedy of her dead lover, Michael Furey. The text, which seems innocent, does not reveal this until the closing pages of the story. And it is one of the strategies of this story to systematically strike at the bastion of male ego until it crumbles at the very end. Thus the very attempt at falsification as well as nullification of the identity of Gretta recoils upon the presumptive male. It is remarkable that Gretta's silence as to the object of her thinking allow Grabriel to live in a world of illusion. It is also ironical that inspite of his death Michael Furey still lives in the mind of Gabriel's wife whereas his identity merges in the plethora of other voices. This is because Gabriel tends to appropriate his wife in terms of conventional discourse. He needs to re-think his vision of womanhood. Once he does that he will be able to return to his original self. The triumph of the narrative lies in its compelling the male to participate in the sufferings of the woman while at the same time wringing from him the recognition of Gretta as a living individual, freed from the context of male possessiveness:

> Generous tears filled Gabriel's eyes. He had never felt like that himself towards any woman, but he knew that such a feeling must be love. The tears gathered more thickly in his eyes and in the partial darkness he imagined he saw the form of a young man standing under a dripping tree. Other forms were near. His soul had approached that region where dwell the vast hosts of the dead. He was conscious of, but could not apprehend, their wayward and flickering existence. His own identity was fading out into a gray impalpable world: the solid world itself, which these dead had one time reared and lived in, was dissolving and dwindling. (*D* 220)

The text balances two modes of vision, two desires, that of Gabriel for Gretta and of Gretta's for Michael Furey. And, if we talk about self-realisation through a discovery of real identity we must relate it to the achievement of desire. But Furey is dead and Gretta's love remains unfulfilled. Her admission that Furey "did not want to live" not only haunts her, but also Gabriel and the text. With the postponement of desire, the achievement of selfhood is infinitely deferred. Like Gretta's wound which remains opened through which flows grief, similarly Gabriel's wound in his manhood can never be stopped. This consciousness brings about a critique and a parody of Gabriel's earlier self which had exulted in his pride possession:

> He saw himself as a ludicrous figure, acting as a penny-boy for his aunts, a nervous, well-meaning sentimentalist, orating to vulgarians and idealizing his own clownish lusts, the pitiable fatuous fellow he had caught a glimpse of in the mirror. (*D* 216-17)

Again, as he gazes at Gretta sleeping: "He watched her while she slept, as though he and she had never lived together as man and wife" (*D* 219). This fracture of his earlier solipsistic, selfish self is never healed. Gretta's sleep, Furey's death, the soft snowfall endlessly descending emphasise an inconclusiveness underlined by Gabriel's routine gesture of lying beside his wife. The uncertainty lies in man's self which, as "The Dead" proves, is elusive in character. Thus, as the two above excerpts illustrate, Gabriel discovers something in both his wife and himself, which was not apparent earlier. Return to his original self necessitates a new language and unless Gabriel discovers it, his identity will remain eternally deferred. In one of his letters to Gretta he therefore questions: "Why is it that words like these seem to me dull and cold? Is it because there is no word tender enough to be your name?" (*D* 211).

A Portrait of the Artist as a Young Man (1916-17)

8

"The artist, like God of creation, remains within or behind or beyond or above his handiwork, invisible, refined out of existence, indifferent, paring his fingernails" (*P* 215). Stephen's observation on authorial detachment has been the occasion of a host of theses and counter-theses among critics. The prominent narratologist, J.P. Riquelme in his "Teller and Tale in Joyce's Fiction" suggests that along with Portrait, Stephen is also the author of both *Dubliners* and *Ulysses* (Riquelme 1983: 95). He notes that Portrait is the result of corporate authorship of both Joyce and Stephen:

> Many critics who have written on *A Portrait* interpret that work autobiographically, claiming that it is based on details of Joyce's youth. Generally, they adduce the title as evidence for the link between the life and the work of art: the portrait is of the artist who writes the book. Unquestionably, strong evidence supports this kind of autobiographical reading. But an autobiographical interpretation of a different sort is also possible, one that sees Stephen Dedalus as the teller of his own story.... In *A Portrait*, we discover that the fulfillment of the process of becoming an author occurs in the act of writing, a belated activity in which character and narrator may be one. Implicit in the story of Stephen Dedalus's growth to maturity is the process by which this book emerges from previously existing texts that Stephen knows, some of which he has written himself. *A Portrait* is both the author's autobiographical fiction and the autobiography

> of the fictional character. It provides the portrait of both artists. (Riquelme 1983: 51)

Any perceptive reading of Joyce, however, involves firstly a recognition of the pivotal role of *Portrait* in the Joyce cannon, without which any approach to his later work would be fragmentary. Secondly, a notion of identity must also take into account, as Robert Young points out in his introduction to Maud Ellmann's essay on *Portrait*:

> The materiality of writing in the novels: at all points, Joyce's texts resist their appropriation back into the discourse of realism, of representation, because of the oddness and opacity of their language. What is perhaps most remarkable, in view of the challenge which Joyce's novels present, has been the tenacity with which they have been read as windows on to the world or into the mind. (Young 1987: 189)

It is precisely here that the binary approach to language and discourse which sees Stephen's position as incessantly alternating between the twin polarities of classical realism (mirror) and romanticism (lamp) seems to be too glib. The materiality of writing is inextricably linked with identity.

Robert Young explains:

> In—"Disremembering Dedalus", Maud Ellmann shows how in *A Portrait* language does not seek to express, represent, reconstitute or describe "experience" or "reality". But to the fiction of transparent language, the subject, here the subject of (autobiography). If the novel is a portrait, a representation, at all, it is, because it shows the becoming of the subject in writing (biography). Rather than portraying the well-rounded "character", it shows the fading of the subject as serial. (Young 1987: 189)

This idea of the decentred self runs counter to the conventional approach to *Portrait* which sees Stephen's identity as slowly maturing through the pose of artistic isolation and detachment from the debilitating influences of family, religion and nation.

Thus:

> *A Portrait* presents a Stephen Dedalus who is disremembering, not developing but devolving, not achieving an identity but dissolving into a nameless scare. A full and self-present consciousness, "His Majesty the Ego" as Freud put it, gives way to the self-mutilation of the subject in and as metaphor. (Young 1987: 189)

Thomas' essay "Stephen in Process/Stephen on Trial: The Anxiety of Production in Joyce's *Portrait*" highlights the manner in which the novel "puts Stephen en process, positions him in the space opened up by the question of productive anxiety—is, of, and about language and the body—the way Joyce articulates Stephen's anxiety of production so as to disarticulate and disperse his own" (Thomas 1990: 285). The notion of the "decentred self" brings into play "the radical heterogeneity and play-of-difference of all signifying practice" which:

> insures that no subject position is fixed: the subject, who can only signify himself within such practices, is never fully present to himself or to the Law but is rather always put en process—a term that Kristeva uses to signify both "in process" and "on trial". (Thomas 1990: 284)

In *Portrait*, Joyce puts Stephen "en process", positioning him in the space opened up by the question of productive anxiety especially with reference to Catholicism, nation and art. For instance, Stephen's ambivalent attitude to religious belief and the church has a reification on his attitude to art. His critique of logocentric patterns of thought in Catholic belief fosters a rethinking of the authorial perspective, locating him nowhere and yet everywhere in discourse. Indeed, through the novel the fluidity of the subject is largely the result of a loosening of the bonds of authority in terms of paternity, both legal (earthly) and religious. The productive anxiety is to be found in Stephen's search for his origins which eludes him always. The fluidity of images, and of discourse enacts this perennial search for paternity and in this way the realization of identity becomes a never-ending process. In chapter nine of

Ulysses, for instance, Stephen alias Telemachus has a question relating not only his earthly father but also the father in heaven:

> Fatherhood, in the sense of conscious begetting, is unknown to man. It is a mystical estate, an apostolic succession, from only begetter to only begotten. On that mystery and not on the Madonna which the cunning Italian intellect flung to the mob of Europe the church is founded and founded irremovably because founded, like the world, macro and microcosm, upon the void. Upon incertitude, upon unlikelihood. Amor matris, subjective and objective genitive, may be the only true thing in life. Paternity may be a legal fiction. Who is the father of any son that any son should love him or he any son? (*U* 179)

If fatherhood is founded upon void and incertitude, it also questions the authorship of texts. As Maud Ellmann in her essay "Polytropic Man: Paternity, Identity and Naming in *The Odyssey* and *A Portrait of the Artist as a Young Man*" points out that "Where do texts come from may be another variation of the question 'Where do babies come from' and in this sense not only Joyce and Homer but also Freud may be involved in the issue of parentage" (MacCabe 1982: 76). As trace of parentage begins to get blurred similarly we begin to question whether the word/work actually reflects the author or whether the self of Joyce may be seen within his fictional successor, Stephen. That is to ask whether the text assumes a transparency through which a linear equation may be made between itself and the author. Maud Ellmann observes in the same essay:

> Dismembered of his mouth or tongue, condemned to "hasitense" or silence, the fallen father of the Wake can neither speak his thoughts nor name his tots. No more can tots like Stephen Dedalus find out their fathers, the authors of their strange un-Irish names. With the fall of the father, the question of the origin of texts and babies thoughts or tots becomes at once rhetorical and inexhaustible. The word in search of a speaker—the letter in search of a scribe—the thought in search of a thinker—the son in search of a sire: all these orphans

> circulate through Joyce's writing, adrift as the itinerant Odysseus, unappeased as fatherless Telemachus. Their wanderings bear witness to convulsions in the order by which fathers beget sons, authors beget thoughts, and gods beget worlds. (MacCabe 1982: 76)

The notion of identity and its relationship to paternity is posited right at the inception of Portrait. Simon Dedalus is heard narrating a story beginning with:

> Once upon a time and a very good time it was there was a moocow coming down along the road and this moocow that was coming down along the road met a nicens little boy named baby tuckoo.... His father told him that story; his father looked at him through a glass: he had a hairy face. He was baby tuckoo. (*P* 7)

As the father names his son "baby tuckoo", it signifies Stephen's entry into the narration. Although the "he" wavers between the father and his son so, it also signifies a continuity and unity between themselves. Initially, however, the distinctness of two persons have been emphasized by describing the father who had a hairy face and the son who was baby tuckoo. As the narrative progresses Stephen's separate identity gathers momentum. He sings his song. He wets his bed which first gets warm but then turns cold.

This sense of attachment and separation from his bodily flow which makes his bed uncomfortable invites his mother's supervision, who changes his oil sheet. Stephen states that "His mother had a nicer smell than his father. She played on the piano the sailor's hornpipe for him to dance. He danced..." (*P* 7). Already Stephen's estrangement from his father has begun. The germ of his fear—fear of dispossession and loss of paternity—which culminates later in his conscious alienation from his real identity, can be detected in the initial pages of the novel. Calvin Thomas comments:

> And yet, in this movement from paternal narration to the mother's music, the problems of identification and separation, of Stephen's "telling himself" both from and through significatory practice, have only been figured in

> roughcast. The problem of separation, not of Stephen from his mother's body but of Stephen from himself, is prefigured in the sentence "when you wet the bed first it is warm then it gets cold". To give Kenner a qualified echo, I would venture that it is not a complete exaggeration to say that every theme in the life work of James Joyce is figured in this one sentence from *A Portrait*. Here I post the flat surface of the bed as blank space, a scene of writing, and the urinary stain itself as a transitional part-object, an inscription, a signifying trace. (Thomas 1990: 287)

According to Derrida, "the trace is the erasure of selfhood, of one's own presence, and is constituted by the threat or anguish of its irremediable disappearance, of the disappearance of its disappearance" (Derrida 1978: 230). This erasure which is likened to death itself parallels the indelibility of certain traces in the unconscious, where "nothing ends, nothing happens, nothing is forgotten" (Derrida 1978: 230). It is within this context that the ambivalence of the author presents itself in *Portrait* in the absence of any fixed standpoint. Stephen's authorship is denied any referentiality in the text itself because the writing becomes a "self-reflexive" process, "a perpetual displacement of sense in a play of forms without resolution" (Attridge and Ferrer 1984: 36). Stephen Heath in his essay "Ambivalences: Notes for Reading Joyce" points out how:

> This irresolution is the very wager of *A Portrait*; the carrying through of two fictions, that of the doxa (Dublin, the Church, the family) and that of the paradoxa (the artist), without the writing being committed to either. The writing of the book is thus a tourniquet between the two fictions and it is in this mobility that the writing hesitates irresolvably. (Attridge and Ferrer 1984: 36)

Thus, the perpetual hesitancy brought about in writing deconstructs not only the logocentric closure of authority in traditional institutions but also does away with the conventional notion of the "bildungsroman" presenting the development of character by stages. The novel systematically reduces the character of Stephen to a plethora of positions, which suffer perpetual modification. From the very first to the penultimate lines of the novel, Stephen is disinclined to commit himself to any fixed static point of view. "Freedom" becomes his motto. Cranly reminds him of his previous determination: "To discover the mode of life or of art, whereby your spirit could express itself in unfettered freedom" (*P* 246). To this end he abjures any form of institutional authority which is likely to codify his freedom within a fixed scale of values:

> I will not serve that in which I no longer believe, whether it calls itself my home, my fatherland, or my church: and I will try to express myself in some mode of life or art as freely as I can and as wholly as I can, using for my defence the only arms I allow myself to use—silence, exile, and cunning. (*P* 247)

As Stephen turns himself loose from all moorings in society, the artist faces his self-imposed isolation and his writing becomes self-reflexive. Here the artist faces two forms of anxiety. As the dispossessed artist, his search for his true origins lead him nowhere with the result that his true self eludes his realization. This leads to his struggle for "identity-in-language", a perpetual scripting of his self in writing (Thomas 1990: 282). It also encourages Stephen to play various fictional roles, which are primarily designated to mislead people but also serve to land Stephen into existential doubt as to the true nature of his own self. Throughout the novel, he betrays an anxiety of losing his essential identity and which conversely forces him to use the weapons of silence and cunning. At school when Wells asks him whether he kissed his mother before going to bed, he answers in affirmative. But when his friends start laughing he recants and says that he did not. Still they laughed and Stephen becomes confused. He falls into doubt: "What was the right answer to the question? He had given two and still Wells laughed. But Wells must know the right answer for he was in third of grammar (*P* 14)".

The entire point of the episode lies in the pattern of discourse. In these lines the prose follows Stephen's thought but earlier it becomes non-committal since it records Wells' statement which is shown in the form of a repetition:

> Tell us, Dedalus, do you kiss mother before you go to bed? Stephen answered:
>
> ...I do. Wells turned to the other fellows and said:
>
> .... O, I say, here's a fellow says he kissed his mother every night before he goes to bed.

The other fellows stopped their game and turned round, laughing. Stephen blushed under their eyes and said:

> ...I do not. Wells said:
>
> .... O, I say, here's a fellow says he doesn't kiss his mother before he goes to bed.
>
> They all laughed again. Stephen tried to laugh with them. (*P* 14)

Stephen's insecurity and uncertainty is positioned between a positive and a negative assertion. Wells' hazing of Stephen is also placed between a positive and a negative term. But as Stephen indicates, Wells knows the correct answer while he does not without taking sides the prose exposes Stephen' vacillation and hesitancy. This becomes all the more ironic when we remember that it is supposed to be Stephen's own prose as he is composing his own autobiography. As the invisible author, Joyce then allows Stephen to form his own critique although unconsciously. In this sense, Joyce's irony which might be well termed "hesitancy" may be said to lack any centre: "it knows no fixity, and its critique is not moral, derived from some sense, but self-reflexive, a perpetual displacement of sense in a play of forms without resolution" (Attridge and Ferrer 1984: 36). The elusiveness of this irony which Stephen Heath explains in "Ambivalences" may be expanded further.

Stephen's uncertainty and infirmity of purpose with regard to kissing his mother has just been noted. His basic insecurity is again seen when he visits the prostitute at the end of chapter two. He is seen recovering his firmness and confidence in the arms of the woman. At first Stephen exults in his newly discovered freedom: "Tears of joy and relief shone in his delighted eyes and his lips parted though they would not speak" (*P* 101). His sensibilities illustrate a complex range of reactions. It shows his usurpation of authority in terms of assertion of his sexual prowess. He tears himself loose from his origins because he negates the authority of both his earthly father and the father in heaven. In this sense, he illustrates the profane joy of a sinner who exults in his sexual knowledge. His fall may be likened to Adam's usurpation of knowledge by partaking of the forbidden fruit.

But before yielding to her charms he must be reassured of his identity which he constantly fears that he might lose. The woman asks for a simple kiss but,

> his lips would not bend to kiss her. He wanted to be held firmly in her arms, to be caressed slowly, slowly, slowly. In her arms he felt that he had suddenly become strong and fearless and sure of himself. But his lips would not bend to kiss her. (*P* 101)

Here as before Stephen positions himself between doing and not doing between self-assertion and self-negation. His ambivalence ends when,

> with a sudden movement she bowed his head and joined her lips to his and he read the meaning of her movements in her frank uplifted eyes. It was too much for him. He closed his eyes, surrendering himself to her, body and mind, conscious of nothing in the world but the dark pressure of her softly parting lips. They pressed upon his brain as upon his lips as though they were the vehicle of a vague speech; and between them he felt an unknown and timid pressure, darker than the swoon of sin, softer than sound or odour. (*P* 101)

It is to be noted that the prose not only reveals Stephens' inner desires and motivations but it also varies between impersonal narration and lyrical effusion. It is all the more remarkable if we feel that the language enacts the joy of a sinner in the sexual act prefigured by the moment of kiss, without imposing any moral restraint. At the same time the prose becomes uncertain, hesitating, without properly clarifying the knowledge gained from sin. If it signifies joy, it also signifies torpor:

> It was his own soul going forth to experience, unfolding itself sin, by sin, spreading abroad the bale-fire of its burning stars and folding back upon itself, fading slowly, quenching its own lights and fires. They were quenched and the cold darkness filled chaos. (*P* 103)

The prose shows its lack of a firm point of view in its portrayal of Stephen's soul both "unfolding" as well as "folding back upon itself": "spreading abroad the bale-fire" and also "quenching its own lights and fires". The process of writing therefore decentres the wholeness and totality of identity in a number of ambivalent postures.

The woman's kiss at the end of the previous chapter is again subject to re-writing in a new context when Stephen utters the glorification of Mary through prayer. Theological and sexual implications converge in an ambivalence of signs which makes both the performance and the writing of sin full of mystery. Kissing, therefore, signifies both the profane and the sacred in the domain of love. Joyce's irony of suspended sense is seen in the falsity of Stephen's posture as prefect in the college of the sodality of the Blessed Virgin Mary.

> The falsehood of position did not pain him. If at moments he felt an impulse to rise from his post of honour and, confessing before them all his unworthiness, to leave the chapel, a glance at their face restrained him. The imagery of the psalms of prophecy soothed his barren pride.... When it fell to him to read the lesson towards the close of the office he read it in a veiled voice, lulling his conscience to its music. (*P* 104-05)

This passage shows how Stephen's sinning nature is held captive by religious practices. Simultaneously, the prose exposes Stephen's ambiguous role. He participates in the ritual but all the while positions him outside the discourse. He effaces the trace of his identity in both cases. Earlier, in his encounter with the prostitute we noted how "his brain and his lips" become "the vehicle of a vague speech", thereby yielding his self to "an unknown and timid pressure". Presently, we notice how Stephen is forced to restrain himself, to forego his true identity in favour of another. Indeed the prose very insidiously prevents him from indulging in a true confession which might have reconciled him to his true self.

The ambiguity deepens with Stephen's negative refuge in the act of sin: "His sin, which had covered him from the sight of God, had led him nearer to the refuge of sinners" (*P* 105). But the ideal of Mary forestalls any emancipation of self. Here religious discourse becomes ambivalent "Her eyes seemed to regard him with mild pity; her holiness, a strange light glowing faintly upon her frail flesh, did not humiliate the sinner who approached her" (*P* 105). The profane and sacred in Stephen's prose intermix, making the act of writing impersonal:

> If ever his soul, re-entering her dwelling shyly after the frenzy of his body's lust and spent itself, was turned towards her whose emblem is the morning star, bright and musical, telling of heaven and infusing peace, it was when her names were murmured softly by lips whereon there still lingered foul and shameful words, the savour itself of a lewd kiss. (*P* 105)

Stephen cannot understand how his lips could be signifier of things, bearing opposite value. If it is so his self becomes a prey to whimsical forces. This fear of losing his identity makes his prose self-reflexive and turn back on itself.

Towards the end of *Portrait* when Cranly asks Stephen about his beliefs in the Eucharist, the latter gives an evasive answer: "I neither believe in it nor disbelieve in it" (*P* 239). When Cranly further enquires:

> Many persons have doubts, even religious persons, yet they overcome them or put them aside; Cranly said. Are your doubts on that point too strong?
>
> I do not wish to overcome them, Stephen answered. (*P* 239)

Stephen's ambivalence with regard to his belief and unbelief not only illustrates his lack of commitment but also his act of perpetually deferring the certainty of things. It is curious to note that when Cranly asks whether he loves his mother (a question that he had earlier faced in school), Stephen expresses his consternation and dilemma as to the actual meaning of the word "love". This distrust of language comes from the notion that terms can never provide a proper signification of anything. His meaning becomes clear in his answer to Cranly's question. When Cranly asks, "I ask you if you ever felt love towards anyone or anything?", Stephen answers, "I tried to love God.... It seems now I failed. It is very difficult" (*P* 240).

Stephen finds it difficult to give assent to propositions without determining the precise signification of a term or an act. Principles, texts, identities never rest within any single code of definition. That is way for Stephen the search for true paternity becomes a fiction. When Cranly asks him his father's identity, he feels at a terrible loss. He was, Stephen states:

> ...a medical student, an oars man, a tenor, an amateur actor, a shouting politician, a small landlord, a small investor, a drinker, a good fellow, a story-teller, somebody, a Secretary, something in a distillery, a tax-gatherer, a bankrupt and at present a praiser of his own past. (*P* 241)

Cranly cannot understand his friend's tentative approach to such a secure thing as a mother's love. According to him, any person must feel a sense of belonging by affirming himself in his parents; in whom also one finds a meaning for his existence:

> .... Whatever else is unsure in this stinking dunghill of a world a mother's love is not. Your mother brings you into the world, carries you first in her body. What do we know about what she feels? But whatever she feels, it, at least, must be real. It must be. What are our ideas or ambitions? Play. Ideas! (*P* 241-42)

Stephen's answer is ironical, indicating the ambiguity of a mother's kiss:

> .... Pascal, if I remember rightly, would not suffer his mother to kiss him as the feared the contact of her sex. (*P* 242)

The paradox of identity is carried further when Cranly asks Stephen: ".... Did the idea ever occur to you, Cranly asked, that Jesus was not what he pretended to be? The first person to whom that idea occurred, Stephen answered, was Jesus Himself" (*P* 242).

Stephen's ambivalence towards Catholicism is underscored by Cranly when he tells his friend:

> .... It is a curious thing, do you know, Cranly said dispassionately, how your mind is supersaturated with the religion in which you say you disbelieve. Did you believe in it when you were at school? I bet you did.
>
> .... I did, Stephen answered.
>
> .... And were you happier then? Cranly asked softly, happier than you are now, for instance?
>
> .... Often happy, Stephen said, and often unhappy. I was someone else then. (*P* 240)

Stephen, as Cranly finds out, is never thoroughly anti-Catholic, rather he is a sceptic. Indeed his scepticism takes him to such lengths that he considers happiness and unhappiness as the obverse and reverse of life, viewing both with equanimity. The mature Stephen is not only anxious in debunking but even disowning his earlier identity. The idea that in childhood he was "someone else" does away with the linear development of a character in the best traditions of the "bildungsroman" and with the notion of continuity in time. Stephen consciously and unconsciously cuts himself loose from his moorings, his unknown origins; he must deny and annihilate himself in order to become himself. Joyce allows Stephen to search for his true identity in the process of writing. This ceaseless action of writing/rewriting destroys the centre of logocentric authority and the arbitrary closure of texts as well as subjecting to endless scrutiny the authorial self.

Stephen's writing records the movement of transgression or sin especially in chapter three. This section as well as the last section of previous chapter presents a breaching or opening up of Stephen's psyche to new experience. At the same time, his conscience forms a critique of his newfound sexual knowledge.

In a sense, his knowledge of sex can be understood in Freudian terms as a wounding of paternal authority. With his initiation into sex, Stephen rivals and deconstructs the tyranny of his father but in the process cuts himself loose from his ancestral origins. In a different sense, Stephen wounds himself as he inflicts punishment on him by his obeisance to God. In the action of self-chastisement, which originates from fear, he experiences a sadistic pleasure, while at the same time enjoys the pleasure of being tortured. This paradoxical joy of the sinner therefore co-exists with the joy of the sexual act:

> A cold lucid indifference reigned in his soul. At his first violent sin he had felt a wave of vitality pass out of him and had feared to find his body or his soul maimed by the excess.... Instead the vital wave had carried him on its bosom out of himself and back again when it receded; and no part of body or soul had been maimed but a dark peace had been established between them. The chaos in which his ardour extinguished itself was a cold indifferent knowledge of himself. He had sinned mortally not once but many times and he knew that, while he stood in danger of eternal damnation for the first sin alone, by every succeeding sin he multiplied his guilt and his punishment. (*P* 103)

The prose here seems to equivocate between contradictory impulses. As Stephen feels "a wave vitality pass out of him" he also notes that the "vital wave" again receded and instead of the body or soul being in danger of "maimed by the excess" a somewhat "dark peace" begins to lull him into serenity. His newfound knowledge is posited against "eternal damnation" and while he exults in sin, he multiplies his guilt and punishment.

It is remarkable to note that Stephen takes pride in his act of sin and in his refusal to serve the Christian God ("non servim") he shows his denial of logocentric authority:

> A certain pride, a certain awe, withheld him from offering to God even one prayer at night, though he knew it was in God's power to take away his life while he slept and hurl his soul hellward ere he could beg for mercy. His pride in his own sin, his loveless awe of God,

> told him that his offence was too grievous to be atoned for in whole or in part by a false homage to the All seeing and All knowing. (*P* 104)

As the long retreat begins, Stephen gets unnerved. Positioned against the unknown, august and awesome power of God, he gives in. Fear of self-dissolution makes him think of confession:

> Could it be that he, Stephen Dedalus, had done those things? His conscience signed in answer. Yes, he had done them.... How came it that God had not struck him dead? The leprous company of his sins closed about him.... Creatures were in the field: One, three, six: creatures were moving in the field hither and thither. Goatish creatures with human faces.... Soft language issued from their spittle lips as they swished in slow circles round and round the field.... They moved in slow circles, circling closer and closer to enclose, to enclose, soft language issuing from their lips... (*P* 137-38)

Using conventional images of hellish creatures the prose enacts a systematic torture to entrap Stephen's psyche with the result that the act of repentance becomes a hysterical show, verging on parody. He jumps out of his bed and starts vomiting profusely. The parody of confession is once again portrayed by means of physical images as he gives vent to his own sins before the priest: "His sins trickled from his lips, one by one, trickled in shameful drops from his soul, festering and oozing like a sore, a squalid stream of vice. The last sins oozed forth, sluggish, filthy." (*P* 144).

The deceptivity of the prose strikes us again when it enacts Stephen's devotion hysterically through the medium of sensuous images:

> His life seemed to have drawn near to eternity; every though, word and deed, every instance of consciousness could be made to reverberate radiantly in heaven; and at times his sense of such immediate repercussion was so lively that he seemed to feel his soul in devotion pressing like fingers the keyboard of a great cash register and to see the amount of his purchase start forth immediately in

> heaven, not as a number but as a frail column of incense or as a slender flower.
>
> The rosaries, too.... Transformed themselves into coronas of flowers of such vague unearthly texture.... (*P* 148)

It may be observed that as Stephen's viewpoint fluctuates, the prose becomes deceptive and ambivalent reflecting things which are binary in nature without offering any direct comment. In this way, the Angel's trumpet blast which stirs his evil impulses in order to purge them is balanced by the trumpet blast of a girl's carefree laughter: "As he crossed the square, walking homeward, the light laughter of a girl reached his burning ear. The frail gay sound smote his heart more strongly than a trumpet blast..." (*P* 115).

The malleability of the prose which reflects Stephen's irresolution is also seen in chapter two where he tries to hold his own and re-write his own identity against a host of inimical powers. The voices of logocentric discourse try to impose on him the codified norms of various institutions but he succeeds in entrammeling himself from their tyranny:

> While his mind had been pursuing its intangible phantoms and turning in irresolution from such pursuit he had heard about him the constant voices of his father and of his masters, urging him to be a gentleman above all things and urging him to a good Catholic above all things. These voices had now come to be hollow-sounding in his ears. When the gymnasium had been opened he had heard another voice urging him to be strong and manly and healthy and when the movement towards national revival had begun to be felt in the college yet another voice had bidden him be true to his country and help to raise up her language and tradition. In the profane world, as he foresaw, a worldly voice would bid hit raise up his father's fallen state by his labours and meanwhile, the voice of his school comrades urged to be a decent fellow.... (*P* 84)

Stephen's vocation led him away from these "hollow-sounding" voice which necessitated a commitment to a certain way of life. But he knew that he was unlikely to yield the sovereignty of his self in the interests of a certain discipline.

Chapter Two focuses on Stephen's search for his true identity as he accompanies his father to Cork; a journey which contains his attempt (as Maud Ellmann notes) to "Cork identity" (MacCabe 1982: 81). He knew that he is in danger of being dispossessed: "He knew, however, that his father's property was going to be sold by auction, and in the manner of his own dispossession he felt the world give the lie rudely to his fantasy" (*P* 87).

Stephen is gripped by a terrible fear, which contains a premonition that his quest might lead to a revocation of his actual origins. As the train moves on to Cork he feels that the neighbourhood of unseen sleepers unsettle him "as though they could harm him and he prayed that they might come quickly" (*P* 87-88). Maud Ellmann in her essay "Polytrophic Man" observes:

> The journey culminates in a search for the initials which identify the father and the son: "S.D." But remembering gives way to a dismemberment: these initials, rather than substantial origins, present themselves at last as living scars. What is more, another scar, or letter, or best of all, "scarletter"...another scarletter precedes these initials in the narrative, and in a sense preempts the name that they imply. This wound, or word, is Foetus....
>
> So, flaunting an originary fullness of identity, these scars will not be corked, will not be stoppered. They infringe the unity and self-containment that the word "identity" has come to imply. (MacCabe 1982: 81)

As Stephen and his father enter the portals of the college where the latter had received his education, his "restlessness had risen to fever" (*P* 89). With the aid of the porter Mr. Dedalus searched for his initials which he had inscribed on a desk, but instead they find the word "Foetus" carved on the dark stained wood. Joyce writes,

> The sudden legend started his blood: he seemed to feel the absent students of the college about his and to shrink

> from their company. A vision of their life, which his father's words had been powerless to desk. A broad shouldered student with a moustache cutting in the latter with a jack-knife, seriously. Other students stood or sat near him laughing at his handiwork....
>
> Stephen's name was called. He hurried down the steps of the theatre so as to be as far away from the vision as he could be and peering closely at his father's initials hid his flushed face (*P* 90). Not only does Stephen feel his loss occasioned by his dispossession of his legitimate fatherhood but he thinks that the sanctity and privacy surrounding his genesis has been rudely violated. Further the "scarletter" also exposes his deep primordial urges within his subconscious: "The letters cut in the stained wood of the desk stared upon him, mocking his bodily weakness and futile enthusiasms and making him loathe himself for his own mad and filthy orgies." (*P* 91)

The word "Foetus" may be said to annul the "concept of primariness", which may be seen as a "theoretical fiction" (Derrida 1978: 203). In this way, Stephen's precise origins may be said to be infinitely deferred. This "recognizing difference at the origin" implies that the exactness of definition cannot be traced. Derrida in his *Writing and Difference* points out that anything: "Originary must be understood as having been crossed out, without which difference would be derived from an original plenitude. It is a non-origin which is originary" (Derrida 1978: 203).

On the other hand, Stephen suddenly experiences the unleashing of potential forces in his "id", which later culminates in his sexual release in the arms of the prostitute. His experience therefore, is pivotal in the sense that "Foetus" releases him from the thrall of paternity and subjects his identity to a notion of "difference". Differing as well as being eternally deferred, Stephen is not only engaged in the process of scripting but also as the middle portion of the novel illustrates, it impels him towards an endless search for his own identity in terms of sexual knowledge. In one sense (we have seen that) the joy of the sinner leads to a "brisure" of the self, in Maud Ellmann's term and action of "splitting" and "joining or embracing" within the term "cleaving", as she explains it in her essay "Disremembering Dedalus" (Young 1987: 192). On the other hand the liberation of self from self in terms of sexual bliss also has creative implications because it culminates in the achievement of "The scholastic quidditas, the whatness of a thing" (*P* 213).

As Stephen explains to Lynch it leads to:

> the instant wherein that supreme quality of beauty, the clear radiance of the esthetic image, is apprehended luminously by the mind which has been arrested by its wholeness and fascinated by its harmony is the luminous silent stasis of esthetic pleasure.... (*P* 213)

Without the mediation of woman, Stephen can never be an artist and gain an apprehension of the proper idea of beauty: the "Whatness" of thing. The re-writing of sin through the medium of Stephen's body has a different connotation from the conventional one. It is imperative that the artist falls and in his fall resurrects his own soul:

> The snares of the world were its ways of sin. He would fall. He had not yet fallen but he would fall silently, in an instant. Not to fall was too hard, too hard; and he felt the silent lapse of his soul, as it would be at some instant to come, falling, falling, but not yet fallen, still unfallen, but about to fall. (*P* 162)

Like Adam, the artist loses his innocence and purity in his fall but unlike the archetype he performs his own redemption. Stephen must learn to come to terms with his own flesh through his knowledge of others. "He was destined to learn his own wisdom apart from others or to learn the wisdom of others himself wandering among the snares of the world" (*P* 162).

This "brisure" of self, therefore not only leads to a "scarification" as Maud Ellmann notes but also to "a complex circulation of sexual and textual economies which both flow out of Stephen and into him" (Young 1987: 192). What passes out as "semen, blood, urine, breath, money, saliva, speech and excrement" is balanced by what flows into him in an "economy of influence" (Young 1987: 193). Although Ellmann locates food, which she compares with the bread and wine of the Eucharist and odours, which enter Stephen in the form of "economy of influence", other senses must also be taken into account. She reminds us that "influence" retains its literary implications: Stephen inhales the literary tradition and re-members it in his secretions (Young 1987: 193).

For Stephen, therefore, mutilation of his own body means a resurrection of his own self. As he himself confesses to Mat Davin, that the soul has a very "slow and dark birth, more mysterious than the birth of the body" (*P* 203). This points to what Derrida has called a "solicitude and solicitation of Being, a historico-metaphysical threatening of foundations" (Derrida 1968: 6). For this purpose, the recurrent pattern of fall and resurrection is essential to the arts:

> To grasp the operation of creative imagination at the greatest possible proximity to it, one must turn oneself toward the invisible interior of poetic freedom. One must be separated from oneself in order to be reunited with the blind origin of the work in its darkness. This experience of conversion, which founds the literary act (writing or reading), is such that the very words "separation" and "exile", which always designate the interiority of a breaking off with the world and a making of one's way within it, cannot directly manifest the experience; they can only indicate it through a metaphor whose genealogy itself would deserve all of our efforts. (Derrida 1978: 8)

It is through his own experience that the artist, therefore, fashions his own artefact. As Stephen reaches back to his blind origins he becomes conscious of his paternity, neither legitimate nor religious but mythical. As he separates himself from his colleagues who invite him to swim in the sea, he remains conscious of "the mystery of his body" (*P* 169). As he is called by his friends he "seemed to hear the noise of dim waves and to see a winged form flying above the waves and slowly climbing the air" (*P* 169). It reminded Stephen of his own vocation:

> a prophecy of the end he had been born to serve and had been following through the mists of childhood and boyhood, a symbol of the artist forging anew in his workshop out of the sluggish matter of the earth a new soaring impalpable imperishable being? (*P* 169)

It is remarkable to note that the prose enacts the resurrection of the artist-Stephen "from the grave of boyhood, spurning her grave-clothes" (*P* 170). Thus:

> His heart trembled; his breath came faster and a wild spirit passed over his limbs as though he was soaring sunward. His heart trembled in an ecstasy of fear and his soul was in flight.... An ecstasy of flight made radiant his eyes and wild his breath and tremulous and wild and radiant his wind swept limbs. (*P* 169)

> Stephen's promise to "create proudly out of the freedom and power of his soul, as the great artificer whose name he bore, a living thing, new and soaring and beautiful, impalpable, imperishable" culminates in his apprehension and expression of the beauty of the girl on the stream. (*P* 170).

The "luminous silent stasis of esthetic pleasure" is felt by Stephen when he perceives the "whatness" in the beauty of the girl by comparing her alternately to a beautiful sea bird and a dove (*P* 213)

Her long and tapering legs are likened to that of a crane, her linen as soft as feathers and her bosom is compared to the "breast of some dark-plumaged dove" (*P* 171).

The question which most of the critics generally bypass in an analysis of the novel is what lies behind Stephen's detached and calm appreciation of beauty, that is the stasis of perfect "esthetic pleasure" (*P* 213). Part of the answer lies in the girl's response.

As Stephen admires her beauty she calmly returns his gaze without any suggestion of shame or wantonness. The other half of the answer lies in Stephen's outburst of profane joy.

The prose maintains a remarkable neutrality, keeping the narrator's emotions well under control, thus contributing to the stasis of feeling. "The first faint noise of gently moving water broke the silence, low and faint and whispering...and a faint flame trembled on her cheek" (*P* 172). It must be observed that throughout the *Portrait* Stephen's encounter with women has been shown in ambiguous terms. Women are mysterious beings. She is like "a bat-like soul waking to the consciousness of itself in darkness and secrecy and loneliness" (*P* 220). And yet she is a becoming creature, shining in her innocence. This alterity of the Woman as virgin/ temptress allows him no fixity or rest. Stephen for once beings to feel that he had wronged his girl friend, Emma Clery: "A sense of her innocence moved him almost to pity her, an innocence he had never understood till he had come to the knowledge of it through sin, an innocence which she too had not understood while she was innocent..." (*P* 222).

The next moment she is portrayed as a temptress, alluring him: "Conscious of his desire she was waking from odorous sleep, the temptress of his villanelle. Her eyes, dark and with a look of languor, were opening to his eyes" (*P* 223).

At other moments, he thinks that Emma would rather "unveil her soul's shy eternal imagination, transmuting the daily bread of experience into the radiant body of everliving life" (*P* 220).

On the other hand, we note that as prefect of the college of the sodality of the Blessed Virgin Mary, Stephen is overcome by the imagery of the Psalms and "glories of Mary held his soul captive" (*P* 104).

In fact, what strikes us is that the true identity of the woman is being eternally deferred without a proper resolution. It is only in the instance of the girl in the stream that the ambiguity is kept in abeyance. Stephen's outburst of "profane joy" illustrates the nebulous balance enacted in his mind between the woman as temptress and as a virgin. The feminine figure here acts in the capacity of a mediatress and which has its origin in the Blessed Virgin Mary. Just as the Virgin Mary enfleshed the divine word in her womb, thus making possible the Incarnation of Christ, similarly the girl in the stream incarnates the creative potentialities of the artist by making possible his re-birth: "Her image had passed into his soul forever and no word had broken the holy silence of his ecstasy. Her eyes had called him and his soul had leaped at the call. To live, to err, to fall, to triumph, to recreate life out of life" (*P* 172).

But the artist's incarnation can only be made possible when he receives the call of the Word. Only when he hears the call of "Stephenos Dedalos! Bous Stephanoumenos!" from a voice from beyond the world only then would his transformation be complete (*P* 169). The call, as B. Schossman points out in his study "Joyce's Catholic Comedy of Language",

> is crystallized in the feminine image posited as the subversion of sin. In Catholic logic, God takes on human form through the intermediary of the Virgin. At the end of the fourth chapter of the *Portrait*, the Incarnation is condensed in the instant of the call, the signifier coming fourth, establishing the temporal break of before/after. With a symbolic gesture, the feminine receptacle becomes the vessel of the Word; her glance rendered as a sign, marks the spiritual flight of Stephen with her heterogeneity. As a womanly figure at the edge of the sea (the significant element of reproduction, the biological site) and as a Daedalian bird (the paternal sign of artistic flight), the bird-like girl calls Stephen to creation.... (Schlossman 1985: XXIII)

Thus, the prose comments: "A wild angel had appeared to him, the angel of mortal youth and beauty.... To throw open before him in an instant of ecstasy the gates of all the ways of error and glory" (*P* 172). And as Schlossman notes that in "his erotic relation to the Virgin, Stephen surrenders once again to the flesh that will give him life.... This birth is metaphorised through images of light, colour, and the cyclic rhythms of poetic language projecting Stephen toward the jouissance of art" (Schlossman 1985: XXXIII).

The prose enacts the birth of the artist. Stephen's soul experiences an incarnation, symbolically portrayed by the efflorescence of a flower trembling and unfolding itself, petal by petal, leaf by leaf (*P* 173). The language releases emotion through the flow of mellifluous consonants:

> A soft liquid joy like the noise of many waters flowed over his memory and he felt in his heart the soft peace of silent spaces of fading tenuous sky above the waters, oceanic silence, of swallows flying through the sea dusk over the flowing waters. (*P* 225)

With the intersection of time and space, of sky and sea, and of noise and oceanic silence, the ambiguities of things have been endlessly prolonged in a continuous rhythmic pattern. There is no final rest in identity and its quest can only be likened to the confused babble of waters, a medley of persona in memory and the one becomes many, a polyphony of selves in the racial unconscious. Here the very term "oceanic silence" is deceptive because it contains "the noise of many waters" (*P* 225). As Stephen illustrates, any assumption of identity becomes deceptive. When Emma asks him whether he was composing poems, Stephen counters with a question "About whom?" The crisis of identity is once again broached in a repetitive pattern: "I though I thought and all that I felt I felt, all the rest before now, in fact..." (*P* 252). For the millionth time Stephen must needs recreate the conscience of his race from the context of his experience with the help of the "Old father, old artificer" who can equally be God, his earthly father as well as the mythical Dedalus (*P* 253).

Ulysses (1922)

9

The conclusion of *A Portrait* pointed towards a decentring of the individual; a solicitation of self, inclusive of the activities of splitting and joining through the alternate movements of loss and renewal, departure and return, cessation and a beginning, death and rebirth (Derrida 1978: 6). *Ulysses* expands this theme of the decentred self, giving it a human, vegetable, animal, cosmic dimension, extending in and out of both time and space. Through the ceaseless activity of writing, there occurs a perpetual deferral of self and meaning. Writing counterpoints themes, personalities, myth and fact, past and present, Judaic as well as Homeric and modern, different varieties of literary styles, the word and flesh, religion as well as politics and aesthetics, giving the production of text an infinite extension, spilling over the conventional notions of the genre.

The hesitancy of meaning is also effected by the lack of any fixed point of view as the narrator slips inside and outside of monologues, considering everything from both subjective and objective viewpoints, diluting the demarcations of self and the other. Finally, the narrator refines himself to such an extent that he allows persons, things, objects, both animate and inanimate to move and express themselves independently and which inculcates in the reader an effect of hallucination. Realism as a mode of perception is exploded because language becomes primary; it is given a will of its own and becomes almost like a living being. It enacts, portrays and creates its own world. This delinking of the narrator and language later achieves its culmination in *Finnegans Wake* in a continuous flow of discourse. In *Ulysses,* discourse not only liberates the authorial self from its narrow confinement but also grants the principal text freedom to combine with other subtexts. This process of permutation and combination of texts was at first noted by both T.S. Eliot and Ezra Pound but its implications were realised later in the interpretations of post-structuralists.

Eliot in his essay "*Ulysses*, Order and Myth" which appeared in *The Dial*, November 1923, indicated Joyce's innovative employment of the Greek myth. He explained that:

> In pursuing the myth, in manipulating a continuous parallel between contemporaneity and antiquity, Mr. Joyce is pursuing a method, which others must pursue after him.... It is simply a way of controlling, of ordering, of giving a shape and a significance to the immense panorama of futility and anarchy which is contemporary history. (Eliot 1972: 177)

Eliot's observation gives rise to a number of suggestions. First of all, it must be noticed that the notion of parallelism for Joyce does not merely imply a permutation of the modern story with respect to the Homeric saga. But it also indicates an infinite extension or referentiality of the self in terms of Christian theology and the human anatomy, not to mention the multiple echoes of Western history, philosophy and art. Ellmann in his study *Ulysses on the Liffey* (1972) notes the literal, ethical, aesthetic and anagogic aspects of Joyce's use of myth (Ellmann 1972: XII-XIII).

What needs to be stressed is the effect of Joyce's use of multiple myths inside the main text on the issue of identity. To take Bloom as a test case we note the very ambivalence, which creeps in the conception of his character right from the beginning. He is not portrayed as an anachronism, that is to say he is not an archaic survivor from a Homeric or a Jewish world of antiquities. He is definitely a modern man but with a difference. In his study, Ellmann notes Bloom's uniqueness:

> Bloom must register, with Jewish characteristics, the same impress of Christianity that, as Stephen indicates (and as Joyce had noted in his alphabetical notebook), everyone now must, so he gave Bloom a history of easy

> minded conversion to Protestantism and Catholicism, and of course situated him in a Catholic country. In this way, he pillowed Judaeo-Christian tradition upon the Hebrew-Hellenic one. But Bloom had also to be a twentieth-century man, and Joyce therefore conferred upon him the grace of unbelief. As a free thinker Bloom is post-Christian, just as, being a Christian convert, he is post-Judaic, and being Judaic-Christian he is post-Homeric. Joyce's book comprehends layer upon layer of the past. (Ellmann 1972: 3-4)

As the book unfolds, we are fascinated by Bloom's scepticism, which gives a contextual basis to the multi-layered tradition, which is his cultural ambivalence. He becomes everyman and no-man. This chequered heritage also makes his personality a complex one from another perspective. Ellmann draws our attention to the fact that:

> Joyce felt an incongruity between his genetic origins in a shiftless father and an orthodox mother, fond of them though he was, and his imaginative origins in Ibsen, Flaubert, Dante, and D. Annunzio. Without abjuring their actual parents, he and Stephen doted on the mystery of multiple parentage. Behind Joyce's characters lie other created characters, behind his creative acts other creators throng lending a hand when they can. They concede continuity, they confirm the centrality of Joyce's undertaking. They constitute an invisible but companionable congeries of presences, an ancestry. (Ellmann 1972: 5)

On one level, this stimulates on the level of personality an incessant flux of divergent identities which may be attuned by the force of a common referentiality but which do belong to different traditions. Penelope, Callidike, Calypso, Gea-Tellus for instance become versions of Molly. Bloom also has a fascination for hiding under the pseudonyms of Henry Flower or Rudolph Virag. This becomes all the more complicated in the quest for paternity. Thus Bloom not only becomes the symbolic father of Stephen but reaches back farther in time, containing traces of the mythic Dedalus as well as Odysseus and also the biblical Noah, not to speak of his Shakespearean heritage, that is, the father of Prince Hamlet. In this sense, the search for paternity becomes a fiction. This is paralleled in the case of the son also. Thus, Stephen becomes a variation of Telemachus, Icarus, Japhet as well as Prince Hamlet. It is indeed remarkable that this centrifugality which decentres the very notion of personality as a self-contained unit is located in the multiplicity of discourses within the text itself.

Joyce's radical technique which opened up the discourse to other texts, thereby subjecting the self to a process of breaching was thereby subjecting the self to a process of breaching was earlier noted by A. Walton-Litz in his study *The Art of James Joyce* (1961):

> This movement from "centripetal" to "centrifugal" writing during the evolution of *Ulysses* mirrors a general change in Joyce's artistic stance. A process of selectivity harmonizes with his early notion of "epiphany", which assumes that it is possible to reveal a whole area of experience through a single gesture or phrase. In shaping the Portrait Joyce sought continually to create "epiphanies", and to define Stephen's attitudes by a stringent process of exclusion; later in his career he attempted to define by a process of inclusion. The earlier method implies that there is a significance, a "quidditas", residing in each thing, and that the task of the artist is to discover this significance through language. Thus in the *Portrait* a single gesture may reveal a character's essential nature; but in *Finnegans Wake* Humphrey Chimpden Earwicker's nature is established by multiple relationships with all the fallen heroes of history and legend. (36-37)

In *Ulysses* the methods of inclusion is manifested by the processes of intertextuality, which work through various ways. It establishes a to-and-fro correspondence between leels of discourse and serves for a comic reduction of attitudes as well as an extension of referentiality. In this way, the relationship of "the primary and secondary texts can lead to a process of" distortion and contamination by which the parody subverts the text from within (Attridge and Ferrer 1984: 105). Andre Topia in his essay "The Matrix and the Echo: Intertextuality in *Ulysses*" explains that the problem involves the relation between the original and the series of copies. Either a distinction is maintained between the original and the copies or else the copies usurp the place of the original. Topia raises the issue of the 'gap' or the 'supplement' which crops up in the conflict of intertextuality as well as writing in general. Quoting from Derrida's essay "Plato's Pharmacy", he points out that:

> As soon as the supplementary outside is opened, its structure implies that the supplement itself can be 'typed', replaced by its double, and that a supplement to the supplement, a surrogate for the surrogate, is possible and necessary. The danger arises when the duplicate ceases to be a simple copy, identifiable as such, and becomes so similar to the original text that it is no longer possible to tell them apart. The devaluation then works in both directions. This problem is at the centre of what we could call the "vertical" analysis of the intertextual network: the essential moment is in fact when the borrowed text, extracted from its original context, begins to deny its origin and filiations. (Attridge and Ferrer 1984: 105)

In this context, intertextual space might be defined as the tension existing between different units, which might be either one of equivalence or of opposition. Topia reminds us that it is essential to notice whether the reader considers the initial paradigm, at the moment of reading. According to him, there are two ways of going through a Bloomian text. Either one can take it as a locked text where the permutations and combinations of myth and fact have been predetermined or one could consider it as a mobile and open text where all items are subjected to the forces of flux. The referentiality of meaning suffer infinite expansion because of both the liner horizontal order which permits the text to move onward through the montage technique and also due to a vertical order which establishes a linkage between the code and its actualization. Each word or item of discourse becomes ambiguous as it carries traces of its origin from a corpus of extant texts or rhetorical matrices as well as being incorporated within the present discourse—"the actual typographical block of the page in *Ulysses*". On this ambiguous nexus, the Joycean text form itself (Attridge and Ferrer 1984: 108).

Another point of importance is the disappearance of quotation marks, which tends to eliminate "all typographic indicators permitting the distinction of the different levels of discourse" (Attridge and Ferrer 1984: 108).

Not only do they blur the originary nature of utterance but their assemblage with the Bloomian discourse opens it to the processes of distortion and perversion to a greater or lesser degree. As Topia comments:

> Thus the text becomes a configuration within which both orphaned and hypercoded discourses circulate. The reactivated text, having lost a large part of its original denotative function (the context of which its functional legitimacy was based), finds itself in a sort of nomadism. The reader is thus confronted with what one might call a surplus of code, a supplement of code. Far from offering a preconscious reverie, the Bloomian interior monologue provides us with the code pure and simple, but a code without an immediate end, one might almost say an aimless code, ready for every adventure and vulnerable to every distortion. (Attridge and Ferrer 1984: 108-09)

In *Ulysses*, the notion of intertextual space becomes operative when we try to comprehend the manifold types of discourse offered by different personalities and which make us aware of their rich potentialities. The book opens sedately with a description of Buck Mulligan, reflecting the serene mood of the surroundings:

> Stately, plump Buck Mulligan came from the stairhead bearing a bowl of lather on which a mirror and a razor lay crossed. (*U* 3)

The mood suddenly changes with the summoning of Stephen. Muligan usurps the role of a priest: "He faced about and blessed gravely thrice the tower, the surrounding land and the awaking mountains" (*U* 3). At the sight of Stephen the "fearful Jesuit" Mulligan "made rapid crosses in the air, gurgling in his throat and shaking his head" (*U* 3). Within the space of a few lines the narrator has indicated the undercurrent of hostility between the two. However, "the tensions of this colloquy" between them are established only when the narrative voice constantly adds "weights on each side of the scales throughout this part of the chapter" (Hart and Hayman 1974: 2). Ben Stock in his essay on "Telemachus" shows how Joyce preserves his impartiality by allowing the antagonism between the two characters to surface naturally. From Mulligan's point of view, he is seen to cover up his bowl "smartly", speak "sternly"; cry out "briskly" and look "gravely" (*U* 3). Whereas Stephen with his sleepy appearance leans his arms on the top of the staircase and looks coldly at this companion who tries to assume supremacy. The varying pattern of discourse shows Mulligan gaining ascendancy over his friend.

When Mulligan deliberately offends Stephen by parodying the Eucharist and makes rapid crosses in the air to ward off the devil in Stephen, the discourse emphasizes the Christian undertones implicit in Mulligan's action: "He peered sideways up and gave a long slow whistle of call, then paused awhile in rapt attention, his even White teeth glistening here and there with gold points. Chrysostomos" (*U* 3).

"Chrysostomos" is the Greek word for "golden mouthed" but here Stephen has in mind St. John Chrysostomos. The irony as Benstock points out, lies in the suggestion of affluence through the presence of gold in Mulligan's mouth, whereas Stephen's is full of decayed teeth. By extension "Buck is also playing the role of the Precursor, John the Baptist" (Hart and Hayman 1974: 3). The parody continues on two levels. On one level Stephen's Jesuit ancestry becomes the butt of Mulligan's jokes. On another level, Buck satirises Stephen's stubborn and inflexible stance. As a contrast Buck's flexibility and his ability to accommodate himself in a variety of roles as an usurper is emphasized.

In the first chapter, as M. Hill in a recent essay "*Amor Matris*: Mother and Self in the Telemachiad Episode of *Ulysses*" points out that the:

> Sea/mother represents a powerful "other" who longs to engulf the self. Again, the mother is seen only in relationship to the male child who is fearful of being sucked in. The theme of creativity and fertility reveals a similar pattern. Here again the mother is seen as frighteningly omniscient. She is representative of Eve, "standing from everlasting to everlasting" (3: 43-44). She is the first source of identity; her stamp on the child is that of the navel which marks his as hers forever. The concept of "amor matris", or mother love, displays the power of the mother's fertility.... Yet her power, like the ghoulmother and the sea, becomes something sinister and threatening. The womb imagery, which proliferates throughout the Telemachiad, is indicative of this. Jeanne McKnight notes that the womb is represented as tempting darkness in which all identity is lost. (Hill 1993: 334-35)

Elsewhere in chapter three the sea is likened to the "oomb, all-wombing tomb" (*U* 40).

Thus, when the narrator describes the transformation of Cyril Sargent's mother from a loving parent to a ghoul, a chewer of corpses, the two ambiguous identities as both creator and destroyer merge in one entity. Such images tempt Stephen to rebellion and denial of the mother-figure: "No, mother/Let me be and let me live" (*U* 9). As M. Hill explains that only by simultaneously sustaining these negative images of his mother "within his consciousness and actively denying their power can Stephen bolster his sense of identity" (Hill 1993: 335).

Ulysses is dotted with these images of denial and return, showing Stephen's loss and search for identity. Like "the fox burying his grandmother under a hollybush" only to dig her up again, Stephen constantly flees from his mother only to return to her once again (*U* 22). In "Nestor" or chapter two, the prose focuses on this oscillatory movement:

> She had saved him from being trampled underfoot and had gone, scarcely having been. A poor soul gone to heaven and on a heath beneath winking stars a fox, red

> reek of rapine in his fur, with merciless bright eyes scraped in the earth, listened, scraped up the earth, listened, scraped and scraped. (*U* 23)

The notion of the Other dominates Stephen's search for identity. The mother can only be defined in relation to the child and *vice versa.* Thus, Amor matris: subjective and objective genitive. "With her weak blood and wheysour milk, she had fed him and hid from sight of others his swaddling bands" (*U* 23). The pattern of discourse subjects the notion of selfhood to a process of flux. The mother's position in bed becomes the vehicle by which her cycles of existence had been noted: "Bridebed, childbed, bed of death, ghost candled" (*U* 40). This later expands into the figure of the universal woman: "A tide westering, moondrawn, in her wake. Tides, myriadislanded, within her, blood—not mine, oinopa pontoon, a winedark sea. Behold the handmaid of the moon" (*U* 40).

When Stephen remembers a comment by Mulligan with respect to his mother ("O, its only Dedalus whose mother is beastly dead") we realize that animal imagery provides one of the major motifs of the book and which paves the way for the many transformations of identity. Stephen becomes known as dogsbody and also the drowned man to be washed ashore at Bullock harbour. Mulligan possesses an equine face, Haines is known as the "oxy chap" and Clive has a scared calf's face while Stephen is an avatar of Icarus who rose and fell.

On another level, although Homeric parallels which become major corollaries later in the book are still relatively dormant, it will be well to remember Mulligan's Homeric role as Antinous, the chief suitor who threatens Stephen's dispossession. This chapter also posits three parallels in the father-son relationship; drawn from the Bible (Noah-Japhet, God the Father-Christ) from the classics (Odysseus-Telemachus) and from Shakespeare (King Hamlet-Prince Hamlet) (Hart and Hayman 1974: 12). Finally, this chapter initiates the inimitable discourse of the sea constantly subjected to forces of flux: "Wavewhite wedded words shimmering on the dim tide" (*U* 8). This later gives over to the "fourworded wavespeech" in chapter three ("Proteus").

> Listen: a fourworded wavespeech: seesoo, hrss, rsseeiss, ooos. Vehement breath of waters amid seasnakes, rearing horses, rocks. In cups of rocks it slops: flop, slop, slap: bounded in barrels. And, spent, its speech ceases. It flows purling widely flowing, floating foampool, flower unfurling. (*U* 41)

The incessant ebb and tide of waters parallels the creation and flow of speech. Language contains infinite possibilities and it is with time that these potentialities are translated into actual speech and things. Just as Martello tower was the dominant symbol of chapter one, suggesting space similarly, the presiding category of "Nestor" or chapter two is time. The narrative follows the fluctuations of things, speech as well as thought processes. Like the wind weaving evanescent patterns, time actualizes the "infinite possibilities" in history and creates a chequered pattern of human life:

> It must be a movement then, an actuality of the possible as possible. Thought is the thought of thought. Tranquil brightness. The soul is in a manner all that is: the should is the form of forms. Tranquillity sudden, vast, candescent: form of forms. (*U* 21)

As E.L. Epstein shows in his essay on "Nestor" that the problem in this chapter is "the proper way to regard the stream of human history" (Hart and Hayman 1974: 27). The narrator locates history between the ambiguities of divine and human worlds, between God and Caesar. But both are founded on cruelty, upon wars of oppression and destruction, whether they are fought for secular or spiritual motives:

> In Caesar, Stephen finds a history of oppression of the Irish; in Christ, oppression of the Jews. Mr. Deasy sees no incompatibility in regarding the manifestation of God as history's goal, and in endorsing anti-Semitic persecution.... Stephen will render nothing unto God or Caesar, for nothing is really theirs. (Ellmann 1972: 22)

Stephen's attitude to the flux of human history is pessimistic. His interpretation is correct but he "suffers intensely from the emotional confusion brought on him by his own 'history', the circumstances of his mother's death and of his anomalous position in Dublin" (Hart and Hayman 1974: 27). As the forces of history attack him, he becomes distant and takes refuge in his plight which is that of the fox burying his grandmother under a hollybush (*U* 22). As Stephen's identity is assailed by the forces of history, the theme of loss and return is once again broached. He differs from Mr. Deasy's interpretation of history as moving "towards one great goal, the manifestation of God" and is eager to escape from its forces: "History, Stephen said, is a nightmare from which I am trying to awake" (*U* 28).

This theme of departure and return has been subtly interwoven in the structure of the book providing the necessary intertextual space which imparts to the three personalities of Stephen, Bloom and Molly an infinite referentiality unparalleled in modern literature. The theme harmonizes the book's main narrative analogues like *The Odyssey*, the story of Shakespeare's life and the Bible. It also influences the structure of the plot as well as a number of individual sentences. Vicki Mahaffey in her study underlines the implications of this theme in the structure of *Ulysses*:

> If Bloom realizes the movement from departure to return, displaying its attendant satisfaction and dissatisfaction, it is Stephen who showcases its theoretical importance. In "Schylla and Charybdis". Stephen argues that Shakespeare, both in his life and his work, used the strategy of exodus and return as a way of finding "in the world without as actual what was in his world within as possible" (*U* 1041-42), seeing life and art as a double mode of recovering one's own alienated images. What any wanderer traverses, and returns to, is always the variousness and singularity of the self.... Departure and return, Stephen suggests, serves as a Paradigm for all cognition.... To follow the book's many departures and returns is to participate in a cognitive paradox of the most disconcerting kind, a paradox that forces us to experience the stress as well as the release of understanding. *Ulysses* not only recapitulates a congeries of motifs of exile that have been central to western

> thought, but it reinterprets the relationship between departure and return as disturbingly complex, suggesting that the two actions like all convenient oppositions, are identical as well as opposed. (Mahaffey 1988: 134)

Ulysses is almost unique in offering its readers an imaginative odyssey, promising the spectre of a home but deferring it infinitely in the process of discourse. The shadows of both Homer and Shakespeare loom large over the narrative because they both deal with the theme of banishment and exile. There is something common in the same restless and meaningful experience, dominated by the opposed cycles of centrifugal and centripetal motion noted earlier, where loss and gain, proximity and estrangement have been balanced in an endless movement of delay. The attempt to locate the point of origin, the "key" signature ends in failure because Joyce's method undermines any desire to equate "return" and apocalypse, or to anticipate absolute closure:

> Joyce's apparent affirmation of reincarnation has little or nothing to do with mysticism; it is simply a compressed reminder of the simultaneous identity and difference between beginning and ending, of the doubleness of each. In the Odyssey of interpretation, too, resolution is necessarily double; although we may think of it as single and final, the various meanings of the word itself illustrate the identity of difference, since "to resolve" is not only "to reduce by analysis" but also to break up, separate. (Mahaffey 1988: 135-36)

It is to be noted that Stephen's search for self involves on his part a proper selection of a mode of discourse and as Colin MacCabe insists in his essay "The Voice of Esau: Stephen in the Library". It rests on "a performance which will both wrest a meaning from Shakespeare and confer an identity on himself within the Irish Literary Movement" (MacCabe 1982: 111).

In chapter one, Mulligan brings to our notice Stephen's queer theory of Shakespeare. Stephen "proves by algebra that Hamlet's grandson is Shakespeare's grandfather and that he himself is the ghost of his own father" (*U* 15). Buch adds another dimension to Stephen's quest for paternity by commenting that the latter may be seen as a variation of Japhet in search of his father Noah in the Bible. The exact reference made by the pronominal "he" is here not clear. "He" might refer to Shakespeare, Hamlet, their respective grandfather or grandson, or Stephen himself. On the one hand as MacCabe indicates, the pronoun "he" can be interpreted:

> either anaphorically, referring back to some previous element in the text, or exophorically, referring outside the text. Writing must depend on anaphor as the written text's situation is too variable for exospheric reference. But this written account of speech hesitates, like Haines, in giving too simple an identification. (MacCabe 1982: 112)

The problem may be understood in the following manner. In terms of his theory Stephen attempts to fix an identity for both Shakespeare and Hamlet but in the process he creates his own identity, "placing himself within a literary tradition which will provide him with the father he so desperately seeks" (MacCabe 1982: 112). And yet this very search as MacCabe points out becomes in itself "the paralysis he tries to above".

As Stephen walks about on the beach at the inception of chapter three, he becomes the centre of an obsessive interpretation of his world. Questing after a hermetic fantasy of total interpretation of things, he mutters to himself: "Signatures of all things I am here to read" (*U* 31), but it is one of the central lessons of the "Proteus" episode that through the "ineluctable modality of the visible" and "the ineluctable modality of the audible" Stephen must open himself to a perpetual re-assessment and re-interpretation (*U* 31). It is here that paternity, identity and language become inseparable. Thus,

> to assume an identity, to recognize and be recognized by the father, is to refuse the possibility of re-interpretation. It is to so fix oneself that interpretation is finished, brought to an end in a moment of paralysed centrality, a moment which...is intimately linked to Stephen's reading of Shakespeare. (MacCabe 1982: 113)

In *Ulysses*, subject and language have been liberated in the process of formal re-writing that allows the book to return repeatedly to its own events, negating any final interpretation. It is especially in the "Circe" section that language turns on itself, underlining this theme of return. In this way the entire text is "re-written to allow an escape from the nightmare identifications imposed by history" (MacCabe 1982: 113)

Stephen's identity is threatened by the forces of change in the "Proteus" section. After locating himself in the palpable world of nature all around him he observes two midwives carrying a bag. This sets him thinking on the facts of his birth and then the creation of the first parents, Adam and Eve and finally the details of Christ's birth and Incarnation:

> One of her sisterhood lugged me squealing into life. Creation from nothing. What has she in the bag. A misbirth with a trailing navelcord.... The cords of all link back, strandentwining cable of all flesh.... Gaze in your omphalos. Hello! Kinch here. Put me on to Edenville. (*U* 32)

Stephen becomes obsessed by the mystery of paternity and he broods on genuine fathers, "ghostly fathers, church fathers, and father priests who in chalices throughout the world bring God once more to birth. His thoughts about women's role in creation also extend from Mary to Eve to Magdalen to the moon" (Ellmann 1972: 24). Without properly ensuring the basis of his affinity and unsure about his orientation, Stephen identifies himself with a host of personalities like Aristotle, Boehme, Hamlet, Blake, to a certain extent Lessing and Gutzkow and an inverted Berkeley. His language modulates into Greek, Italian, German and is also subjected to linguistic inversions. J.M. Morse in his article on "Proteus" tries to show the various transformations of Stephen. In one place, he is changed into a basilisk: a monster hatched from a rooster's egg by a snake. According to Morse, the basilisk seems to be a conglomeration of John Calvin with a reformer of more humane temperament, William of Ockham—to say nothing of Elisha Joachim, Swift, and the swimming priest of "Telemachus" (Hart and Hayman 1974: 39).

The change is not restricted to Stephen. It points to the dissolution of matter. This is highlighted in the transformation of the dog into various animals like hare, horse, seal, wolf, calf, fox, leopard, panher and vulture (*U* 38-39). This flux of identities reaches its climax in the progressive decay of God through the change of matter. Thus, "God becomes mad becomes fish becomes barnacle goose becomes featherbed mountain" (*U* 41-42).

The transformation of matter spills over into the next few chapters. In "Calypso" or chapter four for instance, the corruption of the human flesh into that of animals and the vegetable world is to be noted. The girl living next door to Bloom is compared to "sound meat" as that of a "stalled heifer" (*U* 48). The human, the corporeal and the carnal as well as the animal comes alive when Bloom walks behind the girls' moving hams, comparing her to "prime sausage" (*U* 49). In "Calypso" Bloom faces a loss of manhood. The spectre of castration looms large as he fantasies his wife carrying on an affair with Blazes Boylan, the musician who has planned a concert tour in which Molly is supposed to sing. The prose enacts Bloom's paralysis of will, his voyeurism and his resignation: "A soft qualm, regret, flowed down his backbone increasing. Will happen, yes. Prevent. Useless: Can't move. Girl's sweet light lips. Will happen too. He felt the flowing qualm spread over him. Useless to move now" (*U* 55).

The notion of transubstantiation of identity is operative on multiple levels in the next chapter, the "Lotus-Eaters". Molly's supposed tryst with Blazes Boylan is here counterpointed by Bloom's tryst with Martha. Here, Bloom undergoes a change of identity; he becomes Henry Flower. Symbolically the discourse reflects the changes from the human to the vegetable realm. Bloom is shown reflecting on Martha's letter, which is composed in a "language of flowers":

> Then walking slowly forward he read the letter again murmuring here and there a word. Angry tulips with you darling mayflower punish your cactus if you don't please poor forget me not how I violets to dear roses when we

> soon anemone meet all naught nightly stalk wife Martha's perfume. (*U* 64)

Ellmann notes that in this section the consonance between the human and vegetable worlds are effected through the narcotic influence of drugs and metaphors: "Most conspicuously, flowers and petals stand as botanical equivalents of skin and external organs.... The union of men and plants is also suggested by the human use of nicotine, opium, and other vegetable substances" (Ellmann 1972: 39).

P.F. Herring in his article on "Lotus Eaters" points to the complex origin of the title and suggests that Joyce followed Victor Berard's explanation of the term in his notes on *Ulysses* (Hart and Hayman 1974: 87). According to Berard, the Greek poet had made a pun on lotus and Lethe and the consequence was the "fruit of forgetfulness". Herring notes that Homer might not have been aware of the semitic origin of the work, which referred to "perfume". He concludes that Joyce:

> ...seems to have borrowed from Berard one concept of specific importance in formulating a modern symbolic equivalent for lotus—the dietary-racial one. The diet that unites Catholic Ireland racially, Joyce concluded, is the communion wafer—"opiate of the masses". It is ironic that what unites the rest of Catholic Ireland should exclude a different kind of "lotus eater", Leopold Bloom. (Hart and Hayman 1974: 88)

It is of vital importance to note that the idea of the communion wafer suggested by eating of the lotus and its version in the physical persona of Bloom a lotus-eater is given multiple meanings in this section. As Bloom watches the sacrament being administered by the priest, he becomes immediately receptive to its confectionary, sexual and cannibalistic undertones:

> The priest bent down to put it into her mouth, murmuring all the time. Latin. The next one. Shut your eyes and open your mouth. What? Corpus: body corpse. Good idea the Latin. Stupefies them first. Hospice for the dying.... Rum idea: eating bits of a corpse. Why the

> cannibals cotton to it.... Now I bet it makes them feel happy. Lollipop. (*U* 66)

As the ceremony is going on, the sound of iron nails being hammered in Christ's body is heard. The subject and the object merge in the idea of the communion, the sinner beholds himself also as the sufferer. At once the multidimensionality of the communion wafer becomes apparent when through the motif of the flowers Bloom's body in the bath is transubstantiated into the host of the Eucharist. Here also there is a synthesis of the earlier connotation of the lotus as perfume in a creative, regenerative as well as a procreative context. Bloom's loss of identity in the very process of transformation has, therefore been given a sexual, procreative, mythical as well as a religious dimension. And this has only been made possible by the collusion of different texts:

> He foresaw his pale body reclined in it at full, naked, in a womb of warmth...he saw his trunk and limbs rippled over and sustained, buoyed lightly upward lemon yellow: his navel, bud of flesh: and saw the dark tangled curls of his bush floating, floating hair of the stream around the limp father of thousands, a languid floating flower. (*U* 71)

The next section, "Heads" consists of conflicting discourse patterns. On the face level, the prose enacts a panorama of death and corruption, of the putrefaction of flesh and general dissolution. On another level the prose parodies the conventional notion of death as destruction. Personal hygiene and cleanliness, along with soaps and shampoo figure in the description of the dead. Funerals coincide with the slaughter of animals so that death becomes universal. Whereas the meat of animals including their hide, hair, horns and skin are used for purposes of trade, the corpse of men do not spell profit. The sight of Paddy Dignam's corpse rolling about on the road becomes a comic subject. The parody of death may be seen in Joyce's description: "Funerals all over the world everywhere every minute. Shovelling them under by the cartload double quick" (*U* 83).

And again: "Every mortal day of fresh batch: middle-aged man, old women, children, women dead in childbirth, men with beards, bald-headed businessmen, consumptive girls with little sparrows breasts" (*U* 86).

References to the gravediggers in Hamlet, the burial of Julius Caesar, Friday's burial of Robinson Crusoe, Egyptians embalming mummies in catacombs abound in the text. In the process the meaning and significance of death has been suspended. The text destroys the conventionality of death because processes signifying both death and life are paralleled on the grounds of both identicality and difference. This section is almost unique because it posits a relation between opposite things in the best traditions of Giordano Bruno. As each object yields to its opposite, the processes of death have been deprived of any finality extending once again into the portals of life. The "coffinband" some times becomes the "navel cord" (*U* 92). As identities become unstable and are threatened with change the narrative poses a question: "If we were all suddenly somebody else" (*U* 91).

The flux of identities begins with Joyce himself. R.M. Adams in his essay on "Hades" points out that Macintosh is Joyce himself, who was fond of wearing a dirty raincoat (Hart and Hayman 1974: 102). He is also Theoclymenos, as well as Mr. James Duffy of "A Painful Case" (*Dubliners*), who has returned to haunt Mr. Sinico's grave. He may also be likened to the Wandering Jew, and Christ on the road to Emaus. Finally, he is also the unknown and unrecognized God. Thus "his being in this sense Everyman, in no way conflicts with his being in another sense, No-man" (Hart and Hayman 1974: 103). The notion of the decentred self may also be found in Bloom's changing identities. He is "not only Leopold Bloom but also L. Boom, C.P.M. Coy.... Macintosh and Dear Henry" (Hart and Hayman 1974: 109). Actually, as Adams notes:

> In effect, Bloom is a diffused personality—not merely dim and hazy around the edges, but with chunks of other personalities incorporated with his, and *vice versa*. In later chapters of the book, he will turn transparent, become mythical, and disintegrate entirely; in this chapter, he is being built up, but the negative process of dissolution is already under way in selected spots around his

> periphery. When other people's words turn up in Bloom's monologues, or his in theirs, it isn't a "dropping out of character" but a deliberate dropping of character into some other continuum. (Hart and Hayman 1974: 110)

The problem of identity is once again focused in the next section "Aeolus". Throughout *Ulysses* the nexus between God the Father, God the Sun and God the Holy Ghost has been dealt with in a variety of ways. Hodgart pertinently points out in his essay on "Aeolus" that at the inception of the book the Trinity is separated and Bloom the Father and Stephen as the Son, symbolising Christ are alienated, proving that the sources of creation have turned sterile. The artist has been divided into two, Stoom and Blephen. It is only at the very end that the two halves of the artist, the subjective Stephen and the objective Bloom, the inexperienced and the mature pesona, the agent and the patient recognize their consubstantially as well as their mutual dependence. It is, however, the inspiration provided by the Holy Spirit which provides the necessary fusion through its pattern of discourse. (Hart and Hayman 1974: 118).

In "Aeolus" Joyce equates Charles Stewart Parnell with Moses, who attempted to break the hold of the British on his countrymen. Hodgart reminds us that:

> The figure of Moses is central to the political theme of Ulysses, and to the sustained parallel between the Jews and the Irish political figure whom Joyce admired, and his aloofness set Joyce's own lifestyle: he is the archetype of both the God of Creation and of the Artist, "paring his fingernails". Joyce also equates him with Christ. The implication is that there can be no true victories in the world of politics, and the only triumphs are those of the creative imagination, the equation "Stephen = Christ = Moses = Parnell" is fundamental to *Ulysses*. (Hart and Hayman 1974: 119-20)

They are of the "Aeolus" episode is rhetoric, signifying the venture of writing but without any ulterior signification. The rhetoric follows the rhythm of breathing, inspiration and expiration. The art follows a similar pattern, the airy grandiloquence of the earlier headlines of newspaper suggests inhalation while the later comic reduction of flatulent rhetoric signify exhalation.

It is an endless process signifying the oscillation of meaning, forwards and backwards:

> Grossbooted draymen rolled barrels dullthudding out of Prince's stores and bumped them up on the brewery float. On the brewery float bumped dullthudding barrels rolled by grassbooted draymen out of Prince's stores. (*U* 6)

The ambiguity of the rhetoric implies an oblique comment on the author's own ambivalence with regard to the materiality of writing. Writing both reveals and conceals the self. Thus, the actual authorship of the various styles of discourse is placed under doubt. It might belong to the fourth estate or to the voice of the omniscient author (Ellmann 1972: 73). However, it might be, the headlines along with the movement of prose debar any precise comprehension of reality.

As *Ulysses* unfolds, the status of the omniscient narrator is often placed under doubt. In the next section "Lestrygonians" he is only intermittently visible and even the mode of discourse becomes more suggestive, inclining more towards poetry. Joyce as narrator has no separate identity. He neither uses the third person narrative technique ("he did", "he said", "he though") as employed by Virginia Woolf nor does he indulge in explicit comments like Stendhal, Dostoevsky, Austen and others (Hart and Hayman 1974: 132). An example of Joyce's impersonal style may be seen in the following passage in which language has been empowered to enact and express Bloom's particular mood without authorial intrusion:

> A warm human plumpness settled down on his brain. His brain yielded. Perfume of embraces all over him assailed. With hungered flesh obscurely, he mutely craved to adore. Duke Street. Here we are, Must eat. The Burton. Feel better then. (*U* 138)

Here even language signifies sex. The text produces its own brand of sexuality. Through the act of feeding, men become transformed into animals:

> A man spitting back on his plate: half masticated gristle: gums: no teeth to chewchewchew it. Chump chop from the grill. Bolting to get it over.
>
> .... Hungry man is an angry man. Working tooth and jaw. Don't! O! a bone! That last pagan king of Ireland Cormac in the schoolpoem choked himself at sleety southward of the Boyne. (*U* 138-39)

Even the dead and the living are juxtaposed in the association between the corpse of Dignam, "Dignam's potted meat" with the title of an advertisement; "Plumtree's potted meat" (*U* 140). It also contains the suggestion of cannibals feeding themselves on buried divinity: "Cannibals would with lemon and rice. White missionary too salty. Like pickled pork" (*U* 140).

The flux of images within discourse shows that "nature abhors a vacuum" and that even the solidity of the physical world may be transformed by the torrential flow of words (*U* 135). Like trams passing on rails, cities pass away: "other cityful coming, Passing away too: Other coming on, passing on. Horses, lines of houses, streets, miles of pavements, piled up bricks, stones Changing hand's" (*U* 135). In this way any ulterior signification becomes lost, only the signifiers march forwards and backward: "Useless words" (*U* 134). In the materiality of writing identities become subjected to a process of flux: "No—one is anything" (*U* 135).

In this sense as M.J. Friedman has noted in his essay on "Lestrygonians", the narrator:

> becomes "absolutely colourless and anonymous" and the "syntax has completely broken down" and grammatical safeguards have deserted the language. In fact, it is seemingly more removed from logical controls and closer to a kind of post-symbolist poetry than the bits of Bloom's inner monologue. (Hart and Hayman 1974: 132)

This narrator—he might also be called an "implied author" (Wayne Booth's expression)—performs only limited service in "Lestrygonians".... He can, as we have seen above, remain perfectly detached or else lose identity in the flow of Bloom's monologue. The important thing to remember is that he never speaks for himself.... He is emphatically not a shaping influence on the principal narrative movement of supplying it with an external dimension (Hart and Hayman 1974: 132-33).

The author's relationship with his creations has been given novel expression in chapter nine. In this section "Scylla and Charybdis" Stephen's "theolologicophilological" theorising posits the consubstantiality of himself and Joyce, showing their oneness as well as their separate identities. The idea of aesthetic trinity comprises both identity and difference. That is to say, the creator does not intrude in his creations, he is rather his own ghost; his own person being subject to the temporal order of things. Robert Kellogg notes that:

> Bloom's life has elements in common with Stephen's version of Shakespeare's life and with Joyce's own. The relationship between Stephen and Bloom cannot really be "proved by algebra" because it is not produced entirely by a simple logical analogy, but by some deeper pattern of imagination, some "entelechy, form of forms" which unites Stephen, Joyce, and Bloom in life and in art. It is here in "Scylla and Charybdis", in Stephen's argument about Shakespeare as father, that Joyce tells this reader in effect: "I too, am the father, the older man whom this young artist would one day become". (Hart and Hayman 1974: 167)

The notion of the artist being the father and mother of his creation is central to an understanding of Joyce's standpoint in *Ulysses*. Here Joyce and Shakespeare, including the divine Father provide parallels. If the sexual act is taken as the essence of all artistic and natural creation then the artist must be thought of as an androgyne, combining within himself the double nature of the victimizer as well as the victim, of Iago as well as Othello. God himself combines in himself the role of mother and father to Christ. As Stephen says:

> The playwright who wrote folio of this world and wrote it badly.... Is doubtless all in all in all of us, ostler and butcher, and would be bawd and cuckold too but that in the economy of heaven, foretold by Hamlet, there are no

> more marriages, glorified man, an androgynous angel, being a wife unto himself. (*U* 175)

Ellmann in his penetrating analysis points out how the androgyne combines in himself both aspects of sex; male and female qualities in this episode like "ashplant and hat, flag and pit, Prospero's buried staff and drowned book, and also the categories of time and space...the present and the possible, the now-here and there-then, Stratford and London, Dublin and Paris, land and sea" (Ellmann 1972: 87). The creative process is hereby compared to a "deflowering, a brutalisation of the soul by experience" and all acts of the brain become variants of both the "ravished" as well as the "ravisher" (Ellmann 1972: 87).

The theme of exile and return, noted earlier become one of the central preoccupations of both Shakespeare and Joyce. In Shakespeare:

> The note of banishment, banishment from the heart banishment from home, sounds uninterruptedly from The Two Gentlemen of Verona onward till Prospero breaks his staff, buries it certain fathoms in the earth and drowns his book. It doubles itself in the middle of his life, reflects itself in another, repeats itself, protasis, epitasis, catastasis, catastrophe. (*U* 174)

Similarly, all of Joyce's heroes become victims of usurpation, exile, adultery. Socrates, Christ, Fox, Ulysses, Parnell are all exiled figures who are united with Joyce, either in his different fictional disguises as Stephen, Richard Rowan (*Exiles*), Leopold Bloom or as James Joyce, the ghostly hunter from abroad (*U* 167).

Judge Eglinton summed up that the truth lies "midway". Shakespeare is both "the ghost and the prince. He is all in all" (*U* 174). In this manner, "the boy of Act One becomes 'the mature man of Act Five. All in all.... He acts and is acted on.... His unremitting intellect is the hornmad Iago ceaselessly willing that the moor in him shall suffer" (*U* 174).

The artist strives to pursue a middle path, enacting a fusion signified by the opposed symbols of Scylla, signifying the male or the classical temperament as well as the truths of prosaic reality and that of Charybdis, implying the female or the Romantic qualities as well as the pursuit of ideal truths beyond this world. For Joyce perfect artistry involved the "imagination's simultaneous contemplation of both the truth of its own being and the truth of the visible world" (Hart and Hayman 1974: 157). Here we note a divergence between the mature Joyce and the inexperienced Stephen. In *Ulysses*, Stephen shuns the airy idealism of Russell and Blake in favour of a concrete approach to reality:

> Unsheathe your dagger definitions. Horseness is the whatness of allhorse. Streams of tendency and eons they worship. God: noise in the street: very peripatetic. Space: what you damn well have to see. Through spaces smaller than red globules of man's blood they creepycrawl after Blake's buttocks into eternity of which the vegetable world is but a shadow. (*U* 153)

A distinction, therefore, ought to be made between the artist and his creation. Although the analogy between God, Shakespeare and the artist has been made explicit through the theme of exile, the underlying implication is that author and text can never be equated. Throughout *Ulysses* we have noted the vacillation and ambivalence of discourse. The fluidity of discourse fractures the authority of the text into several possible positions. In the next section "The Wandering Rocks" the uncertainties of discourse have been multiplied with the result that the mind is poised upon doubt and incertitude just as the world hangs over a void. In this "hostile environment" as Joyce termed it in his *Linati Schema* the:

> world, as Emerson in another context announced, "lies broken and in heaps" in eighteen little heaps and a coda, to be precise; the number of this episode's parts duplicates the total number of episodes in *Ulysses*, like a distorting mirror image, to challenge the book's order. (Ellmann 1972: 91)

Actually, the vicious insertion of an uncertainty principle in this chapter represents a development of the earlier negation and dissolution of logocentric discourse, which challenged a stable world-pattern. We had seen earlier in the section on *A Portrait* how Stephen's artistic creed had helped him in cultivating an impersonal attitude with respect to the various forms of logocentric authority in society like religion, family and nation. In *Exiles*, we had seen how Richard nurtured in his soul a "restless living wounding doubt", which may not be healed, living forever under the spectre of his wife's infidelity (*PJJ* 626). The creative role of doubt becomes apparent in this section, which is based on the scepticism and unknowability of Hume's universe. In the earlier section Joyce and played off Aristotle against Plato, here he counterpoints Hume against Aristotle. Although Hume agrees with Aristotle and Stephen in his conviction that:

> memory is a source of personal identity, he insists that "all the nice and subtle questions concerning personal identity can never possibly be decided, and are to be regarded rather as grammatical than as philosophical difficulties". Against Stephen's theory of persons and things having each its signature, Hume refuses to concede uninterrupted identity. (Ellmann 1972: 95)

In the twelfth chapter, "Sirens" the "mythic inversion of paternity" is enacted whereby both Simon and Stephen Dedalus exchange identities (Hart and Hayman 1974: 232). The usurpation of role and identities, which forms one of the primary themes of the book, has been given a new twist in this section. The senior Dedalus is changed into Icarus whereas Stephen usurps the status of Simon Dedalus, thus enabling him to escape the nets of pride and all forms of authority. J. Cope points out:

> Dedalus that was in giving way to Dedalus that will be, Simon bowing out "high in the effulgence symbolistic" to allow Icarus to become Dedalus; but offering to the new father Bloom the idiom by which Stephen can be trained to transcend himself, to soar-music, the sound of the past, unfamiliar, not consubstantial, transcendent as the "mystery of paternity".... Leopold Bloom has become the mediator of the mystery by which mythic fate can be averted. Stephen will later lie in the street

> unconscious and become fused with little Rudy. Here Bloom accepts paternity from a drowned Simon Dedalus: met-him-pike-hoses. (Hart and Hayman 1974: 232-33)

The mysterious "apostolic succession" of fatherhood, which Bloom receives, prepares him for his climactic meeting with Stephen at the National Maternity Hospital later on. In this section, the ambivalences or the hesitancy of writing is exposed in the ironic status of Bloom. On the one hand, the narrative portrays characters like Douce and Kennedy, Lenehan and Boylan, Simon Dedalus, Dollard and Cowley, Richie Goulding who are seen, heard and described by Bloom without his active interference. On the other hand, Joyce allows the reader an omniscience and a superior insight which enables him to probe beneath Bloom's actions and wisdom without the knowledge of the character (Hart and Hayman 1974: 224-25). In this way, the discourse accepts the legitimacy of Bloom's account while at the same time it questions his ultimate validation in the narrative.

In the next section, "Cyclops" Joyce establishes a multiple narrative pattern which introduces an infinite variety in the discourse. Four narrative points of view clash and interact, as the theme of the Cyclops requires two one-eyed narrators and the one-eyed citizen. The two Cyclopeans, Thersites and Pangloss provide events with a double vision, forming the dialectic of the episode. Bloom, who, represents the two-eyed Ulysses counteracts the "Citizen's chauvinism, Thersites" of Bloom may be noticed in his medial position. He is both the centre of action as well as its passive recipient. He is both Everyman, the complete person and also the comic convention as No-man (Hart and Hayman 1974: 249).

It is important to note that in the "Nausicaä" section we are introduced to a female-dominated world. The soft cadences of the prose initiate us into the reaches of the feminine mind here signified by Gerty MacDowell. With her idealistic and inexperienced youth but lame and wasted passion she typifies one aspect of womanhood, the other symbolized by nature, passionate and down-to-earth Molly Bloom. The text shows a gradual domination of feminine discourse-patterns. At the end of both "Nausicaä" (chapter thirteen), and "Ithaca" (chapter seventeen) Bloom falls asleep and the prose deviates into a dream language where masculine control over discourse yields to an incessant flow of images, words and memories. Fritz Senn in his essay on "Nausicaä" comments:

> Tucked between enveloping folds of feminity, the meeting, interacting, parting of Bloom and Stephen are circumbeloped by a darkness that both does and does not comprehend them. They are thus "wombed in sindarkness" (38.10). The image of an enfolding womb within which the most significant action takes place is more than a convenient analogy. Regression into uterine security is at the core of infantile notions of illusory escape, as in "Nausicaä"; the same local anatomical habitation is necessary for the positive interpretations concentrating on birth and rebirth or for Stephen's concept of a creative womb of the imagination. A womb is included in the word "wombfruit" at the beginning of the "Oxen of the Sun" chapter (38.4), whose organ is the womb. The last page of "Ithaca", which is symmetrically opposite and in which Bloom disappears, contains a corresponding image: "the manchild in the womb". (Hart and Hayman 1974: 283-84)

The ambiguity of "womb" has already been indicated at the beginning of the section. It is significant that the term figures both at the inception and towards the close of the book. "Womb" signifies a tempting darkness in which there occurs a loss of identity. But the mother as a loving parent also represents the birth of new life in the son. Here these contradictory terms merge in Joyce's ambiguous woman-image. Earlier we had noted how the images of the mother/Virgin/ temptress become alternate prefigurations of the woman. Moreover, in one important sense the "womb" indicates artistic creativity. The artist transubstantiates the facts of his experience into art; he transforms flesh into the word. Human birth and the creation of art are obverse and reverse of the same originary act of creation. Creation and post-creation are thereby balanced: "In woman's womb word is made flesh but in the spirit of the maker all flesh that passes becomes the word that shall not pass away" (*U* 320).

Therefore, the act of sexuality, the authorship of texts as well as the creation of the world act as parallels. Here the question of identity is of vital importance. The materiality of writing fractures, as we have seen, the authorial self into multiple personas but there is always an attempt to return to the originary dark night of creation from where the text issued. In the process, however, the author comes to terms with the contradictions within his own person:

> And as the ends and ultimates of all things accord in some mean and measure with their inceptions and originals, that same multiplicity concordance which leads forth growth from birth accomplishing by a retrogressive metamorphosis that minishing and ablation towards the final which is agreeable unto nature so is it with our subsolar being. (*U* 322)

The gradual dissolution of the narrative pattern has been exemplified in the last two chapters of *Ulysses*. Here the technique fuses with the subject matter so as to be indistinguishable. This fragmentation of discourse into discrete aesthetic unities by employing the question-and-answer method may be noted in the second last chapter 'Ithaca'. The form of interrogation has the effect of focusing on both the minute particulars as well as the panoramic expanse of human life. A. Walton-Litz in his essay on "Ithaca" points out that the effect is one of:

> Viewing Bloom and Stephen from a great height, against a vast backdrop of general human action and knowledge, while at the same time standing next to them and observing every local detail. It is this "parallax" achieved by the macrocosmic-microcosmic point-of-view which gives the episode, like Hardy's *Dynasts*, the grandeur and sweep that Joyce certainly intended.... Bloom and Stephen do indeed "become heavenly bodies, wanderers like the stars at which they gaze", but at the same time, their subjective lives penetrate every detail of objective

> description.... While "Ithaca" does "resolve" its human figures into their objective counterparts, at the same time the objective universe is suffused with their personalities. (Hart and Hayman 1974: 396-97)

At last, the discourse has successfully neutralised the distinction between the subjective and the objective, between the personal and the universal. This has been achieved by the use of Homeric myth and Christian symbolism. As Bloom thinks about travel and escape, his ambiguity as Everyman and No-man, Elpenor and Ulysses is underlined. He is gradually transformed into a wandering comet whose orbit leads away from the axis of his own self and makes possible his re-emergence in the mythic garb of Ulysses or Hamlet:

> Would the departed never nowhere nohow reappear? Ever he would wander, self-compelled to the extreme limit of his cometary orbit, beyond the fixed stars and variable suns.... Somewhere imperceptibly he would hear and somehow reluctantly, suncompelled, obey the summons of recall. Whence, disappearing from the constellation of the Northern Crown he would somehow reappear reborn.... An estranged avenger, a wreaker of justice on male factors, a dark crusader.... (*U* 598)

As Bloom retires into the womb of infinite possibilities at the end of "Ithaca" symbolised by a full stop, it signifies his rebirth on the next day as Everyman. The last chapter "Penelope" countersigns "Bloom's passport to eternity" because it signifies his cyclic renewal. The ending of Ulysses signifies both an end and a beginning. Joyce assigned no specific time to the last episode obviously because creation is an endless process. In this section, the materiality of writing takes the reader deep inside the mental processes, beyond the province of referential language.

Riquelme writes:

> By adopting this last style, which presses the mimesis of consciousness toward the non linguistic, both as physical sensation and as the unconscious or the imagination, the teller enables the reader to participate in the books' consummation. (Riquelme 1983: 228)

In these terms, the discourse becomes confessional, presenting what has never been and what can never be written. The fact of writing becomes ironic in itself as it questions the very basis of its existence. As Riquelme in his *Teller and Tale in Joyce's Fiction* notes:

> The final style, the end of wandering, in *Ulysses* is also the end of writing as its teleology: to present as style what no style can actually present. We abandon ourselves to a narration that finishes with the abandoning of language at the margin of narrative. (Riquelme 1983: 228-29)

Joyce's declaration of war on language and on conventional logocentric discourse has a "positive emphasis on literature as transgression, as able to subvert the constraints of all other forms of discourse by its 'difference'" (Young 1987: 11). This "self-reflexiveness", which enables the pattern of discourse to curve back on itself and question its own limits can "evade the exercise of power" (Young 1987: 11). This recoiling of discourse produces a critique of the classic conception of the unitary subject because it not only resists domination by any from of authority but it also defers the notion of the authorial self. This perpetual decentring of the self or the fissuring and retarding of the signified is brought about by Molly's reverie at the end.

Finnegans Wake (1939) 10

Finnegans Wake represents an extreme instance of deconstructive activity which tears apart the centrality of the author into a medley of various discourses:

> Anyhow, somehow and somewhere before the bookflood or after her ebb, somebody mentioned by name in his telephone directory, Coccolanius or Gallotaurus, wrote it, wrote it all, wrote it all down, and there you are, full stop. O, undoubtedly yes, and very portably so, but one who deeper thinks will always bear in the baccbuccus of his mind that this downright there you are and there it is only all in his eye.... (*FW* 118)

> This decentring of the author is due to the fact that each person, place and thing have been subjected to a process of flux in which things not only change but that "the travelling inkhorn (possibly pot), the hare and turtle pen and paper", bring about different degrees of change in the "vocable scriptsigns". (*FW* 118)

Indeed, the text often turns back on itself and questions the authorship of the letter as witnessed in chapter five of the *Wake* where the American scholar-critic finds it almost indecipherable.

Since it is in the form of a "proteiform graph", as William York Tindall reminds us in his *A Reader's Guide to 'Finnegans Wake'* (1969), or a "polyhedron of scripture" (Tindall 1969: 101).

> By turns he employs the methods of textual critics, contextual critics, biographers, paleographers, political and psychoanalytic critics. He examines the handwriting,

> the state of the paper, the punctuation (if any), each letter, sign, and word. In short, he is exhaustive; but what his exhausting analysis amounts to is an unintended criticism of criticism by an intending master of burlesque. (Tindall 1968: 100)

The American's critical methodology represents the rambling pattern of discourse of *Finnegans Wake*, lacking any fixed centre or point of reference. Increasingly, we find as Stephen Heath indicates in his essay "Ambivalences" that the context has been fractured into a "plurality of possible positions", into "a multiplicity of instances of discourse" which can never be reduced to any "single line of a truth" (Attridge and Ferrer 1984: 39). Any consideration of the totality or the message of the text is bound up with the problem of intertextuality. Heath underlines that:

> The practice of writing-reading in Joyce's texts is the recognition of the text not as absolute origin or source (expression of "Reality", expression of the Author, etc) but as intertextual space, dialogue of forms which write it as it writes them. (Attridge and Ferrer 1984: 39)

This violation of the "principles of identity and non-contradiction" which brings about "an infinitisation of fictions of possibilities" may be located in the text of the American's discourse (Attridge and Ferrer 1984: 39). He emphatically indicates that:

> .... We are in for a sequentiality of improbable possibles though possibly nobody after having grubbed up a lock of cold corn above his subject probably in Harrystotalies or the vile will go out of his way to applaud him on the unbiased back of his remark for utterly impossible as are all these events they are probably as like those which may have taken place as any others which never took person at all are ever likely to be. (*F* 110)

The "sequentiality of improbable possibles" which the book enviasages may be grasped on multiple levels. From one point of view Joyce's way of writing may be termed after Stephen Heath as an act of "misappropriation" or after *Finnegans*

Wake, an activity of "raiding" (Attridge and Ferrer 1984: 43). Joyce as Shem/sham/shame become a forger who: "did not study with stolen fruit how cutely to copy all their various styles of signature so as one day to utter an epical forged cheque on the public for his own private profit..." (*FW* 181).

Again: "Who can say how many pseudostylic shamiana, how few or how many of the most venerated public impostures, how very many piously forged palimpsests slipped in the first place by this morbid process from his plagiarist pen?" (*FW* 181-82).

According to Tindall, "Shem the Penmman, the exiled author of *Ulysses* and the *Wake* is a problem" because of the "heavy almost painful-jocularity with which Joyce handles Shem, no substitute for irony or comedy, fails to separate the embracing author from his embraced creation" (Tindall 1969: 131). Actually, Shem's signification lies in his progressive irony. Although he writes about himself and on himself, his writing records a centrifugal movement. In a decentring action, his "plagiarist pen" takes into account the different modes of discourse, the entire course of human history:

> ...and the first till last alchemist wrote over every square inch of the only foolscap available, his own body, till by its corrosive sublimation one continuous present tense integument slowly unfolded all marryvoising moodmoulded cyclewheeling history (thereby, he said, reflecting from his own individual person life unlivable, transaccidentated through the slow fires of consciousness into a dividual chaos perilous, potent, common to allflesh, human only, mortal) but with each word that would not pass away the squidself which he had squirtscreened. (*FW* 185-86)

The movement is not only from the individual plane to "dividual chaos", from personal to the universal but the submerging of personal discourse in the stream of "Cycle-heeling history" which gradually screens the author from his text.

The *Wake* highlights the deconstruction of male authority in the fall of the father, an issue which had been broached by

Joyce at the end of *Ulysses* where the flow of feminine discourse had dissolved the author's logocentric control over the narrative. Joyce the narrator contributes to his fracture of self. According to him, the artist is both female and male personalities, comprising in himself both the man who suffers and one who creates. He is actually a prototype of the androgyne. In *Ulysses*, Stephen's theory of Shakespeare focuses on this central ambiguity in the artist, who both "acts and is acted on":

> It is in infinite variety everywhere in the world he has created, in *Much Ado about Nothing*, twice in *As You Like It*, in *The Tempest*, in *Hamlet*, in *Measure for Measure*.... The truth is midway, he affirmed. He is the ghost and the prince. He is all in all.—He is, Stephen said. The boy of act one is the mature man of act five. All in all. In *Cymbeline*, in *Othello* he is bawd and cuckold. He acts and is acted on. Lover of an ideal or a perversion, like Jose' he kills the real Carmen. His unremitting intellect in the hornmad Iago ceaselessly willing that the moor in him shall suffer. (*U* 174)

Finnegans Wake illustrates the decentring of the author into the male and female principles symbolized by the two parents Humphrey Chimpden Earwicker (H.C.E.) and Anna Livia Plurabelle (A.L.P.) respectively. The family attains completeness with their pompous son, Kevin (Shaun), the rebellions son Dolph (Shem) and their flirtatious daughter, Isabel. Although Norris is of the opinion that in the *Wake* the family "serves as the paradigm of a primal social structure" it is one of the high points of the quadraphonic text that it is torn by incest and parricide (Norris 1976: 54).

Humphrey Chimpden Earwicker's family affairs, however, creates a "hubbub caused in Edbenborough" because it has social repercussions (*FW* 29). This crime which has a detrimental effect on society is compared to the curse on the house of Atreus, the fall of Troy and Adam's Original Sin: "The house of Atreox is fallen in dust (Ilyam, Ilyum, Maeromor Mournomates!) averaging on blight like the mundibanks of Fennyana, but deeds going arise again" (*FW* 55).

Indeed, out of the ten Viconian thunders three (seventh, eight and ninth) focus on the fall of the father. In the *Wake* life becomes: "a wake, livit or krikit, and on the bunk of our breadwinning lies the cropse of our seedfather, a phrase which the establisher of the world by law might pretinately write across the chest front of all manorwomanbanborn" (*FW* 55).

The figure of the father, the lawgiver, is superseded by the universal mother or Anna Livia Plurabelle. Thus as M. Norris in her penetrating study, *The Decentered Universe of Finnegans Wake* (1976) notes:

> In contrast to the father, ALP, the mother, embodies the law as a lack. She does not arrange, regulate, designate, or judge, but merely gathers together her children and the fragments of her fallen husband. The linguistic correspondence of her function is the potentiality of language for an infinite number of combinations within a finite system. (Norris 1976: 69)

Joyce's handling of the Viconian thunder has in it a suggestion of the polyvalence and complexity of the elements of a dream. M. Norris aptly points out that:

> Both kinship system and language, instituted by the clap of thunder in Vico's myth, serve the foundation of civilization by introducing those distinctions that linguistically and socially constitute meaningful systems. The source of this meaning in the myth is the voice of the thunder, which is Eliot's Wasteland spoke its humanising commands, and which, interpreted as the voice of God by "the dumb beasts", functions as a version of the theological Word or Logos. (Norris 1976: 56)

The significance of the thunder in the Wake lies in its multivalent associations as well as in the hundred letters of its name. As has just been noted, it is associated with the fall of the father: "the hindering blundering dander funder of plunder sundered manhood" (*FW* 596).

Within this noise, however, lies concealed the suggestion of sin or guilt. It also reveals its onomatopoeic character in recording the sound of falling down a ladder....

"Drumstrumtruminahumptadump..." (*FW* 314). It also suggests a door being closed forcibly following Humphrey Chimpden's retreat from an outrageous mob: "....Lukkedoerendum... andurraskewdy looshoofermoyporter...." (*FW* 257), or the reassuring close of the door by Anna Livia after her chickens have returned: "Thingcrooklyexineverypastures..." (*FW* 113). Referring to the sixth thunder, Tindall reminds us that "Lukkedoer" means "shut the door" in Danish, "unandurras" dun and doras, in Gaelic, and "fermoyporte" in French (Tindall 1969: 165). The thunder also refers to Shaun's cough as well as the sound of defecation (first and second thunders) and the sound of the father being shot. It is clear that all of these thunders have their origin in Wakean sins or guilt which have come down to us from time immemorial.

Norris in her study remarks:

> *Wake* thunder, unlike Vico's thunder does not function as the civilising command of God. On the contrary, instead of promoting matrimony, the thunder words themselves express obscenities ".... Foul...whore.... Strum.... Porn.... Kocks.... Tupper.... Strip...." (90, 31). James Atherton coalesces thunder and stutter as symptom of the original sin of God, "Joyce is suggesting that the original sin of God, "Joyce is suggesting that the original master builder is God and that He stutters when his voice is heard in the thunder—thus proving that He is conscious of having committed a sin!". (Norris 1976: 56)

If Vico's God thunders to bestow law, the *Wake*'s thundering H.C. Earwicker actually breaks laws. The thunder in one sense may be understood as the language of the father, either as the Logos, creating life or as fallen or sinning. In either terms thunder as discourse might be creative or destructive depending on the context. In the *Bible*, the Word signifies logocentric authority. God is father may then be said to dominate the pattern of discourse is assigning a name (Yahweh) to himself, in positing his function and in creating his own identity. According to Lacan, the father has always been identified with the law. The idea of the Mosaic God creating his own identity is important as Norris indicates in understanding the nature of the Wake's discourse:

> The prototype of the Symbolic father is therefore the Mosaic God, whose justification as the source of law resides in the tautology of his name, the inviolable certainty of his identity. The Symbolic father, "The who is ultimately capable of saying 'I am who I am'" is the center or pivot who defines, names, and gives meaning to the constellation of personages around him. Finnegans *Wake* contains numerous references to the Yahwistic "I am", as well as to the naming ritual of baptism, by means of the recurrent verbal motifs "mishe mishe" and "tauftauf". (Norris 1976: 57)

Logocentric discourse established the identity of each person, indicating a stable world order. But the "marry voicing" prose of the Wake with its breakdown of the individual self into a "dividual chaos" illustrates the decentring of the logos which is the sole source of authority as well as the breakdown of law. (*FW* 186). Chaos reigns supreme with the fall of the father.

> In *Finnegans Wake* then the Viconian myth of social and linguistic origin is essentially reversed: in Vico, the thunder creates language and kinship laws while in the Wake the stutter serves as a symptom of linguistic breakdown and incestuous wishes. (Norris 1976: 57-58)

Incest is responsible for the violent disruption of the social order. One of the main themes of the book is the confrontation of the young with the old. This is hinted at quite early in chapter one where Parnell substitutes old Isaac Butt (*FW* 3) and Shimar Shin replaces old Willingdone (*FW* 10). This theme reaches its climax later in chapter eleven where Buckley shoots the old Russian General (*FW* 353). Joyce grasped the Freudian possibilities of this theme of the son challenging the father's authority. The son actually replaces the father and marries the mother. But this Oedipal interpretation of the conflict between the young and the old decentres the notion of identity. As husband/son/father/brother, the individual destroys the fixed loci in familial relationships. Like Oedipus, Humphrey Chimpden is guilty of a heinous crime, which is of an ancient nature "ages and ages after the alleged misdemeanour" (*FW* 35). The problem lies in the nature of quest for the search for the wrongdoer leads to hesitation and uncertainty:

> It is nebuless an autodidact fact of the commonest that the shape of the average human cloudyphiz, whereas sallow has long daze faded, frequently altered its ego with the passing of the showers (Not original!). Whence it is a slopperish matter, given the wet and low visibility (since in this scherzarade of one's thousand one nightnesses that sword of certainty which would indentifide the body never falls) to indentifide the individuone.... (*FW* 50-51)

Norris rightly points out that "this matter of the uncertainty and indeterminability of HCE's identity deserves special consideration because it is too easily dismissed as merely an aspect of his archetypal function, his embodiment of multitudes and subsequent lack of individuality" (Norris 1976: 59).

Any question of identity must begin with an account of Humphrey Chimpden's portrayal in the *Wake*. Here we note parallel echoes between Bloom and Humphrey. Both are portrayed as having more than one identity: they are both everyman as well as no man. Humphrey Chimpden is portrayed variously as:

> An imposing everybody he always indeed looked, constantly the same as and equal to himself and magnificently well worthy or any and all such universalisation.... (*FW* 32)

> "But how transparingly nontrue, gentle writer! His feet one is not a tall man, not at all, man. No such parson. No such fender. No such lumber. No such race." (*FW* 63)

> "...a manyfeast munificent more mob than man" (*FW* 261). First you were Nomad, next you were Namar, now you're Numah and it's soon you'll be Nomon. (*FW* 374)

But the basic difference between *Ulysses* and the *Wake* is that in the latter the father figure is pitted against himself. He breaks laws rather than assign them. As a fallen father, he dissolves the laws of kinship and family's. Humphrey's uniqueness lies in the fact that he himself provides the context for a rebirth at the very end of the Wake. But this notion of resurrection occurs at the inception of the book also. As we notice how this Christian conception flanks the Wake both at the beginning and at its end, we miss the notion of finality in death or a constant flow of life in the "Chaosmos" which defers the attainment of selfhood.

At the beginning Humphrey is described as an "overgrown babeling" a supine tower or a big baby lying "flat". This sleeping giant is awakened by oboes and "flittaflute in tricky trochees" (*FW* 7). As Anna Livia wakes him up, she is accompanied by Stella, Vanessa, Swift and Peter, Jack, Martin from *A Tale of a Tub* (*FW* 7). Humphrey however, is not merely a fallen giant; he is also the risen Christ or the Host in the Eucharist (*FW* 7). The audience proceed to eat him sacramentally. The idea of transubstantiation has been employed to indicate the change occurring in Humphrey, who wakes from his sleep into a "brontoichthyan form" (*FW* 7). Matter changes but the spirit of Jesus/Humphrey Chimpden is preserved in the new form/the Host.

The penultimate end of the book focuses once again on the change of form in Humphrey. In Anna's monologue we find that he is initially labelled as a "wordherfhull ohldhbhoy!" (wonderful old boy), then termed "cooloosus" (*FW* 625) and a "bumpkin" (*FW* 627) and finally into the sea. Containing both the Shem and the Shaun aspects within him he can change within the "twinngling of an aye" (*FW* 620). In his volatile state, he is never at peace within him. Anna also thinks of him as a "wonderdecker" or Vanderdecken, the Flying Dutchman "somebalt that sailder" or Sinbad the Sailor, Patrick Sarsfield (Earl of Lucan) and the Iron Duck of Wellington (*FW* 620) among others (Tindall 1969: 327). At the last moment he changes again to become the sea emptying into the ocean where Anna Livia already flows, being transformed likewise. But H.C. Earwicker rapidly alters to become the "sonhusband", who will take a new wife "a daughterwife from the hills" (*FW* 627) after replacing his father. In short, as Tindall explains:

> Shaun-H.C.E., and Nuvoletta-Isabel—A L.P. will take the place of their parents. Nuvoletta? After the river enters the sea, the sun sucks water up into a cloud which, according to cyclical necessity, will drop a tear into the river, and so for river and ever. (*FW* 328)

On the other hand, Anna changes into a daughter to be united once again with her father, Humphrey Chimpden, who has been already transformed into a sort of Neptune before becoming Finnegan again:

> I am passing out. O bitter ending! I'll slip away before they're up. They'll never see. Not know. Nor miss me. And it's old and old it's sad and old it's sad and weary I go back to you, my cold father, my cold mad father, my cold mad feary father, till the near sight of the mere size of him, the moyles and moyles of it, moananoaning, makes me seasilt saltsick and I rush, only, into your arms. (*FW* 627-28)

Here once more we run into the theme of incest, of Anna rushing into her father's arms. This thematic turn about or return to the beginning of the novel which expatiates on H.C. Earwicker's sin reiterates a continuous flow of discourse harping on the same theme. Stephen Heath in his essay "Joyce in Language" pertinently remarks:

> That Anna Livia's flow occupies the same structural place as Molly's monologue, at the end of the book, underlines the force of the pressure in evidence in the latter but also shows up the difference from the one to the other, exactly the rewriting and displacement. With Anna Livia we are in the whole question of the writing of the Wake, where syntax—the logic of subject—predicate—is overtaken by "sin talks" (*FW* 269), the constant transgressive underrunning of accepted orders, rules of stability, the laws of language and identity—"the farmer, his son and their homely codes" (*FW* 614). Anna Livia's ending of the *Wake* is an epitomising moment of this transgression general to its writing, brought to a head again and again in the theme of incest: Anna Livia

> rushes indefinitely into her father's arms, the river running out and losing itself in the vast ocean, a fearfully ecstatic loss of self.... (MacCabe 1982: 135-36)

But the origins of sin lie far back in racial memory. The Wake itself records the attempt to remember, but the very effort to memorise is ultimately defeated. Behind the present sin of Humphrey lies other sins, sins of mankind, reaching back to the primal sin. Similarly behind him lies an infinite series of paternal figures stretching back to Adam and even to the Logos. The Wake represents an attempt to dig up the origins of Humphrey and Anna through delving deep into the strata of racial memory, in the pre-conscious, the unconscious as well as the collective unconscious. It symbolizes night, the formless and amorphous dark just like *Ulysses* represents day with its "ineluctable modality" of the visible and the audible (*U* 31). There is nothing ineluctable about the Wake. The very act of memory ("mememormee" [*FW* 628]), as the term indicates, is ironical because it is not founded on subjective centre or the individual's knowledge which can impart coherence. It is an act of disremembering or dismembering with respect to both the individual's memory as well as his identity. As the term "riverrun" (*FW* 3) suggests a continuity in terms of flow, the flowing of feminine discourse, so the act of writing may be said to displace identity.

In these terms, the *Wake* may be considered as "That letter selfpenned to one's other, that neverperfect ever-planned?" (*FW* 489). From Humphrey's "dream monologus" (*FW* 474) or 'the steady monologuy of the interior's (*FW* 119) the movement is towards "his drama parapolylogic" (*FW* 474). Therefore, the process of remembering by myself ("mememormee") brings about a decentring of logocentric discourse which always refers back to a central authority. The disruption ("para") of "polylogic" which has begun in *Ulysses* especially in the last five chapters leads to a questioning of the classic novelistic discourse based on certainties of character and plot. Here the position of the woman as noted by Stephen Heath is functional:

> The woman is the other, thus to write to one's other, to drop from an established coherence of the self—oneself,

> the self as one—to the heterogeneous production of a subject of which that coherence is simply an identifying and stabilizing version, a fiction of unity, is to write "feminie" (so HCE, central figure of the Wake, is simultaneously identity and process, "feminisible name of multitude". (*FW* 73) (MacCabe 1982: 137)

It is all the more remarkable when we notice the narrative turning back on itself and questioning its own origins:

> And so they went on, the fourbottle men, the annalists, unguam and nunguam and lunguam again, their anschluss about her whosebefore and his whereafters and she was lost away in the fern and how he was founded deap on deep in anear.... (*FW* 95)

The *Wake* begins with the river flowing and ends with the river returning back. Within this circularity of discourse the writing proceeds in a continuous hesitation:

> And that was how framm Sin from Son, acity arose, finfin funfum, a sitting arrows. Now tell me, tell me, tell me then !
>
> What was it ?
>
> A ... !
>
> ?... O ! (*FW* 94)

The teller/tailor's answer is highly ironic because it comprises a tow or dots between the Alpha (A) and Omega (O) of discourse, with a question mark in between, implying that it can signify everything and nothing simultaneously.

In the *Wake* the centrality of the narrator has also been fractured into multiple points of view through the four historians known collectively "Mammon Lujus" or "Mamalujo", comprising the authors of four gospels, Matthew, Mark, Luke and John as well as the authors of a history of Ireland, Annals of the Four Master. These four apostles record history in all its manifestations, both sacred and secular. The narrator, however, undermines their historic role and often produces a parody of their functions. Imitating the gospel order in the Bible for instance, these four apostles narrate the gospel truth about secret happenings inside a bedroom (Tindall 1969: 285). The man is seen with his nightcap in hand, preparing for bed, while the woman is busy with her curlpins. Matthew's view takes into account the "side point of view" or the "First position of Harmony" wherein the male partly masks the female (*FW* 559).

The comic scene is highlighted by the man's "beastly expression" exhibiting rape in contrast to the woman's "haggish expression" exhibiting fear (*FW* 559). Mark's view which is the "second position of discordance" involves a look from behind as "the male entail partially eclipses the femecovert" (*FW* 564). The "third position of concord" comprises Luke's view from the front where we notice "Female imperfectly masking male" (*FW* 582). Finally, John's view is from above, which is the finest because both woman and man are seen in their proper dimensions in the very act of coition: "While the queenbee he staggerhorned blesses her bliss for to feel her funnyman's functions Tag" (*FW* 590). The point to note is that in the Bible, Mark, Matthew and Luke, who are the authors of the synoptic Gospels along with John proclaim the "Kingdom of God" on earth (Brown 1968: II, 782-84). However, the apostles emphasize different aspects of Christ's teaching. According to E.J. Mally in "The Gospel According Mark", Mark thinks that Jesus reveals his mysterious identity as an evangel (Brown II: 23). J.L. MacKenzie in "The Gospel According to Matthew" states that Matthew stresses the sufferings of Christ as the Son of Man (Brown II: 117). According to B. Vawter in "Johannine Theology", John underlines the role of God as the Father: the sole authority to whom the Son returns after completing his mission on earth (Brown II: 836).

Joyce's intention is burlesque. Depriving these apostles of their sacred functions, they are assigned the role of voyeurists, and their act of sin is made comparable to the "peeping Earwicker" as well as the three soldiers who follow his example. Thus, as Tindall notes, "while father peeped at this two girls in the Park, those soldiers peeped at him..." (Tindall 284). By extension the reader, as he is permitted to peep through the four apostolic cameras, also participates and shares the same sin. This universalisation of the concept of sin leads us back to the sin of the father, that is, Humphrey C. Earwicker and as Stephen Heath notes, it harks back to primal creation of woman in the Bible, which: "tells us that at the beginning there is incest, father and wife-daughter born from his side, which is where Finnegans Wake ends as it begins again, Anna Livia in her father's embrace as the runs back" (MacCabe 137).

The *Wake* resembles an encyclopaedia, dealing with myths, stories, references, focusing on certain documents, asking questions, conducting interviews of people, excerpts from theatrical performances, accounts of films and so on. That is to say the writing comprises all these factors, forming a network of events, allusions and cross-references on which the question of identity and of origins are displayed. One of the most interesting questions on man's identity is asked in Chapter VII, towards the middle of the book. Sphinx's riddle to Oedipus asks: "when is a man not a man?" (*FW* 170). The answer is before he was even a man, that is, his unknown origins in the mother's womb. Heath explains:

> Before (he is "sinse"), when he was in the night of the womb or the flow of the river, a fluidity pre-form, pre-indiviudal. ALP, Anna Livia Plurabelle, is, of course, the writing's imagination of this, river and mother (in Turkish, for example, ana means precisely "mother"), source and site of the generation of life as the children's diagram reveals ("A is for Anna like L is for live"). (*FW* 293) (MacCabe 1982: 139)

The attempt to find out the origins of identity is as difficult in questing for the unknown source of a great river. Through the process of writing, the Wake illustrates this difficulty especially in terms of the myths of creation and fall.

The introductory chapter for instance deals with times, process, the rise and fall of humanity and conflict. The father or H.C. Earwicker figures under the initials of Finnegan, Wellington, Van Hoother. Here the two voices of Joyce as Shem and Shaun become audible. Creative acts like making love, books and towers are shown. Finnegan building a tower is a Variation of Humphrey C. Earwicker. As he works on the ladder, with his drink in his hand, he falls and dies. The funeral symbolised by the tower which is likened to a big baby, is celebrated when the mourners gather round the corpse and start to eat him up sacramentally. This ritual killing and devouring of the father is significant in showing the Christian's participation in the Roman Catholic Mass where he partakes of the host or Christ (Finnegan/Humphrey C. Earwicker) and in symbolizing the son's establishment of authority over his father.

Among other themes enunciated is the distortion of history and historic conflict portrayed by four historians called Mamalujo or "Mammon Lujius" (Matthew, Mark, Luke and John). History here becomes a family affair with Humphrey C. Earwicker/Finnegan as the head. There is also a merging of races in the vast cemetery which a signifies a collocation of past, historical events, personages. It is significant that this babel of voices and confusing discourses show the interpenetration of history and fable from which the tenuous narrative of Humphrey emerges. The biblical story of creation is connected with Irish myth and history, with the conflict between Catholics and Protestants, of Gael and Gall. The exchange of narratives make plausible the multiplication of identities and the delimitisation of H.C. Earwicker. Thus Earwicker's sin in Phoenix Park ("foenix culprit") (*FW* 23) is likened to Adam's fall, "felix culpa" and Finnegan/Finnimore as both conqueror and keeper of akhan or pub is compared with Guinnghis (Guinness) Khan (*FW* 24) (Tindall 1969: 49).

In the second chapter, Joyce names his hero H.C.E. figure in the first sentence of the book, *Howth Castle and Environs* (*FW* 3). But the fact that he is more than somebody is hinted at by the nickname "Her Comes Everybody" (*FW* 32). The idea of H.C. Earwicker being everyman and no-man is implied by Joyce: "An imposing everybody he always indeed looked, constantly the same as and equal to himself and magnificently well worthy of any and all such universalisation" (*FW* 32).

The narrative of the dream emerges in chapter three, introduction a nightmarish quality by "inconsequence, uncertainty and repetition—the same things insistently over and over again" (Tindall 66). The unitary self is atomized into "centuple celves" (*FW* 49) which by the coincidence of their contraries reamalgamerge in that identity of undiscernibles (*FW* 49-50). The changing pattern is delineated by the prose: "It is nebuless an autodidact fact of the commonest that the shape of the average human cloudyphiz, whereas sallow has long daze faded, frequently altered its ego with the possing of the showers..." (*FW* 50-51).

The fun is apparent when the three soldiers ask Hosty (a minor poet) what has actually taken place in the Park and what has befallen Humphrey. Hosty is unable to answer because both Humphrey and himself have changed quite a lot. By turns Humphrey becomes Christ, Parnell, Caesar (Tindall 1969: 72), Frazer's dying god, Earwicker torn "limb from lamb" (*FW* 58). An English actress associates Humphrey C. Earwicker with the rainbow, Arthur, Cain, Adam, Christ and a tower (*FW* 58-59). Further, both Humphrey and Hosty exchange identities. With both gun ("repeater") and watch ("repeater" and "timespiece"), the composite of Hosty, Joyce, Cad, and Humphrey is now "His Revenances", who, like Arthur and "Our Farfar", will return (52:7, 16-17) may be (Tindall 1969: 69).

The fourth chapter signals the period of reflux after Vico's cycle of three ages: the divine, the heroic, and the human. As the apparent connection comes to light, Humphrey is buried in a special watertight coffin. However he is not presented as a corpse but as sleeping for thousand ages through Vico's cycles of generation and regeneration. Identities shift and Earwicker manifests himself in his changing sons: "As Shawn, he is given an ovation, and as Shem that stinker, he goes off into exile. Distinctly different were their duasdestinies" (Tindall 1969: 90).

Suddenly, we are reminded of Earwicker's trial at the old Bailey in London but the proceedings of the lawsuit become as insubstantial as a dream as the witness, lawyer, prisoner and judge exchange identities. Later Earwicker is suddenly metamorphosed into a fox, pursued hotly but the multiplicity of allusions extend his referentiality even further. Not only Reynard the Fox but Mr. Fox (as Parnell was known when he concealed himself from his enemies) as well as Joyce himself when he was hounded into exile by compatriots have been implied through

Earwicker's transformation. In this chapter Anna L. Plurabelle's important functions have been underlined. She is portrayed as the Great Mother or the Geatellus of Ulysses who picks up the ruins of Humphrey C. Earwicker after his fall, picking up his pieces like a hen, ensuring his safety later when the sixth thunder falls. The motif of letter/litter is also continued from chapter one where references to dump and letter occur after the battles of Waterloo and Clontarf: "A pattern is beginning to emerge. Dump, litter, letter, letters, and Wake are depositories and vestiges of our living and dying—and part of their rhythm" (Tindall 1969: 90-91).

In the next chapter, the theme of the letter which was enunciated in chapter one and carried through chapter four, reaches a climax. This litter/letter which was enunciated in chapter one and carried through chapter four, reaches a climax. This litter/letter which was an "allaphbed" (FW 18) in chapter one becomes the alpha ('A') and omega ('O') of litter/literature (*FW* 94). To give an idea of the universality of literature, references are made to the Bible, Shakespeare, Walter Pater, Gay, Pope, Sheridan, Ibsen, Eliot and Pound. Over this creativity in terms of writing Anna Livia is seen to preside. This renewal is also portrayed in terms of the flow of a river and signals the genesis of Vico's divine age. Here the contents of the professor's letter and the Wake become identical, implying the reign of "chaosmos" (*FW* 118) where everything constantly changes, reflecting the chaos of "scriptsigns" in the book itself; a "riot of blots and blurs and bars and balls and hoops and wriggles and juxtaposed jottings linked by spurts of speed: it only looks as like it as damn it" but surely we ought to be thankful for having something "written on with dried ink scrap of paper at all to show for ourselves,..." (*FW* 118). According to Samuel Beckett:

> This writing that you find so obscure is a quintessential extraction of language and painting and gesture, with all the inevitable clarity of the old articulation. Here is the savage economy of hieroglyphics. Here words are not the polite contortions of 20th century printer's ink. They are alive. They elbow their way on to the page, and

> glow and blaze and fade and disappear. (Beckett 1972: 156-16)

The fluidity of language reflects the decentring of logocentric discourse and authority. It illustrates the command of language over meaning, of letters over persona, of the signifier over the signified. This central uncertainty or 'hecitency' in Humphrey C. Earwicker (*FW* 119) is explained by Beckett:

> H.C. Earwigger, too, is not content to be mentioned like a shilling—shocker villain, and then dropped until the exigencies of the narrative require that he be again referred to. He continues to suggest himself for couple of pages, by means of repeated permutations on his "normative letters", as if to say: "This is all about me, H.C. Earwigger: don't forget this is all about me!" (Beckett 1972: 16)

In this context, Anna's function over the "allaphbed" or letter may be grasped. It is she who brings about the renewal or wake of Humphrey in the anagrammatic play of letters, "the ever present movement (agitation) of the wake of difference" (Attridge and Ferrer 1984: 54), in the figure of the "doomed but always ventriloquent Agitator" (*FW* 56) or the "herewaker" (*FW* 619). According to Stephen Heath,

> HCE, "those normative letters" (*FW* 32), give, in their expansion and the transformations they determine, a constant insistence of the signifier in the signified, breaking the linearity of the context and opening onto the logic of the signifier. Why HCE? Evidently because these are the letters of "He Cit Ency"...linking forgery and strategy of hesitation in the ways defined above and reflecting the hecitency of the subject and "his" meaning in this permutation of letters. (Attridge and Ferrer 1984: 54)

In chapter six, H.C. Earwicker assumes universal proportions. He is even "larger than life, doughtier than death" (*FW* 132); "you and I are in him" (*FW* 130), He falls, rises, builds; he is hero, king, giant, mountain, tree, fish, politician, Adam and so on (Tindall 1969: 112). He is, in other words, both everyone and everything as well as Finn MacCool. He is identified with all the Norse gods, all the Danish kings (*FW* 130, 132). He fuses in him the four elements (*FW* 127) and, in Vico's terms "moves in vicous circles yet remews the same" (*FW* 134).

Anna matches Humphrey's polymorphous character in chapter eight. She is not only a wife and temptress but also the mother of a "litter" (*FW* 202), "the dearest little moma ever you saw" (*FW* 207). Her plurality is seen in her ability to form a triangle as well as the figure. She is not limited by time, thus: "Anna was Livia is, Plurabelle's to be" (*FW* 215). She symbolizes the course of the river flowing from Wicklow to Dublin Bay (*FW* 202-03; 207-08). But the interesting point of this chapter is its song of renewal, the fall of night, death and the living river. In accordance with this theme, women are seen to be reborn again, becoming transubstantiated to tree and stone. However, "since Shem is tree and Shaun stone, these women, in a sense, are Shem and Shaun" (Tindall 1969: 147).

As identity is subjected to the fluidity of discourse, the meanings of words multiply to such an extent that no stable coincidence between the two can be observed. The discourse is free to engage in a play of signification over the rapid shift of signifiers. In chapter nine, for example, Joyce gives an impression of density by employing the cinematic technique of montage, and portmanteau words. In chapter ten, Joyce confuses us further by employing three commentators on a single text. Multiple interpretations bring a density to discourse. The three commentators are Shem, Shaun and Isabel and they are concerned with grammar, history and mathematics. The topic of their discourse is their parents. Thus, they interpret their father Humphrey through the medium of history and approach Anna by means of geometry. Their attempt at interpretation extend the referentiality of their parents, through the correspondences of history Humphrey becomes "Cornwall" (*FW* 261), that is both Cromwell as well as king Mark of Cornwall. He is also the Eucharist (*FW* 261), the "original sun" (*FW* 263) being both Adam and God (Tindall 1969: 174). On the other hand, Shem shows how geometry or measuring of the earth's surface can lead us to an understanding of Anna or Mrs Bloom who is also depicted sometimes as Gea-Tellus in *Ulysses* (*FW* 293).

In the later portions of the book, a radical change takes place with the replacement of Humphrey by Shaun. In chapter thirteen, Shaun becomes the new Humphrey C. Earwicker as well as Jesus the postman. But as Tindall notes, "this local incarnation, more than Jesus the postman, is Jesus the Guinness barrel" (Tindall 1969: 224). Like Jesus the Messiah, Shaun preaches sermons but unlike that of Jesus, his sermons contain nursery rhymes, fairy tales, fables and parables. Like Shaun as Professor Jones lecturing to his pupils in chapter six and resorting to the fable of the Mookse and Gripes, Shaun-Jesus narrates another fable, that of the Ondt and the Grasshopper. But by doing so he exposes his one-sidedness and his inadequacy can only be made complete when he meets his other half, that is Shem at the end of chapter fourteen. Humphrey C. Earwicker can only be replaced when the two halves of the author Joyce-Shem and Joyce-Shaun merge. The contradictory halves of Shaun and Shem emerge from the fable of the Ondt and the Grasshopper represents time. The rapprochement between Shaun and Shem materialize as the former recognize Shem's "root language" (*FW* 424). Joyce wielding his "plagiarist pen" is seen in Shem's discourse which is an example of the "last word in stolentelling" and in which "Every dimmed letter in it is a copy" (*FW* 424). This is an indirect reference to the multiplicity of discourses in *Finnegans Wake* in which the narrator as teller/ tailor (in the sense of weaving yarns) is quite lost.

Chapter fifteen poses a question about Shaun's identity but the answer is inconclusive since he, like his father, is a polymorphous being. Although, however, questions about identity remain unanswered, what is in him is revealed. As he confesses:

> "I have something inside of me talking to myself" (*FW* 522), his colourlessness, lack of any fixed point of view, otherwise his "He Cit Ency" comes to light. "Each layer of Yawn's unconscious contains a member of the family" (Tindall 1969: 253). Thus, "Isabel, Anna, and Kate emerge to speak through Yawn, their persona...." (Tindall 1969: 253).

In the end, therefore, it is the children Shaun-Humphrey C. Earwicker and Nuvoletta-Isabel-Anna L. Plurabelle, who replace their parents. But as children, however, it is impossible for them to recover their origins because the *Wake* illustrates the notion of the decentred self. Personality becomes the nucleus of multiple discourses. In these terms, as Tindall notes, the Wake:

> as Mamalujo knows, is a "mill wheeling Vicociclometer, a tetradomational" construction, built like Yeats's "gazebo" or a machine Wight "clappercoupling smeltingworks exprogressive process", known to Vico as "eggburst, eggblend, eggburial and hatch-as-hatch can" (religion marriage, burial, and ricorso) or, according to Bruno, a dialectical process of "decomposition" and "recombination" in which the "heroticisms, catastrophes and eccentricities" of H.C.E. are transmitted by the ancient legacy of the past (A.L.P.) "...letter from litter". The course of history, whether flowery peace or war's in humanity, reveals the same old "adomicstructure" of H.C.E., our atomic Adam, "as highly charged with electrons as hopazards can effective it". When the cock crows, you may be sure of breakfast—"as sure as herself pits hen to paper and there's scribings scrawled on eggs (614.27-615.10). (Tindall 1969: 322)

The four old men/Earwicker's judges/historians known as Mamalujo try to equate the old Humphrey C. Earwicker with the new. Their efforts are bound to be unsuccessful because Yawn is not one person but several at once. As a polymorphous being, he not only comprises many personalities but actually becomes a teller of tales, being the scriptor of many narratives. Like the flow of Anna L. Plurabelleat the end of the book Humphrey C. Earwicker/ShempShaun/Joyce becomes the confluence of many discourses. Like the *Wake* with its multiplicity of narrative patterns, he comprises in himself "tales within tales" (*FW* 522).

It is interesting to note that pursuit of selfhood becomes eternally deferred as the characters in the Wake become conscious of their infinite referentiality. This process of writing which turns back on itself is perceived by Tindall. Referring to the Wake, which resembles a "cubical crib" (*FW* 476) in which Yawn/H.C.E. lies, he remarks:

> What the four men are after, then, is not only H.C.E., the Wake's personal concentrate, but the Wake itself. Like a college of critics or critics in a college, examining the levels of a text, they are trying to discover what they are in. (Tindall 1969: 254)

Conclusion

James Joyce represents a unique instance of an artist who uses the materials of art to split open the disparate and conflicting impulses within himself. In this study, the question of artistic detachment has been assessed not only in terms of the author's relationship to his artifact but also in relation to a critical activity which makes him an arbiter of the myriad discourse-patterns within him. This positioning of the artist both outside and inside his discourse establishes a vital linkage between the noumenal and the phenomenal selves without assigning primacy to either factor. In this lay Joyce's distinctive contribution to aesthetic theory. The perception of beauty becomes a critical activity which balances the co-ordination of the subject and object as well as that of matter and form. In Joyce's novels, we notice a gradual loosening up of conventional and formal structures for making amenable the expression of the various discourses within the self. Or rather, the untying of the self leads to an experimentation with formal aspects of art with a view to accommodate the deconstructive activity of the self.

The notion of the artist looking at his own reflection without any illusion has been aptly summarised in Joyce's aesthetics, and it is precisely this which separates his approach to art from that of Pater's or that of the Romantics. It is pre-eminently the plasticity of his art that enables him to perceive any object from all sorts of angles. To exemplify, with him it is this absence of any point of view that has befuddled a generation of critics in thinking that he is either completely indifferent or that "Joyce is everywhere in his books always writing about himself, his family, his country" (Gluck 1979: 117). Actually, what needs to be stressed is that he continually highlights the problems he faces in writing about his own experiences. Joyce's complexity was due to his writing at a certain period when Europe was constantly engaged in war and everything seemed to be subjected to the forces of flux. A singular instance of this is his creation "Dooleysprudence" (1916) which expresses in a comic spirit "the point of view of the badgered yet optimistic individualist living through war, revikytuib abd cinnercuak deoresuib" (Budgen 1989: 206). In this comic fragment, the artist is referred to as the common as in *Ulysses*:

> Who is the funny fellow who declines to go to church
> Since pope and priest and parson left the poor man in the lurch
> And taught their flocks the only way to save all human souls
> Was piercing human bodies through with dumdum bulletholes?
> It's Mr. Dooley,
> Mr. Dooley,
> The mildest man our country ever knew
> "Who will release us
> From Jingo Jesus?"
> Prays Mr. Dooley-ooley-ooley-oo. (*CW* 246-47)

The plasticity of Joyce's art is evident in his portrait of Bloom who has been drawn with an "infinite number of contours" and from all conceivable angles (Budgen 1989: 65-66). Budgen comments on this aspect of Joyce's fictional strategy in his study *James Joyce and the Making of 'Ulysses'*:

> The multiplicity of technical devices in *Ulysses* is proof that Joyce subscribed to no limiting aesthetic creed, and proof also that he was willing to use any available instrument that might serve his purpose. It was hardly likely that, having denied all religious dogma and having carefully avoided all political doctrine, he would submit

> to artistic limitations. There are hints of all practices in *Ulysses*—cubism, futurism, simultanism, dadaism and the rest—and this is the clearest proof that he was attached to none of the schools that followed them. (Budgen 1989: 198)

In this respect although Barbara Reich Gluck in her illuminating book *Beckett and Joyce*, notes that the basic difference between these two avant-garde writers in the 1930s lay in Beckett's "losing identity in that of his characters" whereas Joyce "is capable of distancing himself through irony from even such an autobiographical character as Stephen" still she misses the point when she equates him with his fictional creations in *Finnegans Wake* (Gluck 1979: 117). Actually, the materiality of Joyce's writing creates opportunities for the representation of a series of his possible selves, which are at all events critically weighed and sometimes ironically detached from his real self. Indeed, the facility with which Joyce could move in and out of his fictional representations has been noted affectionately by S. Gilbert in his recollections of the author. Often Joyce was wont to display during the innumerable tea parties given by Nora, the "Stephen Dedalus" mannerisms and "fin de sicle attitude" in public (Letters I: 35). And this was noted by Nora with delicate irony and indulgence.

Again, the keen alienation felt by Joyce as an artist is also paralleled by the theme of the betrayed artist which runs right through his work and is often harped on his essays as diverse as "Ireland, Island of Saints and Sages" (1907), "Oscar Wilde The Poet of 'Salome'" (1909), "The Shade of Parnell" (1912) and so on. In his essay on Ireland Joyce felt:

> compelled to point out that his country had its history of betrayals, of eloquent inactivity, of absurd and narrow belief. His attitude, though he calls it objective, wavers between affectionate fascination with Ireland and distrust of her. (*CW* 153)

Mason and Ellmann's introductory note reveals the central ambiguity in Joyce's thought. This is especially evident in his essay on "Oscar Wilde" where he represents the aesthete as a type of the betrayed artist. The paradox may be seen in Wilde's "fame as the spokesman of the aesthetic school" around whom "was forming the fantastic legend of the Apostle of Beauty" (*CW* 202). Joyce delineates how "the cult of the sunflower, his favourite flower, spread among the leisured class, and the little people heard tell of his famous white ivory walking stick glittering with turquoise stones, and of his Neronian hair-dress" (*CW* 202). And yet he finds the "subject of this shining picture" to be more "miserable than bourgeois thought" since often his medals and "trophies of his academic youth" were pawned and his wife had to borrow money for a decent pair of shoes (*CW* 202). Only in his later years did he become rich with his fame as a dramatist only to squander away his hard-earned fortune. The irony lies in the fact that the artist who thought he was bringing back a "Golden Age and the joy of the world's youth" by his insistence on a theory of beauty (which threatened to become a way of life) was actually howled down by a crowd of people who celebrated his condemnation by dancing outside the court.

A similar fate was reserved for Parnell by his countrymen. Parnell's strategy as Joyce outlines in his essay "The Shade of Parnell" was to utilise any English party either liberal or conservative to secure his country's emancipation. To this end, he rallied behind him "every element of Irish life" and forced the Liberal Government in England to restore autonomy to Ireland (*CW* 227). In 1886 Gladstone was forced to "read the first home Rule Bill at Westminster" (*CW* 227). Suddenly, Parnell was discredited owing to his love-affair with a married woman and the Liberals used this situation to their own advantage, negotiating the autonomy of Ireland against Parnell's conviction. At this moment he was betrayed by his own people who castigated him.

Yet, in spite of this fear of betrayal, Joyce was not in the true sense of the term an expatriate. His frequent visits to Ireland testifies to this fact. What is most interesting is his own ambivalence towards the Irish question. It would not be true to say that he did not love Ireland. But it is also a fact that Joyce exhibited a deep antipathy towards the very attitude which may be termed insular or parochial. The regeneration of Ireland must be put in the hands of the avant-garde who will not yield to the demands of popular nationalism but make themselves amenable to literary currents and innovations from the continent.

Much of the same ambivalence may be noted in his attitude to art and the poetic personality. Making much of the concept of artistic detachment, he could never escape a subtle ironic attitude towards both; his characters and to himself. The mystery of the Joycean artist lies precisely in the absence of any artistic viewpoint (No-man), along with his ambiguous presence (Everyman) in his works.

The lack of centrality in Joyce that expresses itself in the decentring of self therefore enables him to take up any position either inside or outside the pattern of discourse. This study elucidates how such a critical distancing on the part of Joyce could be understood as a profound need to understand and assimilate the disparities within a logocentric world-view either in terms of Catholicism, politics, formal aesthetics and restrictive narrative forms as well as the linearity of individual discourse. His uniqueness lay in dismantling the norms of authority in traditional institutions and conventions so as to make possible the confluence of myriad ideologies and thought-patterns which effectively decentre the stable self and point to its referentiality to other selves through history myth, religion and narrative. The fracture of the artist, which is thereby occasioned in the materiality of writing, can be satisfyingly explained through a deconstructionist approach that illustrates through its differential reading, the deferral of any realisation of a final telos in terms of discourse.

Bibliography

Abrams, Meyer Howard (1958). *The Mirror and the Lamp: Romantic Theory and the Critical Tradition*, New York: W.W. Norton and Company, Inc., 1997.

Armstrong, Alison (1973). "Shem the Penman as Glugg as the Wolf-man", *A Wake Newslitter*, 10 (August), 51-57.

Attridge, Derek (1988). "Joyce, Jameson, and the text of history", in Ed. Claude Jacquet, *James Joyce*, 1: *'Scribble' I genèse des texts*, Parris: Letters Modernes, Minard.

Attridge, Derek, and D. Ferrer, eds. (1984). *Post-Structuralist Joyce: Essays from the French*, Cambridge: Cambridge University Press.

Aubert, Jacques (1984). 'riverrun', trans. Patrick O'Donovan, in Eds. Derrek Attridge and Daniel Ferrer, *Post-structuralist Joyce: Essays from the French*, Cambridge: Cambridge University Press.

Barrett, W. (1987). *Death of the Soul: From Descartes to Computer*, Oxford: Oxford University Press.

Barthes, Roland (1980). *Elements of Semiology*, trans. Annette Lavers and Colin Smith, New York: Hill and Wang.

—— (1972). *Mythologies*, trans. Annette Lavers and Colin Smith, London: Jonathan Cape.

—— (1975). *The Pleasure of the Text*, trans. Richard Miller, New York: Hill and Wang.

—— (1974). *S/Z*, trans. Richard Miller, New York: Hill and Wang.

Bateson, Gregory (1972). *Steps to an Ecology of Mind*, New York: Ballantine.

Bauerle, Ruth (1982). "Bertha's role in *Exiles*", in Eds. Suzette Henke and Elaine Unkeless, *Women in Joyce*, 108-31.

Beckett, Samuel *et al.* (1962). *Our Exagimination Round His Factification for Incamination of Work in Progress*, New York: New Direction Books.

Beja, M. (1971). *Epiphany in the Modern Novel.* London: Peter Owen Ltd.

—— (1973). *James Joyce: Dubliners and A Portrait of the Artist as a Young Man:* A Casebook. London: Macmillan. University Press

—— (1992). *James Joyce*: a Literary Life: Columbus: Ohio State University Press.

Benstock, Bernard (1965). *Joyce-Again's Wake: An Analysis of 'Finnegans Wake'*, Seattle: Washington University Press.

—— (Ed) (1985). *Critical Essays on Joyce*, Boston: G.K. Hill & Co.

—— (1991). *Narrative Con/Texts in Ulysses.* Urbana: University of Illinois Press.

Benstock, Shari (1985). "Nightletters: Women's Writing in the *Wake*", in Ed. Bernard Benstock, *Critical Essays on Joyce*, 221-33.

—— (1982). "The Genuine Christine: Psychodynamics of Issy", in Eds. Suzette Henke and Elaine Unkeless, *Women in Joyce*, 169-96.

Bishop, John (1986). *Joyce's Book of the Dark: 'Finnegans Wake'*, Madison: Wisconsin University Press.

Bogel, F.B. (1984). *Literature and Insubstantiality in Later Eighteenth Century.* Princeton: Princeton, University Press.

Bosinelli (Bollettirei), Rosa Maria (1970). "The Importance of Trieste in Joyce's Work with Reference to his knowledge of Psycho-analysis", *JJQ*, 7 (3), 177-84.

—— (1981). "Psychoanalytical Criticism and Metapsychology" *JJQ*, 18 (3), 349-55.

Bowra, M. (1978). *The Romantic Imagination.* London: OUP.

Bottrall, M. (1975). *Gerard Manley Hopkins: A Casebook.* London: Macmillan.

Brittain, C.M. (1989). *Logos, Creation, and Epiphany in the Poetics of Gerard Manley Hopkins.* D.A.I. 48: 3756A-3757A.

Brown, R.E. *et. al.* (eds.) (1968). *The Jerome Biblical Commentary* London: Geoggrey Chapman Ltd. 2 Vols.

Brivic, Sheldon (1980). *Joyce Between Jung and Freud,* Port Washington, NY: Kennikat Press.

—— (1985). *Joyce the Creator,* Madison: Wisconsin University Press.

Budgen, F. (1989). *James Joyce and the Making of "Ulysses" and Other Writings.* Oxford: OUP.

Burgess, A. (1965). *Re Joyce.* New York: W.W. Norton and Company Inc.

Campbell, Joseph and Henry Morton Robinson (1947). *A Skeleton Key to 'Finnegans Wake'.* London: Faber and Faber.

Carroll, D. (1987). *Paraesthetics : Foucault, Lyotard, Derrida.* Methuen; New York & London.

Chatman, Seymour (1978). *Story and Discourse: Narrative Structure in Fiction and Film,* Ithaca: Cornell University Press.

Cixous, Hélène (1976). *The Exile of James Joyce,* London: John Calder.

—— (1981). "The Laugh of the Medusa", trans. Keith Cohen and Paula Cohen, in Eds. Elaine Marks and Isabell de Courtivron, *New French Feminisms: An Anthology,* New York: Schocken Books.

—— (1984). "Joyce: the R(use) of Writing", trans. Judith Still, in Eds. Derek Attridge and Danile Ferrer, *Post-structuralist Joyce: Essays from the French,* Cambridge: Cambridge University Press.

Cohn, Dorrit (1966). "Narrated Monologue: Definition of a Fictional Style", *Comparative Literature*, 18.

Coleman, Dorrit (1966). "A Note on Joyce and Jung", *JJQ*, 1 (1), 11-19.

Coleridge, S.T. (1973). *Biographia Literaria.* J. Shawcross. 2 Vols. London: OUP.

Colum, Mary (1922). "The Confessions of James Joyce", *Freeman*, 5 (123), 450-52.

Coulson, J. (1970). *Newman and the Common Tradition: a Study in the language of Church and Society.* Clarendon: OUP.

Crump, I.M. (1991). *Disselving the Individuone: Joyce's Narrative Representations of the Self* D.A.I. 53.V (November): 1514-A. University of California, Berkeley.

Culler, Jonathan (1975). *Structuralist Poetics*, London: Routledge & Kegan Paul.

—— (1989). *On Deconstruction: Theory and Criticism after Structuralism,* London: R & KP.

Cunningham, G.W. (1933). *The Idealistic Argument in Recent British and American Philosophy.* New York: Century Co.

de Beauvoir, Simone (1961). *The Second Sex*, trans. And Ed. H.M. Parshley, New York: Bantam.

Deming, R.H. (ed.) (1970). *James Joyce : The Critical Heritage.* 2 Vols. Delhi: Vikas.

Derrida, Jacques (1973) "Difference", *Speech and Phenomena, and Other Essays on Husserl's Theory of Signs*, trans. David B. Allison, Evanston: Northwestern University Press.

—— (1981). *Dissemination*, trans. Barbara Johnson, Chicago: Chicago University Press.

—— (1986). *Glas*, trans. John P. Leavy Jr and Richard Rand, Lincoln and London: Nebraska University Press.

—— (1978). *Introduction to Edmund Husserl's "The Origin of Geometry"*, trans. Edward Leavey, Hassocks: Harvester.

—— (1974). *Of Grammatology*, trans. Gayatri Chakravorty Spivak, Chicago: Chicago University Press.

—— (1987). *Positions*, trans. Alan Bass, London: The Athlone Press.

—— (1979). "Scribble (writing power)", *Yale French Studies*, 58, 1979.

—— (1978). "Structure, Sign and Play in the Discourse of the Human Sciences", in *Writing and Difference*, trans. Alan Bass, Chicago: Chicago University Press.

—— (1987). *The Post Card: From Socrates to Freud and Beyond*, trans. Alan Bass, Chicago: Chicago University Press.

—— (1984). "Two Words for Joyce", trans. Geoff Bennington in Eds. Derek Attridge and Danile Ferrer, *Post-structuralist Joyce: Essays from the French*, Cambridge: Cambridge University Press.

—— (1985). "Ulysse gramophone: L'oui-dire de Joyce", in Ed. Claude Jacquet, *Genèse de Babel: Joyce et la creation*, Paris: Louis Hay.

—— (1978). "Violence and metaphysics: An essay on the thought of Emmanuel Levinas", *Writing and Difference*, trans. Alan Bass, Chicago: Chicago University Press.

Eagleton, Terry (1970). *Exiles and Émigrés: Studies in Modern Literature*, London: Chatto and Windus.

—— (1978). *Criticism and Ideology: A Study in Marxist Literary Theory*, London: Verso.

Eco, Umberto (1979). *A Theory of Semiotics*, Bloomington: Indiana University Press.

—— (1989). *Foucault's Pendulum*, trans. William Weaver, London: Secker and Warburg.

—— (1962). *Opera Aperta*, Milano: Bompiani.

—— (1982). *The Aesthetics of Chaomos: The Middle Ages of James Joyce*, trans. Ellen Esrock, Tulsa: Tulsa University Press.

—— (1979). *The Role of the Reader: Explorations in the Semiotics of Texts*, Bloomington: Indiana University Press.

Edgerton, William B. (1968). "Szhoising with the Soviet Eliot, T.S. (1972). *Selected Essasy*. Faber of Faber. Encyclopedias", *JJQ*, 5 (2), 125-31.

Eliot, T.S. (1972). *Selected Essasys*. Faber of Faber.

Ellmann Mary (1968). *Thinking About Women*, New York: Harcourt Brace Jovanovich.

Ellmann, Richard (1982). *James Joyce*, Oxford: OUP.

Empson, William (1956). "The Theme of *Ulysses*", *The Kenyon Review*, 18, Winter.

Ferrer, Daniel (1988). "*Archéologie du regard dans les avant-texts de <<Circé>>*", in Ed. Claude Jacquet, *James Joyce 1: 'Scribble 1 genèse des texts*, Paris: Letters Modern Minard.

—— (1984). "Circe, regret and regression", trans. Gilly Lehmann, in Eds. Derek Attridge and Danile Ferrer, *Post-structuralist Joyce: Essays from the French*, Cambridge: Cambridge University Press.

—— (1985). "The Freudful Couchmare of ËD: Joyce's Note on Freud and the Composition of Chapter XVI of *Finnegans Wake*", *JJQ*, 22 (4), 367-82.

Ferrer, Daniel and Derek Attridge (1984). *Post-structuralist Joyce: Essays from the French*, Cambridge: Cambridge University Press.

French, Marilyn (1976). *The Book as World: James Joyce's 'Ulysses'*, Cambridge, MA: Havard University Press.

Freud, Sigmund (1925). *Collected Papers*, trans. Alix Strachey and James Strachey, London: The Hogarth Press/The Institute of Psychoanalysis.

—— (1910). *Eine Kindheitserinnerung des Leonardo da Vinci*, Leipzig and Vienna, trans. as "Leonardo da Vinci and a Memory of His Childhood", trans. Alan Tyson, *The Standard Edition of the Complex Psychological Works of Sigmund Freud*, trans. and Ed. James Strachey in collaboration with Anna Freud *et al.*, London: Hogarth

Press and The Institute of Psychoanalysis, 1953-76, XI, 63-137.

—— (1910). "The Psycho-Analytic View of Psychogenic Disturbances of Vision", *The Standard Edition*, XI, 314-21.

Genette, Gérard (1966) *Figures 1*, Paris: Seuil.

—— (1980). *Narrative Discourse*, Ithaca: Cornell University Press.

Gilbert, Sandra and Susan Gubar (1985). *No Man's Land: The Place of the Woman Writer in the Twentieth Century*, New Heaven: Yale University Press, 2 Vols., Vol. 1, *The War of the Words*, 1988, Vol. 2, *Sexchanges*, 1989.

—— (1985). "Sexual linguistics: gender, language, sexuality", *New Literary History*, 16, 3, 515-43.

—— (1979). *The Madwoman in the Attic: The Woman Writer and the Nineteenth Century Literary Imagination*, New Heaven: Yale University Press.

Gilbert, Stuart (1952). *James Joyce's 'Ulysses'*, New York: Vintage Knopf.

Glashine, Adaline (1954). "*Finnegans Wake* and the Girls from Boston, Mass", *Hudson Review*, 7, Spring.

Goldberg, S.L. (1961). *The Classical Temper*, New York: Barnes and Noble.

Gorman, Herbert (1948). *James Joyce*, New York: Rinehart and Co.

Greimas, A.J. (ed.) (1970). *Sign, Language, Culture*, The Hague: Mouton.

Hart, Clive (1962). *Structure and Motif in Finnegans Wake*, London: Faber and Faber.

Hawkes, Terence (1977). *Structuralism and Semiotics*, Berkeley: UCLA Press.

Hayman, David (1963). *A First Draft Version of 'Finnegans Wake'*, Austin: Texas University Press.

—— (1978-79). "Nodality and the infra-structure of *Finnegans Wake*", *JJQ*, 16 (1-2), 135-50.

—— (1970). "The Empirical Molly", in Eds. Thomas F. Staley and Bernard Benstock, *Approaches to 'Ulysses': Ten Essays*, Pittsbgurgh: Pittsburgh University Press.

Heath, Stephen (1984). "Ambiviolences: Notes for reading Joyce", trans. Isabelle Mahieu, in Eds. Derek Attridge and Daniel Ferrer, *Post-structuralist Joyce: Essays from the French*, Cambridge: Cambridge University Press.

Hegel, G.W.F. (1977). "Preface", *Phenomenology of Spirit*, trans. A.V. Miller, New York and Oxford: OUP.

Henke, Suzette (1982). "Stephen Dedalus and Women: A Portrait of the Artist as a Young Misogynist", in Eds. Suzette Henke and Elaine Unkeless, *Women in Joyce*, 82-107.

Hence, Suzette and Elaine Unkeless (1982). *Women in Joyce*, Brighton: The Harvester Press.

Hjelmslev, L. (1959). *Essais Linguistiques*, Travaux du Cercle Linguistique de Copenhagen, vol. XIII, Copenhagen: Nordisk Sprog-og Kulturforlag.

Holly, Marcia (1975). "Consciousness and Authenticity: Toward a Feminist Aesthetic", in Ed. Josephine Donovan, *Feminist Literary Criticism*, Lexington: Kentucky University Press.

Howe, Florence (1972). "Feminism and Literature". In Ed. Susan Koppelman Cornillon, *Images of Women in Fiction: Feminist Perspectives*, Bowling Green, Ohio: Bowling Green University Popular Press.

Irigaray, Luce (1981). "The Sex Which is Not One", in Eds. Elaine Marks and Isabelle de Courtivron, *New French Feminisms: An Anthology*, New York: Schocken Books.

Jakobson, Roman (1962). *Selected Writings*, 4 Vols., The Hague: Mouton.

Jakobson, Roman and Morris Halle (1956). *Fundamentals of Language*, The Hague: Mouton.

Jameson, Fredric (1972). *Marxism and Form: Twentieth Century Dialectical Theories of Literature*, Princeton: Princeton University Press.

—— (1981). *The Political Unconscious: Narrative as a Socially Symbolic Act*, Ithaca: Cornell University Press.

—— (1982). "*Ulysses* and History", *James Joyce and Modern Literature*, London: Routledge and Kegan Paul.

Joyce, James (1970). *Dubliners*: Middlesex, England: Penguin.

—— (1969). *A Portrait of the Artist as a Young Man*. Middlesex, England: Penguin.

—— (1986). *Ulysses*. Ed. H.W. Gabler, W. Steppe, C. Melchior. London: Penguin Books in association with Bodley Head.

—— (1982). *Finnegans Wake*. London: Faber and Faber.

—— (1985). *The Portable James Joyce*. Ed. Harry Levin. New York: The Viking Press Inc. (rpt.) Middlesex: Penguin.

—— (1959). *The Critical Writings of James Joyce*. Ed. Ellsworth Mason, Richard Ellmann. London: Faber and Faber.

—— (1975). *Selected Letters of James Joyce*. Ed. Richard Ellmann.

—— (1957). *Letters of James Joyce*. Ed. Stuart Gilbert. Vol. I. London: Faber and Faber.

—— (1966). *Letters of James Joyce*. Ed. Richard Ellmann. Vols. II and III. London: Faber and Faber.

—— (1987). *James Joyce's Letters to Sylvia Beach: 1921-1940*. Eds. Melissa Banta, Oscar A Silverman. Bloomington: Indians University Press. Secondary Sources.

Joyce, Stanislaus (1958). *My Brother's Keeper*, Ed. Richard Ellmann, London: Faber and Faber.

Kashkin, Ivan (1968). "Dzhois, Dzhems", *Literaturnaia éntsiklopediia*, III Moscow: 1930, cols. 248-51, trans. William B. Edgerton, "Dzhoising with the Soviet Encyclopedias", *JJQ*, 5 (2), 125-31.

Kenner, Hugh (1978). *Joyce's Voices*, Berkeley: UCLA Press.

Kestner, Joseph (1978-79). "Virtual text/virtual reader; The structural signature within, behind, beyond, and above", *JJQ*, 16 (1-2), 27-42.

Kimball, Jean (1983). "Family Romance and Hero Myth: A Psychoanalytic Context for the Paternity Theme in *Ulysses*", *JJQ*, 20 (2), 161-73.

—— (1980). "Freud, Leonardo, and Joyce: The dimensions of a childhood memory", *JJQ*, 17 (2), 165-182.

—— (1976). "James Joyce and Otto Rink: The incest motif in *Ulysses*", *JJQ*, 13 (4), 366-382.

Klein, Melanie (1950). "Mourning and its relation to manic-depressive states", *Contributions to Psycho-Analysis*, London: Hogarth Press/Institute of Psycho-analysis.

Kornilova, E.V. (1968). "Dzhois (Joyce), Dzheims", *Kratkaia literaturnaia éntsiklopediia*, Moscow: 1964, cols. 654-55, trans. William B. Ederton, "Dzhoising with the Soviet Encyclopedias", *JJQ*, 5 (2), 125-31.

Kristeva, Julia (1970). *La Poétique de Dostoievski*, Paris: Seuil.

—— (1980). *Desire and Language: A Semiotic Approach to Literature and Art*, trans. Leon S. Roudiez, New York: Columbia University Press.

—— (1982). *Powers of Horror: An Essay on Abjection*, trans. Leon S. Roudiez, New York: Columbia University Press.

—— (1973). "The System and the Speaking Subject", *The Times Literary Supplement*, 12 October: 1249.

Leavis, F.R. (1962). *The Great Tradition: George Eliot, Henry James, Joseph Conrad*, Harmondsworth: Penguin.

Lévi-Strauss, Claude (1964) *La cru et le cuit*, Paris: Plon.

—— (1972). *Structural Anthropology*, trans. Claire Jacobson and Brooke Grundfest Schoepf, London: Penguin.

Lyons, J.B. (1973). *James Joyce and Medicine*, Dublin: Dolmen Press.

Makward, Christiane (1976). "Interview with Hélène Cixous", trans. Ann Liddle and Beatrice Cameron, *Sub Stance*, 13.

Mayoux, J.J. (1965). *Joyce*, Paris: Gallimard.

McCarroll, David L. (1969). "Stephen's Dream—and Bloom's", *JJQ*, 6 (2), 174-76.

McHugh, Roland (1980). *Annotations to Finnegans Wake*, Baltimore: Johns Hopkins University Press.

—— (1976). *The Sigla of Finnegans Wake*, London: Edward Arnold.

—— (1968). "A Structural Theory of *Finnegans Wake*", *A Wake Newsletter*, V, 6.

Millet, Kate (1970). *Sexual Politics*, Garden City, NY: Doubleday & Co.

Norris, Margot (1982). "Anna Livia Plurabelle: The Dream Woman", in Eds. Suzette Henke and Elaine Unkeless, *Women in Joyce*, 197-214.

—— (1974). *The Decentred Universe of Finnegans Wake: A Structuralist Analysis*, Baltimore: Johns Hopkins University Press.

O'Brien, Darcy (1976). "A Critique of Psychoanalytic Criticism, or What Joyce Did and Did Not Do", *JJQ*, 13 (3), 275-92.

—— (1968). *The Conscience of James Joyce*, Princeton: Princeton University Press.

Ong, Walter J. (1981). *Fighting for Life*, Ithaca: Cornell University Press.

Peirce, Charles Sanders (1931). *Collected Papers* (8 Vols.) Eds. Charles Hartshorne, Paul Weiss and Arthur W. Burks, Cambridge, Mass: Harvard University Press.

Piager, Jean (1971). *Structuralism*, trans. Chaninah Maschler, London: Routledge and Kegan Paul.

Prince, Morton (1969). *The Dissociation of a Personality: A Biographical Study in Abnormal Psychology*, New York: Greenwood Press.

Prop, Vladimir (1958). *Morphology of the Folktale*, Bloomington: Indiana Research Center in Anthropology.

Rabaté, Jean-Michel (1984). "Lapsus ex machine", trans. Elizabeth Guild, *Post-structuralist Joyce: Essays from the French*, Cambridge: Cambridge University Press.

—— (1985). "Pour une cryptogénétique de l'idiolecte Joycian", in Ed. Claude Jacquet, *Genèsae de Babel: Joyce et la creation*, Paris: Éditions du Centre National de la Recherche Scientifique.

—— (1988). "Le Noeud Gordien De <<Pénélope>>", in Ed. Claude Jacquet, *James Joyce 1 <<Scribble>> 1: genèse des texts*, Paris: Minard.

Rank, Otto (1912). *das Inzest-Motiv in Dichtung and Sage: Grudzüge einer Psychologie des dichterischen Schaffens*, Leipzig: Dueticke.

Saussure, Ferdinand de (1974). *Cours de Linguistique Géneral*, trans. Wade Baskins, London: Fontana.

Scholes, Robert (1982). *Semiotics and Interpretation*, New Haven: Yale University Press.

—— (1972). *Structuralism in Literature: An Introduction*, New Haven: Yale University Press.

—— (1972). "*Ulysses*: A Structuralist Perspective", *JJQ*, 10 (1).

Scott, Bonnie Kime (1987). *James Joyce*, Brighton: The Harvester Press.

—— (1982). *Joyce and Feminism*, Brighton: The Harvester Press.

Shechner, Mark (1976). "Exposing Joyce", *JJQ*, 13 (3), 266-74.

—— (1976). "James Joyce and Psychoanalysis: A Selected Checklist", *JJQ*, 13 (3), 383-84.

—— (1977). "Joyce and Psychoanalysis: Two Additional Perspectives", *JJQ*, 14 (4), 416-19.

—— (1974). *Joyce in Nighttown: A Psychoanalytic Inquiry into 'Ulysses'*, Berkeley: UCLA Press.

Slater, Philip B. (1971). *The Glory of Hera*, Boston: Beacon Press.

Sollers, Philippe (1978). "Joyce & Co", *In the Wake of the Wake*, trans. Stephen Heath and Elliott Anderson, Madison: Wisconsin University Press.

Solomon, Margaret C. (1969). *Eternal Geomater: The Sexual Universe of Finnegans Wake*, Carbondale: Southern Illinois University Press.

Suleiman, Susan Rubin (1985). "Writing and Motherhood", in Eds. Shirley Nelson Garner, Claire Kahane, and Madelon Sprengnether, *The (M)other Tongue: Essays in Feminist Psychoanalytic Interpretation*, Ithaca: Cornell University Press, 352-77.

Sultan, Stanley (1964). *The Argument of 'Ulysses'*, Columbus: Ohio State University Press.

Tall, Emily (1980). "James Joyce Rcturns to the Soviet Union", *JJQ*, 17 (4), 341-47.

Thornton, Weldon (1968). *Allusions in 'Ulysses': An Annotated List*, Chapel Hill: North Carolina University Press.

Tindall, William York (1959). *A Reader's Guide to James Joyce*, New York, Farrar, Straus and Giroux.

Todorov, Tzvetan (1966). "Perspectives Semiologiques", *Communications*, 7, 139-45.

Topia, André (1984). "The Matrix and the Echo: Intersexuality in *Ulysses*", trans. Elizabeth Bell and André Topia, in Eds. Derek Attridge and Daniel Ferrer, *Post-structuralist Joyce: Essays from the French*, Cambridge: Cambridge University Press.

Unkeless, Elaine (1982). "The Conventional Molly Bloom", in Eds. Suzette Henke and Elaine Unkeless, *Women in Joyce*, 150-68.

Van Boheemen, Christine (1987). *The Novel as Family Romance: Language, Gender and Authority From Fielding to Joyce*, Ithaca: Cornell University Press.

Van Dyck Card, James (1973). "'Contradicting': The word for Penelop", *JJQ*, 10 (4), 439-54.

Vico, Giambattista (1968). *The New Science*, Eds. T. Goddard Bergin and M.H. Fisch, Ithaca: Cornell University Press.

Von Phul, Ruth (1959). "Joyce and Strabismal Apologia", *A James Joyce Miscellany*, 2nd ser., Ed. Marvin Magalaner, Carbondale: Southern Illinois University Press.

Walcott, William (1971). "Notes by a Jungian Analyst on the Dreams in *Ulysses*", *JJQ*, 9 (1), 37-48.

Walton-Litz, A. (1961). *The Art of James Joyce: Method and Design in Ulysses and Finnegans Wake*, London: Oxford University Press.

Walzl, Florence L. (1982). "*Dubliners*: Women in Irish Society", in Eds. Suzette Henke and Elaine Unkeless, *Women in Joyce*, 31-56.

West, Alick (1936). *Crisis and Criticism*, London: Lawrence and Wishart, rpt. 1975.

Wight, Doris T. (1986). "Vladimir Propp and *Dubliners*", *JJQ*, 23 (4), 415-33.

Wilson, Edmund (1969). *Axel's Castle*, New York: Charles Scribner & Sons.

Yonge, Charlotte M. (1966). *History of Christian Names*, Detroit: Gale Research Co.